OF LOVE AND LOATHING

OF LOVE & LOATHING

Marital Life, Strife, and Intimacy in the Colonial Andes, 1750–1825

NICHOLAS A. ROBINS

University of Nebraska Press | Lincoln and London

Manufactured in the United States of America

♾

Library of Congress Cataloging-in-Publication Data
Robins, Nicholas A., 1964–, author.
Of love and loathing: marital life, strife, and intimacy in the Colonial Andes, 1750–1825 / Nicholas A. Robins.
pages cm
Includes bibliographical references and index.
ISBN 978-0-8032-7719-9 (hardback: alk. paper)
ISBN 978-0-8032-8450-0 (epub)
ISBN 978-0-8032-8451-7 (mobi)
ISBN 978-0-8032-8452-4 (pdf)
1. Marriage—Boliva—Charcas—History—18th century. 2. Domestic relations—Bolivia—Charcas—History—18th century. 3. Charcas (Bolivia)—History—18th century. 4. Charcas (Audiencia)—History—18th century. 5. Charcas (Bolivia)—Social life and customs—18th century. 6. Charcas (Audiencia)—Politics and government—18th century. 7. Spain—Colonies—America—Administration—History—18th century. I. Title.
HQ591.R63 2015
306.810984'09033—dc23
2015013579

Set in Galliard by L. Auten.
Designed by N. Putens.

This book is dedicated to

Petrona Leaños and Roque Hurtado
María Pasquala Yraola y Sustaeta
and Martín Medrano
Catalina Vera and José Galleguillos
Francisca Torres and Joaquín Buitrago

Persecuted protagonists in this work

Contents

Acknowledgments

The road from an idea to a book is always an arduous one, and I have been fortunate to benefit from the support and guidance of many people along the way. Much of the research for this work was conducted at the National Archive and Library of Bolivia (ABNB), in Sucre, where both the staff and holdings are exceptional. I would like to thank its director, Juan Carlos Fernández as well as his predecessors Ana María Lema and Marcela Inch Calvimonte for their support of this project. Likewise, I would like to express my gratitude to Joaquín Loayza Valda and Judith Teran Ríos, past and present assistant directors of the ABNB, for their assistance.

I also had the privilege of being able to rely upon and consult with the ABNB's Maria del Carmen Martínez López, Nelva Delgadillo Hurtado, Alvaro López Donoso, Cecilia Mardoñez Barrero, María Renee Pareja Vilar, Ana María Nava Gabriel, Lucelia Paniagua Vedia, Gabriel Rivera, Oscar Hurtado Borja, María Elizabeth Mollinedo, Leonor Ferrufino Fernández, and Carlos Castaños. They are not only very knowledgeable staff but also colleagues who embody the highest standards of professionalism.

I would like to thank Avelina Espada, the director at the Archdiocesan Archive-Library "Monseñor Taborga," also in Sucre, as well as former director Edgar Valda, for their support of this work. They, and I, were assisted by Elisabeth Paniagua and, previously, by Margoth Céspedes La Madrid, both of whom are patient and tireless in their dedication to their work.

I would also like to thank Bernardo Gantier, SJ, for clarifying certain aspects of religious rites, as well as Rodrigo Zogbi, who provided insights concerning judicial issues. I am also indebted to María del Rosario Barahona Michel for transcribing several documents, providing insights into many aspects of colonial life, and stimulating discussions. Likewise, I would like to thank William Lofstrom for his comments, insights, and translations of many documents, Domingo Izquierdo for facilitating a visit to the former convent of the Virgin of Los Remedios in Sucre, and Frank van den Hout for his support of my research.

Support for this work did not come only from abroad, and I would especially like to thank William Beezley and Steven Vincent for the support and insights they so generously provided. I am also grateful to Kathryn Sloan, Chad Black, and Marcia Stephenson, all of whom provided very helpful suggestions and welcome encouragement as I prepared the manuscript. Thanks are also due to Robert Robins for his helpful comments on a draft manuscript, and to my wife, Susan Halabi, for her patience and encouragement. Finally, I would like to thank Bridget Barry and Sabrina Stellrecht at the University of Nebraska Press and my copy editor, Jesse Arost, for their support of this project.

While to all I am immensely grateful, I remain responsible for any errors or omissions in the work.

OF LOVE AND LOATHING

Introduction

Tuesday, March 14, 1758, was one of the worst days of Roque Hurtado's life. He had only recently bid an anxious farewell to his lover, Petrona Leaños, their five children, and the peaceful, rural life they had shared for many years. Authorities had issued arrest warrants for them due to their illicit, and adulterous, relationship. Perhaps tipped off that their detention was imminent, they had decided to flee in separate directions. Days before, Petrona and the children had made their way to a friend's home in the city of La Plata. On that Tuesday, Roque was on the run, scampering downstream along a rocky riverside. His time as a fugitive was short-lived, however, and he soon fell into the hands of the *corregidor*, or district governor, and his posse. The corregidor would later suggest that his fruitless five-year search for the couple had been brought to an end because "the Divine Eyes [of God] could no longer tolerate it, and He put him into my hands."[1]

Rather than resulting from divine guidance, Roque's capture was due to new information that made it impossible for the corregidor to continue to turn a blind eye to the illicit relationship. With Roque manacled and placed on a chestnut-colored mule, the corregidor ordered the mayor of the village of Mojotoro to convey the prisoner to La Plata. There a bedraggled, defeated Roque became a spectacle, paraded through the streets to the city jail under an escort of six men. On the way to and through the city, he had plenty of time to ponder the perils, and now-distant pleasures, of illicit love. Beyond his concern for his own fate, Roque agonized over what was in store for Petrona and their family. Within the week Petrona would also be arrested and, like Roque, charged with adultery and ignominiously imprisoned in the city jail, along with her three youngest children. Soon after, she and the children were confined in a cell in the Convent of the Virgin of Los Remedios in La Plata, where they would remain without any external support for over eight months.[2]

Petrona and Roque were former neighbors in the town of Presto who had begun a romance more than five years earlier when Petrona's husband, Simón Tadeo Sánchez y Inojosa, was traveling. The couple ran off to Potosí, spending about a month there before returning to Yamparáez Province, where they took up residence on the Canto Molina hacienda, owned by Roque's friend, Francisco de Torres. Over the next three years, the couple led a quiet life and began their family. Although isolated on the hacienda, news of their relationship reached Corregidor Manuel Victoriano Pérez de Aragón. Acting on the husband's complaint, in March 1753, he sent a commission to the hacienda demanding that Francisco hand over Petrona. With the couple in hiding, their host claimed that they had moved away, insisted that he did not want to "abet any sins," and assured the party that he would report the lovers if they returned.[3]

Despite this close call, the couple continued to live on Canto Molina for two more years. In 1755, Roque found work as a *diezmo*, or tithe, collector for the priest Gabriel de Paniagua, and the family moved to his hacienda. Perhaps Father Paniagua believed they were married or was unconcerned about their status, although it is ironic that adulterers would be sheltered and given employment by a clergyman. By June 1757, they had returned to Canto Molino, but their peace would not last long. Determined to find his wife, Petrona's husband unexpectedly arrived at the hacienda one day, ostensibly to grind a load of grain. There he encountered, and had a verbal confrontation with, Roque. Reporting this to the corregidor, the husband expressed his fear that the couple would flee, or even try to kill him. In his petition he produced witnesses who all agreed that Roque and Petrona had long been "living freely as if they were married."[4]

On the basis of this testimony, the corregidor ordered the arrest of the couple and the seizure of their property. With the lovers now behind bars, the husband sought to have Roque banished to a hacienda twenty-five leagues from La Plata. This request was the result of negotiation between the two, as the property was owned by a friend of Roque's, and the husband agreed to pardon the crime if the sentence was carried out. After Roque spent five weeks in jail confessing his guilt and expressing contrition, the court sentenced him to four years of exile on terms almost identical to those requested by the husband. Simón was less forgiving of his wife, however, and sought to have her perpetually cloistered at her own expense.[5] The court partly acceded to his request, ordering her sequestered for four years in the Convent of the Virgin of Los Remedios in La Plata, which also served as a girls' orphanage. In December 1758, after more than eight months of confinement in a cell with three children, she petitioned the court for her release on the basis that her husband was not supporting her financially. The court initially granted her freedom of movement within the convent walls and later allowed her to have the city of La Plata as her "prison" so that she could support herself and her children.[6] Neither Roque nor Petrona abided by the terms of their release for long. In May 1759, the husband complained that Roque had reappeared in La Plata and that Roque had twice tried to poison him. He also claimed that Petrona had abused her permission to leave the convent and had reunited with Roque. Four months later, the prosecutor agreed to pursue the matter, although the family had disappeared and the case was then abandoned.[7]

Petrona and Roque's story weaves together many elements that defined intimacy in colonial Latin America: ill-chosen or forced marriages, absent husbands, long-standing and socially accepted illicit affairs, illegitimate children, the use of haciendas to avoid public scrutiny, complicit officials, women's confinement in religious institutions, negotiated settlements to restore lost honor, the clergy's insistence on reconciliation, and fears of being murdered by a spouse's lover. How individuals, and couples, navigated the waters of intimacy, and the risks inherent to them, reveals much about both them and the society in which they lived. In the colonial Andes, the Catholic Church and Spanish monarchs sought to impose narrowly defined limits on intimacy that were based on, and sought to reinforce, patriarchal norms, Catholic doctrine, and, ultimately, regal power. Patriarchy formed a vital strand in civil and ecclesiastical notions of morality and found expression both in social and political policies and in quotidian relations in the markets, plazas, homes, and bedrooms of the colonial Andes. While patriarchy was overarching, it was not all-encompassing.[8]

Focusing on the period from 1750 to 1825, this book utilizes case studies to examine the application of late colonial Bourbon policies concerning marriage and intimacy, their effects on people's lives, and how they resisted them to create, and break, intimate bonds in colonial Charcas.[9] This region encompassed present-day Bolivia and parts of Peru, Chile, Paraguay, Uruguay, and Argentina. Laws concerning intimacy underscore the moral, racial, and patriarchal ideals of the time as well as the extent to which they were evaded in daily life. What emerges is an image of a society with considerably more moral latitude than would appear from an understanding based on the primacy of religious doctrine and regal edicts—and one in which free unions, independent women, illegitimate children, and de facto divorces abounded. While such tendencies to some extent reflect the consequences of coerced, abusive, and abandoned marriages, they also highlight the prevalence of women's agency, or their ability to make choices concerning resources, relationships, and movement. That agency, however, was only one side of the coin, because to achieve it women often suffered unhappy unions, severe physical abuse, humiliation, abandonment, reclusion, and social sanction.[10]

Regal efforts to reassert patriarchy in late colonial Charcas actually exacerbated the trends that they sought to reverse. Not only did the crown seek to enforce existing laws concerning marriage, but it also issued successive royal decrees from the 1770s to the early 1800s that granted increasing power to fathers and guardians to influence the marriage choices of those subject to them. Such policies precipitated numerous lawsuits as young couples sought to evade, challenge, or temper these restrictions. It was not only elite fathers who went to court to stop marriages; so too did single mothers and people from the lower classes. Among the unintended consequences of the enhancement of paternal power in marriage choice was a rise in clandestine marriages, highlighting the clash between romantic affinity and a patriarchal, caste-based society. Moreover, the erosion of individual choice in marriage exacerbated the prevalence of abusive marriages, extramarital affairs, illegitimate children, and spousal abandonment, all of which the Bourbon monarchs sought to reduce.

Regal initiatives to reinforce patriarchy and morality included the enforcement of edicts requiring itinerant husbands to return to their wives. Such efforts underscore the degree of population mobility, familial fragmentation, and marital discord that characterized colonial society while revealing a broad, vital, and understudied arena of female agency. The application of these spousal reunification laws was as fragmented as many of the unions they sought to restore, reflecting a lack of enthusiasm on the part of civil officials to enforce them and even less from husbands to comply. Although authorities occasionally utilized the law to end publicly illicit relationships, enforcement frequently responded more to opportunities for political or economic gain, or personal rivalries, than to moral striving. When the order came through to return to one's spouse in a matter of days or face an ignominious trip home as a prisoner, merchants were forced to quickly sell their wares and try to collect debts at a discount, informal unions were imperiled, and people who were in the often interminable process of divorce faced the distressing prospect of reuniting with their spouses. Many husbands had not seen their wives in years, and the paucity of demands by wives for their return suggests that many preferred the relative independence that separation offered.

Among the lamentable consequences of regal and ecclesiastical policies to uphold marriage as an indissoluble and lifelong union were the pervasiveness of recurring domestic abuse and the often insurmountable challenges faced, especially by women, in obtaining a divorce or annulment. Spousal abuse was not only tolerated but legal in colonial society and as a result was underreported in the documentary record. Despite this, its prevalence is shocking, with women often being strung up and flogged, beaten, mutilated, and even murdered by their husbands. As one such victim, María Estrada, put it, one "thing are the events themselves, and another only told."[11] As a matter of policy, clergy urged couples to reconcile, often exacerbating a cycle of abuse. A failed effort of reconciliation was in practice a prerequisite for a divorce petition to be accepted and placed on the docket by ecclesiastical authorities. As a result, many a battered woman was left with no choice but to return to a violent husband who had been only further incensed by his loss of honor as a result of his wife having left him. Even when a divorce petition was accepted, it was costly, advanced slowly, usually involved the woman's reclusion, and usually did not have a clear outcome. Such petitions not only describe a lugubrious side of domestic life but also reveal how women could be coerced into marrying a man they hardly knew or whose face they had never seen.

By examining the enforcement of, resistance to, and jurisdictional rivalries over laws concerning intimacy, this work ties royal and church policy concerning marriage to the individuals who were affected by them and whose personal narratives serve as a window to the daily workings of colonial society. Theirs are stories of passion, resistance to convention, forbidden love, captive sons and daughters, clandestine marriages, familial discords, street quarrels, horrific physical abuse, and informal divorces. Their lives played out in a wider social context where slaves and domestic servants were often the best informed about what occurred behind closed doors, making their testimony especially revealing, and often bitterly opposed. Neighbors not only heard about domestic discord; they often listened to it and in some cases intervened to stop it. It was not just the elite who sought judicial recourse but also common people, of diverse ethnicities and occupations, including tailors, barkeepers, farmers, and even slaves. Their stories also encompass the "Generation of 1780," as several of the protagonists participated in, or were victims of, the Great Rebellion of 1780–82. Some, like Friar Matías de la Borda, were held captive by the indigenous rebels, while others, like Father Dionicio Cortés and Corregidor Juan Antonio de Silva y Acuña, were killed by them. Many more, such as Catalina de Miranda, had their haciendas destroyed in the uprising.[12]

Inextricably entwined with morality and patriarchy was honor. A ubiquitous social touchstone, it indicated one's standing in, and the expectations of, a community and reflected the legitimacy of one's birth, racial origins, occupation, personal integrity, and public behavior.[13] Honor transcended the individual and subsumed the family, magnifying its importance at all levels in society. Beyond the virtue of being true to one's word, the meaning of honor was gender-dependent. For men, it revolved around the exercise of power, both within the family and in society, and was also expressed through sexual prowess. For women, honor was contingent on acquiescence to patriarchal authority, modesty, loyalty, religious devotion, premarital virginity, fidelity during marriage, and chastity in widowhood. An honorable and virtuous woman was expected to be *recogida*, or withdrawn, in her own home and to acquiesce to male authority as expressed at both the individual and social levels. Furthermore, she was to spend her time devoted to her family and spiritual activities and not to leave the home when not accompanied by a male chaperone or servant. Virginity was a commodity inextricably tied to individual and familial honor, as well as to estate perpetuation. While premarital sex was seen as dishonorable, it was common, and the loss of honor was attenuated if the couple was engaged. Even illegitimate children could be legitimated, and thus made honorable, if the couple wed. Alternatively, a man could be compelled to satisfy a "virginity debt," which could involve the payment of a dowry or other compensation, to restore a woman's honor.[14]

In daily life, honor and social standing were communicated by noble and professional titles, dress, seating order, how people spoke to and deferred to a person, and the legal ability to carry a weapon. For both men and women, "racial purity" and honor were directly related, although the degree of racial heterogeneity in society made this a fluid concept depending on location and other signifiers of honor.[15] Within this context, however, being of African or Indian descent was seen as dishonorable, as was working directly in commerce or in manual occupations, such as agriculture or artisanry. While honor could be lost, it could also be regained through duels, legal suits, financial settlement, marrying one's lover, and a *gracias al sacar*, which was a bureaucratic means of changing one's status, for example, of race or birth.[16]

For any person, accusations of criminality, marital infidelity, and religious deviance damaged individual and familial honor, as did a widow remarrying within a year of losing her husband. Among the lower classes—who usually lacked "racial purity," political standing, wealth, or all three—personal integrity and virtue were central tenets of honor. As the eighteenth century advanced, honor increasingly concerned wealth and rectitude as opposed to race and noble origins. It was this tendency, and the social mobility it implied, that led to the series of royal edicts beginning in the 1770s that enhanced parental authority in marriage choice. In these laws, the crown sought to prevent the erosion of family honor through unequal marriages and possible "racial mixing."[17]

The Revolving Door of Recogimiento

Petrona Leaños's husband Simón sought not only to punish his wife and her lover but also to restore his own honor. His request to have Petrona sentenced to perpetual reclusion was central to this design, as was Roque's banishment. Like Petrona, many of the women portrayed in this volume were confined, either in a religious institution or a private home, while facing accusations of immoral behavior, during divorce proceedings or conflicts over marriage choice, or as a result of suffering domestic abuse.[18] When the confinement was in a religious establishment, it was referred to as recogimiento, whereas *depósito* was the term used when a woman was placed in the custody of a respected local resident or family member. In both cases, the intent was to withdraw the woman from society for a period that could run from weeks to years.[19] Reclusion could be voluntary or involuntary under order of civil officials who made a formal request to the archbishop. Its use for both protective and punitive purposes provides an excellent lens through which to analyze both the social control, and also protection, of women in colonial society.

While women could be placed in recogimiento in a convent, in Charcas they were more frequently placed in religious orphanages, or *beaterios*, which were cloistered religious houses for pious lay women. Following the Council of Trent (1545–1563), and thus for most of the colonial period, religious houses that functioned exclusively as convents were not generally used as recogimientos for women accused of immoral conduct, although women in divorce proceedings were still placed there. This was often at the request of a husband who saw the conventual life as a means of further isolating his wife from her family as well as of increasing her hardships, and hence the pressure to return to him or to abandon her case.[20] While some recogimientos served primarily as women's prisons, funded by the crown and administered by religious orders, others, such as beaterios and orphanages, had a more socio-religious focus and diverse populations in terms of age and ethnicity. For example, when Petrona entered the Convent of the Virgin of Los Remedios, in addition to the nun-administrators, she encountered a diverse population that included many orphan girls preparing to enter a convent or to be married; abused women, along with their children, seeking a divorce; and others accused of infidelity or concubinage, such as herself. That many women had an experience with some form of religious confinement is underscored by the fact that in 1700, over 20 percent of the females in Lima resided in some form of religious institution, including a recogimiento specifically for women in the divorce process.[21]

Once confined in a religious house, women required economic support, as well as their bed and clothes, if they were going to avoid hunger, severe discomfort, and being assigned demeaning tasks.[22] Some women were supported by their husbands, often reluctantly and under civil court order, while others were aided by family members, sold jewels or other property, or survived by making handicrafts or cleaning. Whatever the case, they were expected to carry their own economic weight, and many women, especially among the elite, suffered hardships that they had never experienced before.

Compelling a man to support his wife in reclusion was fraught with challenges, as Petrona quickly learned, and she ultimately used this fact to her advantage. Like some men facing divorce, Simón Barrios contended that since his wife, Manuela Guzmán, had initiated the case and brought no dowry, he was not obligated to support her.[23] Others, such as Alejo Ballesteros, defied a court order to pay a hefty twelve pesos a week to his wife, Tomasa Erazu. She had decided to seek a divorce after Alejo was caught hiding under his widowed lover's bed during the night rounds in La Plata. Faced with Alejo's refusal to support his wife, the vicar general allowed Tomasa to leave the recogimiento twice a week to earn a living.[24]

Because a husband was legally required to economically support his wife in reclusion, he had considerable influence over where she was confined and with whom she had contact. Beyond confinement, economic hardship, and physical discomfort, sequestered women were also subject to the pressures of priests and nuns, who in abuse and divorce cases consistently urged reconciliation. Thus, many faced the painful choice of indefinite misery in recogimiento or a return to an abusive and often vindictive husband. Overall, it was much easier to be placed in recogimiento than to get out, as once inside inmates were a source of labor or revenue for the institution, supplementing its income from mortgages and other investments.[25] In contrast, being placed in depósito could range from living a secluded life with one's parents or relatives to being confined or even restrained in a room in the house of a stranger.[26]

Given the hardships and often open-ended nature of reclusion, many women resisted confinement. Like many of her contemporaries, Hilaria Díaz cited her poor health in an effort to be released from recogimiento. She was seeking a divorce in 1764, claiming her husband was abusive and that her father had forced her into the marriage. After nine months in the Puríssima Concepción convent in La Paz, she sought to be released, as she had lost considerable weight and had breathing problems resulting from "the extreme cold and discomfort of the cell."[27] Also in La Paz, the widow Rafaela Valverde had been accused of an illicit romance and by June 1769 had spent two years in recogimiento. In her pleading, she described herself as a "prisoner" who had been enduring "hunger and nakedness," while "suffering from intolerable labors, harm and illness as a result of being destitute and without help."[28] Her attorney argued that if she was guilty she should only have been fined eight ounces of silver, and in any case, her supposed lover had died a few months previously. Perhaps because of the impossibility of a continuing romance, Valverde was finally cautioned and released.[29]

Reclusion, especially in a convent, was commonly used for vengeful purposes by husbands, who wanted their wives to suffer and desist from pursuing legal action against them. Such was the case with María Francisca Barrios, who was in the midst of a divorce proceeding against her husband Ramón Ballivián. After the case had stagnated for years, in 1804 she accused Ramón of forcing his way into her house in La Plata and trying to rape her. As a result, she petitioned the ecclesiastical authorities to be placed in depósito in the home of respected friends, something she would later regret. Ramón denied any ill intent, insisting that he had simply come from La Paz with their four children in an effort to reconcile.

He also opposed her request to be placed in depósito and petitioned the court to have her dispatched to the Santa Clara convent, where conditions were considerably more restrictive than in depósito or an orphanage. He noted that she had been ordered into recogimiento when the case was accepted, although the directive had been rescinded due to her epilepsy. Ramón agreed to support her financially in the convent, where, he asserted, she would be well cared for, and unquestionably protected from him. The church prosecutor, a clergyman whose role was to defend marriage, supported his request, noting that if Ramón was to support her in reclusion, it should be in a place of his choosing. Prior to sending her to the convent, however, the prosecutor suggested that María, once again, be urged to reconcile.[30]

María was without question an independent and tenacious woman, and she flatly rejected the choice between living in a convent or with a man she feared and despised. Her attorney, José Pimentel, played for time, sometimes week by week, through various legal motions. First, he sought to have the prosecutor removed from the case by accusing him of partiality toward the husband, later refused to respond to court orders, and requested the reissuance of various documents. Among them was an often ignored ecclesiastical ruling that stated that married women could be sent to convents only if their lives were at risk from accusations of infidelity, and then only in exceptional cases. As no one had ever made such an accusation against María, Pimentel argued that she could not legally be forced into the convent. Furthermore, he averred, her epilepsy was incurable, and since this was the reason she was not previously forced into reclusion, there was no reason to revisit the issue.[31]

By this time a year had passed, and María continued to live on her own, under increasing financial pressure and always under the specter of imminent confinement. Meanwhile, although her husband Ramón and their children had returned to La Paz, his advocate, Manuel Malavia, continued to aggressively pursue the case. Just when it looked like María was about to lose her liberty, a new ecclesiastical prosecutor was assigned to the case. Unlike his predecessor, he accepted that her illness was chronic and had been the basis for her not being confined years before. He also noted that no one had accused her of infidelity, nor was her life at stake, and that as a result there was no legal basis to place her in the convent. Although the outcome of the case is unclear, the tide was clearly running in María's favor.[32]

Once their wives were in a recogimiento, husbands could protract their suffering through various tactics. Melchora Azurduy experienced this in the Santa Isabel orphanage in La Plata in 1803. Not only had her husband, Manuel Arciénaga, refused to financially support her; he had also failed to respond to or even return the case file that he had received eight months earlier. As a result, she had been "supported . . . by Divine Providence" and asked to be released to her parents.[33] Only when facing the prospect of arrest for refusing to respond to the court did Manuel claim that the case file had been destroyed. Further, he insisted that since Melchora had voluntarily entered reclusion and the divorce petition had never been filed, he was under no obligation to support her financially. This resonated with the civil authorities, who determined that unless she formalized her divorce petition, he did not have to pay her anything beyond the paltry one and one half pesos he had reluctantly provided.[34]

The Legal Framework: Form versus Function

Colonial legal disputes played out in three parallel court systems, reflecting civil, ecclesiastical, and military *fueros*, or independent corporate bodies and jurisdictions. As a result, civil authorities could not compel a cleric to testify nor demand actions of prelates or military officials and instead relied on formal requests for cooperation. Cases that concerned the marriage bond, such as dispensations, divorces, and annulments, came under the purview of the ecclesiastical court. Otherwise, cases such as those concerning physical assault, rape, kidnapping, concubinage, infidelity, or financial support fell under civil authority. Beginning in 1754, some issues, like bigamy, fell under both jurisdictions.[35] Men in the military were subject to martial law as opposed to civil law, although the ecclesiastical court retained preeminence in marital issues. In some cases, petitioners sought to increase the pressure on their adversaries and had related cases pending in different courts. For example, a woman might seek a divorce from an abusive husband in ecclesiastical court while seeking criminal charges for battery or financial support in civil court.[36]

Although a plaintiff could present an initial petition to a magistrate directly, both plaintiffs and defendants were subsequently represented by counsel. This could be in the form of a *procurador*, or an attorney with limited but sufficient legal training to pursue a case before a magistrate of the first instance. Alternatively their advocate could be an *abogado*, or a lawyer with more extensive and formal legal education. Unlike a procurador, an abogado could practice before the *audiencia*, which served as a court of appeal for both civil and criminal cases. Both plaintiffs and defendants could request an indigent attorney, who was either the *protector de los naturales*, for Indians, or the *procurador de pobres* for non-native indigents. For their part, minors were represented by the *defensor de menores*.[37] As a result, the protagonists in this work were generally represented by an advocate who framed their case and presented their argument in the manner that they believed would most appeal to the court. Even when a person had an advocate, they could, and often did, write the respective court directly.

The civil and ecclesiastical systems, upon which this study is based, functioned in a similar manner. In rural civil cases, corregidors, or their lieutenants, served as magistrates in the first instance, while *alcaldes*, or mayors, fulfilled the same role in municipalities. Municipalities had two alcaldes, who served concurrent one-year terms and were elected by the *regidores*, or councilmen, in two rounds of voting. Often there were frictions between the two, reflecting the fact that the alcalde "of the first vote" had jurisdiction over property-owners and the elite, while the alcalde "of the second vote" exercised jurisdiction over the rest of the population. Alcaldes also led the *ronda*, or night rounds, in the company of the *alguacil*, or sheriff, soldiers, pages, and often slaves. Such patrols were intended to maintain public order and ensure morality, and they commonly included surprise domestic inspections. Not uncommonly, they also served as a means of pursuing vendettas.[38]

Cases could be initiated in one of two ways. In one, an alcalde or corregidor could assume the role of complainant and initiate a legal process *de oficio*, or by virtue of his authority. Alternatively, a plaintiff could initiate a suit in either the civil or ecclesiastical jurisdictions by submitting an initial brief stating the accusation. If the case was accepted by the court, the *sumaria información*, or initial phase of testimony, began and was subject to a variable, extendable, but ultimately limited time frame. The plaintiff, or their advocate, specified which questions to ask, and witnesses were sworn under oath to speak the truth. A scribe recorded all testimony, and in the case of Indians two interpreters aided in the gathering of evidence. Those giving testimony were permitted to relate not only what they had seen and heard directly but also what they had been told by, or had overheard from, others, thus making hearsay evidence acceptable.[39] As one witness explained, "As they say, the voice of the people is the voice of God."[40] While civil deponents could be compelled to testify, priests required the permission of their bishop or guardian, and military men that of their superiors. Once it was complete, the witness read their testimony, or had it read to them, ratified it, and indicated their approximate age.[41]

When one side had gathered their evidence, the *translado*, or transfer, occurred, during which the case file was remitted to the adverse party, who could then reply in the *contestación*, or response. This was also an opportunity to delay the case by not responding until repeatedly ordered to do so by the court, or by claiming that the brief had been lost or destroyed. In criminal cases, after witnesses had testified, the accused would make a declaration in which they could also provide an interrogatory for additional witnesses. This translado/contestación process could go through several cycles before advancing to the *prueba* stage. Here, the *fiscal*, or prosecutor, would examine and offer his perspective on the case based on colonial jurisprudence and indicate how he believed the judge should rule. The next stage was the *publicación de probanzas*, in which the judge rendered his verdict. Finally, there was the *sentencia*, in which the judge issued the punishment in cases of guilt.

Either party could appeal a decision made at the municipal or provincial level by presenting it to the audiencia, which also had executive and legislative functions.[42]

In arriving at decisions, civil and ecclesiastical judges had to contend with a bewildering and conflicting array of royal edicts, laws, and canonical doctrines. These ranged from Rome's Justinian Code of 534 and the Siete Partidas of 1251 to the Leyes de Toro of 1505, the Council of Trent of 1545–63, and the 1681 Recopilación de Indias. To assist them, magistrates had recourse to numerous guides, such as the *Instrucción Jurídica* of Joseph Juan y Colom, published in 1736, and the *Teatro de la Legislación Universal de España é Indias*, by Antonio Xavier Pérez y López, first published in 1791. Not all passed royal muster, however, such as the *Anotaciones a la Real Pragmática*, published in 1785 by Joseph Lebron, which contained interpretations that were deemed inconsistent with royal policy and was consequently banned.[43]

Within this context, women had an attenuated legal standing.[44] This is perhaps best illustrated by the fact that for much of the colonial era, the testimony of one Spanish man was equivalent to that of two Indians or three women, and in the case of male and female fraternal twins, the male was always regarded as being firstborn. Moreover, women were banned from attending university and holding public office. Despite structural impediments, women, especially widows and adults who never married, did have formal rights. For example, a widow could buy and sell property, borrow and lend money, serve as an executrix, bring a legal suit, and, except in cases of wills, serve as witness to transactions. In contrast, a married woman required the written permission of her husband for such actions. A married woman did retain ownership of her *arras*, or a gift from a man to his fiancée, and her dowry, and although they were generally administered by her husband, they could not be seized for his debts. Unless a husband willed otherwise, his widow would serve as the guardian of her children, and as head of household, so long as she remained single and led a virtuous life.[45]

Beyond their limited formal rights, which required assertion to have any effect, women's agency was enabled by the custom of allowing them to petition civil courts without the permission of their husbands, which technically they required. This was also the case in Charcas, especially when women sought assistance from the courts on issues of child support, abuse, rape, marriage licenses, dowries, and other domestic issues. Such practices highlight the role of custom in civil court decisions and the wide range of actions available to judges due to the lack of a binding nature of precedent.[46]

In the end, however, domestic power was concentrated in the hands of the husband or father. It was he who made the decisions concerning the children's education and legal affairs and whose consent was required for marriage unless the offspring were willing to suffer disinheritance. In the event of separation or divorce, the father had automatic custody of the children over three years old as long as he had not been convicted of major crimes such as heresy, incest, or sedition.[47] Paternal power was further enhanced by the fact that, in most cases, the age of majority was twenty-five. In addition to being empowered as fathers, as the following pages demonstrate, men were also treated much more leniently than women in cases of concubinage and infidelity.

The cases in this work are largely drawn from archival documents in the National Archive and Library of Bolivia as well as from the Monseñor Taborga Archdiocesan Archive-Library, both in Sucre, Bolivia. With few exceptions, they are legal documents, which include intimate correspondence, filed in either the ecclesiastical or civil courts, and the cases presented in the text serve both as exemplars of other cases cited in the notes and as indicators of broader trends. Informal separations and spousal abuse, for example, were clearly widespread in late colonial society, and for every case filed there were in all likelihood scores of similar potential cases that were not.

Given the nature of the cases, the documents frequently are polemic and one-sided, portray their adversaries in the worst light possible, and often do not present the larger context of the events. This was somewhat less the case with witness testimony as opposed to the initial petitions and briefs submitted by advocates. Despite these limitations, the documents do present both sides of a dispute, often in considerable detail. In addition, the cases, verdicts, and sentences reveal what were considered civil and ecclesiastical transgressions, and their sanctions.

Unfortunately for those involved as well as for later historians, many civil and especially ecclesiastical cases lacked a clear outcome, and the documentary collections are ultimately fragmentary. While many people came to a negotiated settlement out of court, others simply abandoned their cases. This was common with divorces, not only because the church was institutionally reluctant to grant divorce but also because many people could not or did not want to continue to pay the attorneys, scribes, and fees, especially as the husband was usually obligated to pay both his and his wife's legal and living expenses. Also, given the pressures for reconciliation in divorce cases, many abandoned their efforts in an attempt to work things out with their spouses or resigned themselves to abusive marriages. Because obtaining a divorce was an expensive and very time-consuming process with an uncertain outcome, once a case was accepted by the court and the couple physically separated, many were willing to accept the de facto divorce that separation offered.[48]

It was within this context that colonial intimacy occurred, constrained by a caste-based society founded on patriarchy, honor, religious doctrine, and moral double standards for men and women. The narrow confines of morality, the coercion used in its enforcement, and the often insurmountable challenges of choosing one's mate or obtaining a divorce relegated many couples, and their offspring, to the realm of illegitimacy. That realm, however, was so large that illicit relationships, like domestic abuse, were generally socially accepted and often public. Among the most common forms of forbidden relationships were concubinage and adultery, to which we now turn.

CHAPTER I

"Crimes of Sensuality"

Morality versus Affinity

Despite the legal and ecclesiastical insistence on church-sanctioned marriage, consensual unions and extramarital affairs were commonplace both in Charcas and Spanish America. Such unions ranged from transitory, clandestine liaisons to public, long-term relationships. To some degree illicit romance was the consequence of forced marriages or those of economic convenience, yet it also reflected a geographically mobile society. Despite the prevalence and social acceptance of illicit relationships, they carried the inherent risk of both civil and religious sanctions, which could include fines, incarceration, banishment, and excommunication. Beginning in the seventeenth century, concubinage came under the purview of civil authorities, although cases of marital infidelity remained under ecclesiastical jurisdiction. Punishment for concubinage tended to be harsher for the woman, who was generally of a lower social, economic, or racial status than her lover. While she faced the possibility of indefinite reclusion, the man generally only risked a brief incarceration and a fine.[1]

Concubinage and illicit affairs were at the root of the high rates of illegitimate births in Latin America, which exceeded those in Spain, Europe, and the British colonies in North America. In sixteenth-century Spanish America, overall illegitimacy rates reached 50 percent, and up to 80 percent among mestizos, or those of mixed Spanish and Indian ancestry.[2] In Lima's San Sebastián Parish between 1562 and 1689, approximately 37 percent of all mestizos and creoles, or those of Spanish parents born in the colony, were illegitimate, although rates for mestizos peaked at 80 percent.[3] In La Paz, illegitimacy rates during the colonial period generally ranged between 40 and 50 percent.[4] Overall in Latin America, the incidence of illegitimacy was generally higher among mestizos and slaves than among Indians, Spaniards, and creoles and declined gradually in the eighteenth century.[5]

The city of La Plata, which served as the capital of Charcas, appears to have followed a different trend. There, illegitimacy rates among those born to Spaniards and creoles were notably higher than that of Indians, generally exceeded that of mestizos, and sometimes were more than that of slaves. From 1750 through 1820, between 53 and 64 percent of births to Spanish and creole mothers in the city were out of wedlock, compared to between 45 and 62 percent among mestizos. Moreover, these figures underestimate the numbers of illegitimate offspring of Spanish or creole fathers, as those born to a mestizo mother would be classified, and baptized, as mestizos.[6]

In contrast, among those baptized in the largely Indian parish of San Sebastián, which included part of La Plata and the surrounding area, out-of-wedlock births accounted for between 15 and 30 percent of births from 1750 through 1820. Among blacks illegitimacy rates during the same period ranged from 52 to 79 percent.[7] Overall, the higher illegitimacy rates among blacks to some degree reflected the difficulties slaves faced in establishing and maintaining nuclear families.

Baptismal records also indicate much higher rates of secret pregnancies, and hence *hijos expuestos*, or foundlings, among Spaniards and creoles than any other group. This reflected their higher social status and consequent greater concern for maintaining familial honor. For example, in both 1750 and 1760, 32 percent of all children born to Spaniards and creoles were foundlings, an incidence that increased to 37 percent in 1768 before beginning a decline.[8] Overall, in the years examined above, on average 23 percent of those classified as Spaniard or creole were hijos expuestos, compared to 9 percent among mestizos, 3 percent among blacks, and 2 percent in the largely indigenous parish of San Sebastián.[9]

These figures underscore the fact that living with one's concubine, and having illegitimate children, were by no means unusual in the region, especially among Spaniards, creoles, and mestizos. Priests and military and other officials were often fathers of illegitimate children, reflecting the prohibition of clerical marriage and marital restrictions on military officers and royal officials. Beginning in 1578, royal officials were prohibited from marrying in their jurisdiction, and although the ban was widely ignored, in 1764 the crown extended it to their offspring. Beginning in 1728, military officers were required to obtain permission to marry from their commanding officers, and, after 1741, from the monarch or his delegate. The fact that such restrictions were routinely ignored underscores the gap between laws and their enforcement in the colony, which paralleled that between morality and social practice.[10]

Illegitimacy had its consequences, however. For much of the colonial period, men who were illegitimate children were excluded from universities as well as from ecclesiastical and royal service unless they had been subsequently legitimated. Illegitimate daughters often lacked an attractive dowry, and their mothers frequently remained single for life. Unless legally recognized by the father, offspring born out of wedlock generally received little or no inheritance. Although a father who had no other children could bequeath all of his estate to his illegitimate child, if he had other legitimate children, he could dispense of only 20 percent of his wealth as he chose. This did not preclude him, however, from donating money in lieu of inheritance.[11]

Among those born out of wedlock, there was a distinction between an *hijo natural*, or natural child, who was born of single parents and whose father was legally required to support the child, and the more shameful "illegitimate" child, at least one of whose parents was married. Overall, a natural child had less shame and more possibilities for becoming legitimate, as the parents had not broken a marital vow and could marry, amend the baptismal record, and thus legitimate the child. Similarly, a child born of an incestuous relationship, which included one between second-degree relatives, could be legitimated by a dispensation and the subsequent marriage of the parents. A dispensation could also be granted to allow an illegitimate female to enter religious life.[12]

Another path to legitimation was to petition for a gracias al sacar from authorities in Spain. This bureaucratic mechanism allowed one to legally change her or his racial or birth status, as well as to obtain a noble title. It could even be applied retroactively, making a deceased illegitimate person legitimate, thus restoring familial honor. The process was not only time-consuming but also costly. For example, in 1773 the fee to legitimate one's birth ranged from 206 pesos for a "natural" child to 1,512 pesos for a child of a priest, reflecting the amount of disgrace to be erased. As social and economic obstacles increased with the child's age, so did the gracias al sacar petitions. This tendency was exacerbated by increasing discrimination against illegitimate children throughout the eighteenth century as economic growth fostered social mobility as well as elite efforts to limit it.[13]

The distinction between natural and illegitimate offspring was part of a broader "continuum of illegitimacy."[14] A child's place in this spectrum was enhanced if the child's father was listed on baptismal records, had high social status, and supported or recognized the child, either legally or by such indicators as residence, affection, and use of the family name. Illegitimate children were often integrated into the home of one of the parents as a foundling. Overall, it was possible to "pass" as legitimate and "honorable," and even obtain a government position, depending on the local context and prestige of the family. Economic and social opportunities for foundlings increased in 1794 when Charles IV mandated that they be considered as his offspring, and thus legitimate.[15]

While a pregnancy out of wedlock was shameful for the woman and caused consternation within the family, maintaining a secret pregnancy was a common means of preserving the family's public honor and the woman's reputation as a virgin. In the eighteenth century, some estimates suggest that up to one-half of illegitimate children in Latin America were born from secret pregnancy, and as we have seen, between one-quarter and one-third of births to creoles and Spaniards were foundlings. Once born, however, the secret was literally out, and unless handled carefully, the mother's reputation would suffer if she did not marry the father or accept the child into the family as a foundling.[16]

Secret pregnancies were difficult to maintain, as Manuela Tapia learned in La Plata in 1822. Her husband, José Buenaventura Antezana, was seeking a divorce as a result of her numerous adulterous relationships, which had produced at least two children. Manuela was not only a passionate woman but also a jealous one. She betrayed herself one evening at a party when one of her lovers flirted with other women, provoking her to smash "glasses of wine . . . and plates" in a fit of rage.[17] She took more care in concealing the children her affairs produced, one of whom was being raised in the house of her sister under the guise of a foundling. Manuela was also accused of having an older illegitimate child who was born on her sister's hacienda in 1817.[18] In the end, claims of fidelity were shattered when her husband found a cache of love letters between her and three of her lovers.

In one, Manuela wrote to Blas Sevilla, "Reiterating my ardent affection, I ask you to use me as you will, as I am all yours, your lover," while in another she wrote, "It would be better if I were far from your sight, instead of dying of thirst when it would appear that I have water on my lips. Let me stop loving you, let me say what I feel, and if you should chance to read these lines, know that the only remedy that can alleviate my suffering is seeing you. . . . With this note [I] send the heartfelt affection of she who calls herself yours."[19]

Several months later, insolvent and confined in recogimiento, she wrote to another lover, Patricio Hidalgo, confiding:

> I am on the verge of desperation, and am now living with the orphan girls, from which I send these tear-stained doodles. I am almost beside myself, and my sole consolation is the thought of

> kissing you. . . . Even though you may think me crude, please understand that I find myself in lamentable ill health, which obliges me to trouble you, asking you for 50 pesos . . . since I find myself locked in here without any allowance. As soon as my rascal husband left my support was suspended, so you can imagine my suffering, as a stranger [in La Plata] and bereft of any support but yours. . . . I wish you well being, yours to command, Manuela.[20]

Although the documents do not reveal the outcome of the case, the tide was clearly running against Manuela after she admitted writing one of the letters to Blas Sevilla.[21]

In contrast to the pervasiveness of out-of-wedlock births, there are comparatively few cases of mothers demanding child support.[22] Although some fathers supported their illegitimate offspring through informal arrangements, if the father did not acknowledge the child it was difficult if not impossible for a woman to prove his identity. Furthermore, mothers of illegitimate children were frequently of a lower social and economic standing than the father and lacked the resources to demand support or prevail in court.

Some, like the young creole Melchora Gusman, nevertheless courageously made the attempt. She had come to La Plata from her home in Cochabamba in March 1798 with the intention of devoting herself to a religious life. Initially lodging in a private home owned by Manuela Baraona, she planned to enter the Beaterio de Santa Catalina, and then, she hoped, the Santa Clara convent. About a week after her arrival, Melchora began to receive the attentions of the politically well-connected alguacil, Manuel Antonio Tardío. He appeared to be enchanted by her, visiting daily, with much of the time spent together in the privacy of Melchora's room. Soon she was pregnant, and over the next several months Manuel arranged and paid for better lodgings and hired a wet nurse. As the time approached for her to give birth, they went to his hacienda in nearby Yotala, named Ñuccho, where their daughter Josefa was born. After the birth, Manuel continued to support mother and child with four pesos a week and to provide a wet nurse.[23]

Melchora soon realized that Manuel, despite his promises, was neither going to marry her nor acknowledge their child. Her efforts to sue him for child support were stymied, however, by the refusal of many attorneys to take the case, as many were allied with or feared Manuel due to his position as alguacil. Ultimately, in August 1799, the civil court granted her request to be declared indigent and to appoint José Joaquín Quintela as her counsel. Over Manuel's objections, the court allowed the testimony of her servants, all of whom substantiated her claim that Manuel was the father. Although he admitted to visiting her in her lodging, he denied being the father of the baby, insisting that "whom wanted to entered the house."[24] He denied making any financial or marital promises to Melchora and sought to discredit her by claiming that she was not a virgin when they met. Some of his testimony was contradicted by Melchora's servant, who attested that she refused to see any other man and that all of the other residents in the Baraona house were certain that Manuel was the father. His credibility was further challenged when the wet nurse whom he had hired revealed that she was also tending to his other illegitimate children. Despite this setback, Manuel's attorney mercilessly impugned all of Melchora's witnesses, characterizing them as "vile," Indians, or of mixed race and accusing them of lacking any "conscience."[25]

In an ironic twist to the case, Melchora was placed in recogimiento in the Beaterio de Santa Catalina, where she had originally intended to prepare for entrance to the convent. By May 1800, over two years after she arrived, the baby Josefa had died, and the audiencia ordered Manuel to pay her five hundred pesos pending the outcome of the case. His attorney was able to suspend the order, arguing that it was possible that she was pregnant when she arrived in La Plata. He again impugned her integrity, and sought to humiliate her, by demanding a physical examination to see whether she was pregnant again while insisting, "[she] is not, has not been, nor can she be honest."[26]

Although Melchora's attorney was able to prevent the examination, he was unable to have the five-hundred-peso fine upheld. On June 10, 1800, the court ordered Manuel to pay her two hundred pesos and for Melchora to be ignominiously taken, under guard, to her parents in Cochabamba. She successfully appealed being sent home as a prisoner, arguing that it was "too indecorous and injurious to my honor." She also obtained an extension of two months to recover from "a very dangerous flow of blood," which suggested that she had indeed been pregnant a second time and miscarried.[27] Like many women, she had been seduced, exploited, incarcerated, and humiliated and had lost her child, hopes, and innocence in the process. Unlike many women, she challenged the odds, and a very powerful man, in court, seeking not only child support but her lost honor. For his part, Manuel would continue to serve as the alguacil for the remainder of the colonial period and was politically active in the early republic.[28]

Colonial Concubines

The widespread nature of illicit affairs raises the question of why some people were prosecuted for it and others not.[29] It appears that simply having, or even living openly with, a lover was generally not a cause for civil or religious action. Rather, it was usually the result of a complaint from an offended spouse, some other transgression, or a political, economic, or personal rivalry that precipitated action. Indeed, prosecutions for "living in sin" appear to have been more frequently the result of vendettas than of efforts to uphold social mores. When enforcement occurred, a local magistrate would usually arrest the lovers during night rounds.[30]

Sometimes, however, night rounds were not necessary and clergy took the lead despite their lack of formal authority in cases of concubinage. Such was the case in the town of Santiago de Huancané, in Paucarcolla Province. On March 5, 1770, at around 9:00 a.m., Lorenzo Farfán de los Godos was at home with his mistress Hermenegilda, an Indian or mestiza from Puno. They had been living openly together for at least a year, as Lorenzo worked as a tribute collector for his relative, Corregidor Cipriano de Oblitas. That morning, however, was different, as suddenly the village priest, who was a man named Francisco Chávez, the two alcaldes, and four Spaniards burst into his house. Startled and outraged, Lorenzo listened as Father Chávez began to loudly read an order from the bishop of La Paz, Gregorio Francisco de Campos, that had directed him to gather evidence concerning Lorenzo's "execrable" concubinage and the "well known scandal and pernicious example" that it set.[31] The bishop further instructed Father Chávez to place the woman in depósito and excommunicate Lorenzo if he refused to leave town. As Father Chávez read the bishop's order, Lorenzo angrily and abruptly cut him off. Despite the compromising circumstances, he insisted that Hermenegilda was not his lover but rather his servant. He also claimed, correctly, that issues of this nature were subject only to civil jurisdiction.[32]

The threat of excommunication apparently did give Lorenzo pause, as he indicated that he would soon be departing to the town of Vilque to continue his tribute collection. Underscoring Father Chávez's urgency in running Lorenzo out of town, the clergyman ignored the requirement that subsequent notifications be made on different days, something Lorenzo was quick to point out. Instead, he issued a second notification on the same day, and the third and final one two days later. By this time, however, he was having a hard time finding witnesses to accompany him. Later testimony would suggest that Father Chávez had pressured witnesses to testify and altered their statements to make them more incriminating, and at least one witness demanded that his be fully retracted.[33]

Meanwhile, Lorenzo was planning a spirited response. After his third notification, on March 7, 1770, he and four witnesses went to Father Chávez's house around 8:00 p.m. There he read a letter he had prepared, in which he asserted that he was a cavalry officer, and hence subject to the military fuero, and demanded an official copy of the bishop's order so that he could respond to it "in defense of my honor."[34]

Despite this, Lorenzo was almost immediately excommunicated, and, as required, Father Chávez had the notice nailed to the church door. The next day, Lorenzo and twelve supporters gathered on the plaza, read the excommunication order, and again marched to the priest's home, where they intended to present a second letter. The cleric, however, refused to receive them on the grounds that not only was Lorenzo now an excommunicate but also that he had implicitly threatened the priest by arriving in the company of armed men.[35]

By March 22, Lorenzo had gone to La Paz to try to resolve the conflict, demanding that both the bishop and priest be removed from the case, as it was subject only to civil jurisdiction. Lorenzo averred that the cause of the matter was that Father Chávez was jealous of Lorenzo's ambiguous link with the priest's mistress, a woman nicknamed "Angel Mouth Micaela."[36] Bishop Campos remitted the original documents to the audiencia in La Plata. In the process he asserted that Lorenzo "in some way confessed to it," as he admitted that Hermenegilda was his cook and washerwoman and "by these names . . . are known in these parts . . . concubines."[37] By May 1770, despite the legal strength of his case, Lorenzo's hopes of greater sympathy from civil authorities were dashed when the audiencia upheld the bishop's authority on the matter and ordered civil authorities to assist the prelate in enforcing his orders.[38] The fact that the decision was contrary to the law underscores the wide latitude the audiencia enjoyed in issuing rulings. The decision is all the more surprising given that civil and ecclesiastical authorities generally jealously guarded their respective fueros, although in this case the audiencia did not challenge the bishop's intrusion into their realm of authority. It is also possible that there was another dimension to this case that resulted in Lorenzo essentially being abandoned by the audiencia. Nevertheless, this case highlights the tendency for mistresses to be of lower social, economic, and ethnic standing than their lovers and the opportunities domestic service provided as a cover for such relationships.

While Father Chávez's mistress appears to have been at the root of his discord with Lorenzo, prosecutions for concubinage more commonly reflected personal conflicts involving civil officials. One such case, between a merchant and an alcalde in Asunción, in present-day Paraguay, erupted into a larger political dispute involving the regional governor and ultimately the audiencia. In 1780, the prosperous trader Miguel Caldevilla had been having an illicit relationship with a young woman of lesser social standing named Micaela. Informed of the relationship, the alcalde José Antonio Zabala y Delgadillo gathered testimony that indicated that Miguel was regularly seen entering and leaving her residence through different routes, both day and night. One witness, who lived in the room next door, related how Micaela's other lovers were a source of friction for the couple. On one occasion, Miguel was seen beating Micaela in the street before the two went inside the home. Other witnesses noted that she went about the city unaccompanied, and thus at the expense of her honor, while another asserted that despite her work ironing clothes, "from one day to the next she went from being barefoot to wearing shoes, and such finery cannot be had, in my opinion, through any kind of personal labor."[39] In August the alcalde summoned the lovers as well as Micaela's stepmother, who had knowledge of the affair, warning the women to lead honorable lives. Addressing Miguel with "wisdom and love," he also prohibited him from visiting their house.[40]

Despite the admonition, by late October Miguel and Micaela had resumed their liaison, and Alcalde Zabala decided to take stronger action. In the company of a cavalry detachment along with foot soldiers and slaves, they surrounded the house one afternoon as the three o'clock bells rang. Using his staff of office, the alcalde hammered on the door of the shop that occupied the front of the home, prompting a disrespectful reply from Miguel. As the alcalde continued to demand that he open the door, one of his slaves saw Micaela and a *mulata*, or a woman of both African and European descent, running toward a concealed door in the corral, which the slaves had already locked from the outside. Meanwhile, the alcalde ordered his men to break down the front door and entered the shop. Finding no one inside, he then tried to open the door that led to the rest of the house. It was, however, blocked, as someone had placed hay and a horse behind it to impede their entry. Forcing his way past, the alcalde inspected the other rooms while Miguel helped a panic-stricken Micaela over the corral wall.[41]

Although Micaela had escaped and Miguel was not arrested, Alcalde Zabala did detain Miguel's cook, María Petrona Franco. As he was interrogating her concerning Micaela's whereabouts and she was relating how she would serve the couple in bed, an enraged Miguel appealed to the governor of Paraguay, Pedro Melo de Portugal. He complained that the alcalde's actions had been "with great damage to my reputation" and claimed that Zabala had broken down the door before he could get dressed after his siesta. Fearing what his cook might reveal, he also demanded that they release her immediately "without touching a hair."[42] The governor ordered the alcalde to send him the documents concerning the case and later refused to return them, intending to retain them until the New Year, the end of the alcalde's term.[43]

What had begun as a conflict between a merchant and an alcalde had now become a jurisdictional issue between the alcalde and the governor. In late November 1780, with his term of office about to end, Alcalde Zabala presented a letter to Governor Melo, complaining that he was obstructing the case and threatening to take the issue to the audiencia. Although Governor Melo returned the case file, he also fined the alcalde two hundred pesos for disrespect and fined the scribe twenty-five pesos for consenting to write the letter. Less than two weeks before their terms were to end, both the first and second alcaldes ordered Miguel's arrest and the seizure of his property. Miguel again appealed to the governor, arguing that the first alcalde had no jurisdiction in the matter, and the most severe punishment, if he were guilty, would be a fine of one pound of silver.[44]

Governor Melo interceded at this point and had the warrant rescinded. He noted the notorious enmity between the merchant and alcalde and impugned the testimony that the latter had gathered.[45] Further, he acknowledged that Miguel was a well-established and respected merchant, while Alcalde Zabala was known for his "imprudence and violent nature" and habit of accusing or harassing other people in the city.[46] The jurisdictional issue was taken up by the audiencia of La Plata, which in June 1781 accepted the alcalde's argument that a governor could not intervene in a case until the alcalde had issued a ruling. They further agreed that he had not been disrespectful toward the governor and overturned the fine. Despite Governor Melo's appeal and obstruction in the return of the partially paid fine, the audiencia upheld their original decision in February 1782. While their decision put the case to rest, it had been at the cost of Miguel's time and honor. It also demonstrated how political authorities could utilize morality as a weapon, laying bare the local personal, political, and jurisdictional rivalries in the city.[47]

Like Miguel Caldevilla and Micaela, José Galleguillos and Catalina Vera also found that political protection for illicit relationships could only go so far, even when it was enhanced by god-parental linkages. In a concession to social convention, they maintained separate but adjoining residences during their many years of informal union in the highland silver-mining city of Oruro. A secret door connected the homes of these ostensible neighbors, permitting both a largely normal family life within their walls and a ready escape in the event of a raid during the ronda. Despite separate residences, they received visitors together and "all of the town" knew of the relationship, and of the four-year-old daughter it produced. Indeed, the child's godfather was the couple's close friend, and alcalde, Melchor Rodríguez. For unclear reasons, in 1755 Corregidor Miguel de Landaeta determined to put an end to the relationship, targeting Catalina as opposed to José. After his admonition to end the relationship went unheeded, the corregidor decided to arrest her. While leading night rounds in mid-September 1756, he went to her house but she was not there. He decided not to search for her in José's house "to avoid scandal" and instead stationed a sentinel nearby. When the lookout reported that she and her daughter had returned to their house, the corregidor arrested her and prepared to place her in recogimiento in Cochabamba.[48]

Alcalde Rodríguez interceded at this point and persuaded the corregidor to instead remand her to depósito in the home of the silversmith Igancio Coca. Ignacio was also related to José through god-parentage, and his house was adjacent to Catalina's. At daybreak four days later, José helped her escape, and the two disappeared. Suspecting that the alcalde was behind their getaway, the corregidor ordered him to apprehend her or be liable for the four-thousand-peso bond he had posted. There is no record of their subsequent capture, and at this point even the corregidor was uncertain how to proceed. Seeking to avoid a spiraling conflict with the alcalde, he forwarded the case to the viceroy for guidance.[49] While god-parental relationships offered the couple a degree of political protection, it is interesting to note that by maintaining the fictitious façade of separate homes they were able to bridge illicit intimacy and social acceptance.

That is also what Francisco Zea and his young lover María Viviana de Tapia achieved by living together as father and daughter. Around mid-1757, María had been seduced by Francisco, first by promises of marriage, and then in deed, when she surrendered her "virginal jewel."[50] The two soon journeyed to Oruro, where after Francisco introduced himself as a vintner from Arequipa, Peru, and María as his daughter, they began to live together. Facilitating the fiction, María called him father in public, and the two soon found acceptance among the city's elite. Two years later, they relocated to the nearby town of Antequera, where Zea fell ill, and in a deathbed confession admitted that he was already married. As a result of the affair, Oruro's new corregidor, Bernardo Ruiz de Tagle, ordered that María be placed in depósito "under lock and key and . . . [deprived] of all communication" pending her return to her parents.[51] After four weeks of captivity, she was released to her brother, Manuel de Tapia. Not long thereafter, the corregidor learned that she was living with another man, Joseph Rodríguez. Despite briefly being placed in depósito two more times, she continued the relationship, which ultimately resulted in the arrest of her new lover and her escape to La Plata.[52]

These and numerous similar cases in the region highlight several trends. One is the class difference between the men and their lovers, the latter of whom tended to be younger and of considerably lower social, economic, and ethnic standing. A female lover could be readily integrated into the home as a domestic servant, providing sufficient cover to avoid inquiry, if not suspicion. Women also suffered physical abuse by their paramours, who often believed that they were seeing other men. Others found more creative means to maintain both an illicit relationship and the appearance of probity, such as by living in adjoining homes or posing as father and daughter. Finally, despite their power, for many men personal honor was their Achilles' heel. Political and economic strength did not always carry over to the realm of morality, and an attack on their honor had not only social costs but financial ones as well.

Spurned Spouses

Concubinage and marital infidelity often overlapped.[53] Male adultery was not illegal under civil law unless it was with a married woman or household servants, or if it was a public liaison. Barring these conditions, a wife could accuse her husband of adultery only in ecclesiastical court, and in theory had to be represented by a male relative. Underscoring the differential treatment of women is the fact that if a husband caught his wife in the act of adultery, he could legally kill her and her lover on the spot, but not vice versa. Similarly, while a widower was legally free to have a lover, in practice a widow suspected of an illicit relationship could be placed in reclusion and if found guilty was subject to property seizure and the loss of custody of her children.[54]

Night rounds led to the exposure of many extramarital relationships, such as in Potosí on January 8, 1763, when Alcalde Juan Bernardo Inda was leading the ronda, "attending . . . to the many insults that, under cover of night, are committed in this town."[55] At around 8:30 p.m. he encountered Pedro Arrambide and an unnamed married woman huddled in the darkness of a doorway. Inda had learned of the affair from his predecessor, who had warned Pedro to break off the relationship after the woman's socially prominent husband had complained. Encountering the lovers in the darkness and seeking to avoid gossip that would bring further dishonor to the husband, the alcalde ordered his assistants and servants away and proceeded toward the couple with only his scribe to record the events. He then confronted them, ordering the woman to go home and telling Pedro to cease the relationship, move to a difference residence within three days, and not go within four blocks of his lover's house. He also chastised him for taking a risk, saying that "an unfortunate event" could happen if the husband had found them instead.[56] Given that Pedro had been warned by the previous alcalde, Alcalde Inda decided to take testimony on the case from his predecessor under an oath of secrecy, again to protect the reputation of the husband.[57]

The next month, Pedro not only had refused to move to a different house but was also seeing the woman "with greater frequency."[58] When Alcalde Inda warned her to "watch out for your honor and cease offending God," she responded, crying, that "she would follow him even to Hell."[59] The prosecutor noted that in such cases, the punishment for the man for a first offense was a fine of eight ounces of silver and a year of exile, and for the second offense sixteen ounces of silver and two years of exile. As Pedro had been warned by the previous alcalde, the prosecutor viewed it as a second offense and called for the corresponding punishment. To ensure their decision would not be reversed on appeal, the alcalde also consulted with the audiencia in La Plata. The prosecutor there agreed with the suggested punishment, adding that Pedro's property should be seized and urging that his confession be taken in secret to avoid "worse scandals and . . . other pernicious consequences . . . that afterwards cannot be remedied."[60] On February 25, 1763, authorities seized Pedro's goods, fined him, and exiled him to beyond a twenty-five-league radius from Potosí, with the sentence to begin within three days irrespective of whether he appealed. While this was an unusually severe punishment, Pedro had brought it upon himself. The punishment appears to reflect the fact that Pedro ignored the warnings as well as the fact that the affair was overt and involved the wife of a powerful man, and it was also likely compounded by his conflicts with the alcaldes.[61]

While Pedro's indiscretion exposed his affair, love letters often did the same, as Isidro Villanueva found to his chagrin in La Plata in 1794. Lorenzo Coronado had accused him of having an affair with his wife, Lorenza Guarayo, which prompted the counter-accusation from Isidro that Lorenzo was having an affair with his wife, Estefa Guardia. Tensions had been brewing for some time and came to a head one September evening just after sunset when Lorenzo was walking home. On the way, he encountered Isidro and his friends under the arcade of the main plaza. Insults soon gave way to a scuffle, in which Isidro's family soon joined. Isidro's accusation appeared to have merit, as his wife called out in defense of Lorenzo. A crowd quickly gathered before the fight was broken up by a passing Spaniard, leaving Lorenzo lying on the ground with cuts to his face and having lost his hat, handkerchief, and money. He then filed a complaint with the alcalde, who ordered Isidro jailed.[62] The balance further shifted to Lorenzo's side when he produced a letter from Isidro to Lorenza that he had intercepted. The letter, which had been tightly folded many times, perhaps so that it could be smuggled or thrown, read:

> My dearest sweetheart Lorenzita:
>
> I know not how to prove the affection I have for you, my dearest life, since you are all I long for and that which gives satisfaction to my feelings . . . the one for whom I am passionate. I find no satisfaction by day or night as I ponder your beauty. What kind of heart could see and not feel, never finding even a minimum of consolation or relief? And so this sorrow that accompanies me is the reason that I find myself wandering the streets at all hours of the night, if only to find some relief, some consolation. But my luck is so bad that even if we were to meet we cannot be together. So, love of my life, I

> can only tell you again of my feelings for you and the hope that some evening you might give me the pleasure of going with me to walk at the Recoleta. . . . But if you truly care for me, what else can I do but lament my solitude and ill fortune in the company of the beasts and birds of the countryside, lamenting the loss of my lady, with whom I was so happy? I will hush the sorrow and pain within my heart and all ill fortune will cease. I beg you to reply to this bothersome note, and that which goes with it between the lines, so do not disappoint me about our meeting. I will do everything possible to wait for you outside my door, even though I know it is unseemly. I am ever your servant,
>
> *Isidro de Villanueva*
>
> Fly, fly little paper on the wings of confusion, and pluck an answer from your very heart.[63]

As with many such cases, this one comes to an abrupt and unclear end. By mid-December 1794 Isidro was still in jail, though his wife had petitioned for his release.[64]

While love letters could expose illicit relationships, so could an illness, as the mestizo Innocencio Rojas learned. A peon on a hacienda, Innocencio had been in a relationship for three years with María Inojosa before they both contracted leprosy, thus revealing their affair. Seeking to avoid punishment for concubinage, Innocencio persuaded Bernardina Céspedes to marry him in 1811, although the affair with María continued. For the next two years, Bernardina was in essence their domestic servant before she could tolerate it no more. In filing suit against him for abuse, she explained that the lovers "lay about in bed continually and without respite, being served in bed rapidly and attentively . . . while I was stuck with the task of spinning, making *chicha* [a fermented corn drink] and tending the cattle and other animals, at their beck and call . . . all of which I . . . swear under penalty of the whip."[65]

Bernardina was especially fearful of Innocencio's temper, as she claimed that he had beaten two previous lovers to death. On the basis of her accusation, the magistrate arrested Innocencio and María. Bernardina's claims of servitude were substantiated when one of those who arrested the lovers testified that upon arriving at their house, Innocencio was in bed, María was sitting by his side, and his wife was preparing lunch outside. In his confession, although Innocencio denied the accusations of murder, he admitted to the long-standing affair, adding that his wife served them "with much humility."[66] María initially denied the illicit relationship, but when confronted with Innocencio's confession, she insisted that the affair had ended when he married Bernardina. After two weeks in jail, Bernardina petitioned unsuccessfully for her husband to be released but called for María to be perpetually banished for the "horrendous crime of adultery."[67] Ultimately, after she endured five months of confinement, the magistrate exiled María to beyond twenty-five leagues from town and released Innocencio to his wife, his leprosy having advanced to the point where he did not have "a piece of healthy skin."[68]

Like Innocencio, the silversmith Ildefonso Argandoña also found himself behind bars as a result of accusations of infidelity by his wife, Antonia Rojas. In 1795, she accused him of having an affair with a widowed mulata named María in the town of Mizque. She claimed not only that the two had been seen drinking and walking together on the street but also that María sent him food. At her request, the alcalde had Ildefonso arrested while Antonia gathered witnesses. The witnesses testified that while they had seen the two spending time and drinking together, which was highly suggestive of a relationship, none had actually seen any other evidence of an affair. A woman who was María's neighbor testified that she was awakened one day by Antonia's banging on María's door, screaming for her husband to come out, resulting in the witness suffering "a strong headache."[69] Behind bars, Ildefonso characterized his wife as such an extremely jealous and violent woman that no one wanted to come to their house out of fear of her rage. He went on to relate how on one occasion she physically attacked his apprentice, who happened to be María's, and perhaps his own, son. After about a week in jail, Antonia petitioned to have him released so that he could resume working, but only on the conditions that he not see María and that he move his workshop to the same street as their house, presumably to keep a closer eye on him. The alcalde admonished María but had some degree of sympathy for Ildefonso's challenges, as he read him the order releasing him from jail "lovingly."[70]

These cases underscore three tendencies. One concerns the spectrum of discretion and its relation to public versus private space. While in all cases the affairs were uncovered, those that occurred in public spaces, such as the streets, plazas, and dark doorways, appear more likely to be punished than those conducted within the home, because they openly defied social mores. Even if an affair was conducted discreetly, exposure could occur as a result of "physical" evidence, such as love letters, pregnancy, and even a contagious illness. Finally, a wife's complaint could land her husband in jail, giving her leverage in extracting concessions, fleeting though they often were, and demonstrating her ability to use the judicial system to her advantage.

Despite the higher moral expectations and generally harsher punishment of women than men, cases of female infidelity abound.[71] Beyond the opportunities presented by long-absent husbands, it also reflects the greater likelihood that a man would take legal action when faced with a cheating wife in order to defend his honor. If a husband could produce witnesses to demonstrate that his wife had been seen with a man three times after he had forbidden contact, adultery was considered proven. As we have seen above, illicit relationships were also inferred by such things as the exchange of suggestive looks, conversations, walking or spending time alone together, and the sending of food.[72]

Such illicit relationships often resulted in lovers becoming fugitives, as was the case with Micaela Vargas and her mestizo lover, Andrés Ontiveros, in Mizque. They were both married to others, and their year-long relationship had produced a child. Things became even more complicated for them in 1769 when Andrés was accused of the theft of livestock and became a wanted man. The couple fled together, along with their child and two children that Micaela had with her husband. They found refuge in a very isolated, rustic house before they were betrayed by its owner, who perhaps feared he would be considered an accomplice. Soon, the lovers were apprehended by the husband, Sebastián Ferel, and the owner of the stolen livestock and marched as prisoners to Mizque.[73]

Sebastián requested that the alcalde place his wife in recogimiento, as he was certain that she would run off with Andrés again if given the chance. Andrés confessed to the relationship, acknowledged their child, and accepted responsibility for some of the stolen livestock.[74] In an initial sentence, which was apparently not carried out, the alcalde declared that in view of

> such an infamous crime I . . . order that said Micaela and said Andres Ontiveros be given fifty lashes, the woman thirty by the hand of her husband, so that they may serve as a deterrent and example to others, so that they may live in the holy fear of God our Lord, and in respect for Royal Justice. And the woman shall be remanded to the custody of the home of General Dionisio de Arancibia, in order that he keep her under strict custody, while said Ontiveros is to remain in the public jail of this city, in order that the plaintiff may be able to subpoena him if he so chooses.[75]

This did not satisfy Sebastián, who argued that the sentence was equivalent to pardoning the crime. Instead, he called for an exemplary punishment that would better serve as a warning for the entire community, in which, he asserted, such crimes were common. Instead of a lashing, he called for Andrés to be sent as a prisoner to an *obraje*, or textile mill, where in addition to purging himself of his scandalous crime, he would "settle down and temper the excessive love that he has professed for . . . my wife, with whom I still wish to bind myself in a virtuous life."[76] Barring this, he feared that he might kill both Andrés and his wife, or that they would try to kill him. Perhaps at the urging of his priest, he requested that his wife be returned to him once she had completed whatever sentence the alcalde ordered. In the end, Micaela was sent back to her husband and Andrés was sentenced to work as a prisoner for six months in a vineyard, although this was not immediately carried out as he still faced sentencing on the rustling charge.[77] This case shares many of the outlines of other cases concerning a wife's infidelity: the woman was placed in recogimiento, clergy urged reconciliation, and the husband negotiated a solution with his rival that included banishment that was largely accepted by the court.

United We Fall

The frequency of marriages to promote economic and familial interests, combined with the often insurmountable obstacles to divorce, created an environment that was conducive to infidelity and concubinage for both men and women. It also led to the continuation of many preexisting affective relationships outside of marriage. Simply put, some couples were inseparable.[78]

Among them were Roque Hurtado and Petrona Leaños, with whose story this book begins. Petrona's husband, Simón, was not alone in his inability to end his wife's romantic relationship. In 1760, Xavier Durán, like Simón, was unable to stop the open relationship that his wife, Eusebia Córdoba, was having with another man, Juan Bautista. Xavier claimed, and witnesses substantiated, that no sooner would he leave his home than Juan would arrive to "freely use [his] wife."[79] Juan's only occupation seemed to be staking out the house, a ceaseless task in which he was assisted by his lover, who would send him food and blankets, as he was living outdoors. On one occasion, Xavier entered his house, finding Juan "next to my wife," but Juan escaped after a scuffle.[80] On another occasion, he was almost caught just outside of Xavier's house during night rounds, but he was alerted by the barking of dogs and yet again escaped. On a third occasion, two of Xavier's brothers captured and brought Juan to jail, from which he also escaped. Even Eusebia's brother testified against her, revealing that Juan had secretly tagged along during a trip she and Xavier made to Cochabamba, sustained by the food Eusebia sent him. Once there, his furtive visits continued when Xavier would leave the building, although Juan was surprised on one occasion by Eusebia's brother, who found his sister was "braiding his hair, feeding him," and providing "other evident signs" of their amorous relationship.[81] On this basis, an arrest warrant was issued for Juan, although there is no indication he was apprehended or that the relationship ended.

Also like Roque and Petrona, Antonio Villagómez and Josefa Rosas demonstrated that they were willing to pay a high price to be together when they were caught, again, in the act of adultery and arrested in Oruro in April 1778. On the previous occasion, Josefa had been arrested, but she escaped from jail with Antonio's help and the two fled to La Plata. Their time there together was brief, however, as Antonio was apprehended and forced to return to his wife, María Dominga Villafañe. Nevertheless, he and Josefa soon resumed their affair, which led to the April arrest. More enraged than chastened, and speaking to his wife through the bars of his cell, Antonio "threatened to finish her off at knife point, saying she was not really his wife, and that above all he would free his lover from the prison in which she was confined, and that in the face of everyone he would take her as he pleased."[82] Despite this, he managed to convince her to sign a document stating that they were "united and in good harmony" so that he would be released from jail. No sooner was he released than he went to La Plata in search of Josefa, and María called for his rearrest and the return of her property that he had dissipated.[83]

Some relationships began before, and continued after, people were married, such as that between Joaquín Buitrago and Francisca Torres in Cinti. In August 1806, Joaquín's wife, Josefa Calvimontes, filed a complaint with the *subdelegado*, or lieutenant governor and magistrate, Gregorio Barrón, who ordered that Francisca depart in three days to the audiencia in La Plata to face charges of concubinage. When she refused, the *alcalde pedaneo*, or rural magistrate, Domingo Morales, apprehended and dispatched her there as a prisoner, although she escaped in Potosí. In November, Josefa filed a new complaint, and the audiencia ordered a secret investigation and that Francisca be placed in depósito. Testimony confirmed not only that Joaquín spent considerable time in her home but also that the two attended a Christmas party together "as if she was his wife," causing an "unspeakable" scandal that left "people astonished."[84] The alleged outrage apparently did not extend to the alcalde pedaneo, Morales. The couple had visited his house over the holiday, presenting the unusual circumstance in which a fugitive was hosted by her erstwhile captor.

After a week in depósito, Francisca unsuccessfully petitioned to be released on bail, admitting that two of her four children were Joaquín's. Seeking to maintain her honor, she insisted that they were conceived when she and Joaquín were supposedly engaged. Despite her protestations, she was again dispatched to La Plata and ordered into reclusion. Once there, she complained that much of the testimony against her was by Francisca's servants. Because she had four children to care for and no support, she was allowed to leave recogimiento but ordered not to leave La Plata.[85] As was so common, the husband never testified nor was punished, and despite the fact that the relationship was common knowledge in the area, local authorities appeared reluctant to act.

Neither wealth nor liberty was necessary for inseparability, as such couples were also found among Indians and slaves. For example, in 1808 the Indian Andrés Guaca was in a long-standing affair with his wife's cousin and neighbor, Manuela Callisaya. Although his wife, Narcisa Mamami, had caught them in flagrante four times, no one—not the alcalde pedaneo, nor the subdelegado, nor the lieutenant priest, who had given them a "severe lashing"—had been able to separate them.[86] Similarly, in La Plata in February 1780 the slave Antonio Merino filed a suit against another slave, Manuel Valenzuela, over the nine-month relationship he had with his wife, Apolinaria Caraballo. Antonio lamented that they had conducted the affair "with so much effrontery, abandon and insolence that he has not had one day of peace due to their excesses."[87] Not only would the lovers spend days on end together, but even when she was with Antonio, Apolinaria would prepare food and send it to Manuel while refusing to cook for her husband.[88]

Antonio's situation was all the more complicated, as Manuel had a fearful reputation for violence. On one occasion, an altercation erupted between them, which resulted in Antonio fleeing down La Plata's streets to the home of the vicar-general with Manuel at his heels shouting that he was going to "gut" him and ultimately trying to stab him.[89] On another occasion, Manuel broke into Antonio's house, and, not finding his quarry, robbed it instead. Antonio was represented by the attorney for the indigent, who reminded the court that Manuel's threats were to be taken seriously. The previous year he had even attacked an alcalde, who was forced to flee out of a window of the city hall. While on that occasion his owner sent him out of town until the end of the alcalde's term, it does not appear that he was punished for the affair. Apolinaria, however, was ordered to live indefinitely at the Santa Clara convent, where she was to be at the "service" of the nuns.[90] Interestingly, neither owner of the slaves was involved, at least overtly, in the case.

Relationships such as these underscore the tragic challenges individuals faced who simply wanted to share their lives with someone they loved. Marriage as a means of social or economic advancement often left love by the wayside. This only set the stage for wrenching decisions: to follow the heart or social norms. With divorce essentially not an option, people from all walks of life led emotionally unfulfilled lives and accepted unhappy and often abusive marriages. Others defied social and religious convention, and were willing to pay the price, to be with those with whom they felt they belonged.

Excesses and Exile

Banishment was a common method of separating lovers or otherwise removing individuals of ill repute from a region. The term could be perpetual but was generally for a period of years and applied to a radius of a certain number of leagues.[91] As we have seen with the case of Roque Hurtado, it could prove to be a temporary, and largely ineffective, remedy. Despite this, it was a punishment meted out to both men and women whose independence and resistance were a challenge to colonial authority.

One such woman was Paula Sandóval, who in 1767 had been living apart from her husband for the past seven years in Potosí after he had been sent as a royal official to Chile. During this time, she had begun an affair with an unnamed priest, who was consequently obligated by his superiors to leave the city for some time. Upon the cleric's return, Paula did not hide her affection, going so far as to make suggestive comments to him in the company of other clergy and a prelate. This put the governor of Potosí, Jaime San Just, in a bind. While he wanted Paula to leave the city to avoid more scandal, he was, at least initially, reluctant to formalize charges against her that would further dishonor her husband. Seeking a quiet resolution, in late June he sent a scribe to her home, ordering her to depart to her hometown of La Plata within twenty-four hours without "reply [or] excuse."[92] Governor San Just did not conceal his view that the cleric with whom she had an affair was the innocent victim of Paula's "insolent rudeness and sacrilegious audacity."[93]

Paula ignored the order to leave the city, and when Governor San Just encountered her in a private home, he again demanded that she leave, offering to assist her with mules and money for the trip. She initially acceded to his request, yet the agreed-upon day for her departure came and went before she informed the governor that she would only leave under formal judicial order. In July, Governor San Just consulted with the audiencia in La Plata, urging, whatever they decided, that she be banished from Potosí, otherwise "the consequences cannot easily be remedied."[94]

In July or August, Paula finally departed to La Plata, where she took up residence in a private home. Soon after her arrival, a scribe transmitted a secret judicial order preventing her from leaving the city and ordering her to live "with all the modesty, honesty and withdrawal appropriate to her condition and the absence of her husband."[95] She ignored this order as well and soon began a relationship with Juan Antonio Castro, who was married to Manuela Porzel. As a result, on August 22, she was arrested and placed in the Convent of the Virgin of Los Remedios. She complained that her arrest was without "orders, cause, process or justification" and that the "honor of her status" had been tarnished, and she sought to defend herself because "otherwise her life will be at well known risk if (as is quite natural) this event comes to the attention of her husband."[96] She denied that Manuela had caught her and Juan in bed together, insisting that she had been "at mass, as always," and complained of Manuela insulting her and making a scene at her door.[97] The documents do not reveal what happened next, as the audiencia ordered that the file be placed in the secret archive and declared it would issue a ruling "in time," although no record of it has been found.[98]

Like Paula Sandóval, the sisters Antonia and Jacinta Barriga were independent, if disreputable, women. The governor of La Paz, Sebastián de Segurola, sought to put an end to their "scandalous life" in 1788 and placed them in depósito. Although both were accused of maintaining illicit relationships, the precipitating event appears to have been Antonia's liaison with an unnamed man "of honor and distinction" whose wife had left him as a result of the affair.[99] Governor Segurola agreed to release the sisters under bond and the promise that they return to their hometown of La Plata. Although they were seen leaving on the road there in early November, they only went so far as Oruro, where Antonia reunited with her lover and claimed she was too ill to continue the journey. As in other cases involving prominent individuals, the male lover's name was never mentioned in the document, if not to protect his reputation, then that of his wife.[100]

In cases of adultery, negotiated settlements involving exile were not unusual.[101] Nor, however, were violations of the accords, as Antonio Martínez learned in 1782. He suspected that his wife, Manuela Carreón, was having an affair with a young tailor's apprentice named Diego Sánchez in La Plata. His suspicions were confirmed one mid-November evening when Manuela asked for his permission to console a neighbor whose baby had recently died. Antonio granted the request but had a servant trail her. Soon he returned to tell Antonio that he had seen Manuela and Diego "hand in hand" in an alleyway. Antonio immediately left to confront them, and although he saw them, they fled before he could catch them.[102]

He petitioned the alcalde to separate the lovers and produced witnesses, all of whom were aware of the relationship but had never told Antonio about it. They concurred that no sooner would Antonio leave than "said woman would usually amuse herself, in all her looseness, with a ridiculous boy named Dieguito, in a small room that is used as a kitchen . . . all of this without the knowledge of the master [tailor], who was devoted to his work, in the belief that his wife was faithful and constant to him . . . but the reverse was true, because neither the witness or the other artisans or renters wished to [tell the husband] . . . due to the delicate nature of the matter."[103] Another resident of the house, Santos Mendieta, testified that he had also caught Diego beating his lover and had repeatedly chastised the woman for the affair. Following this testimony, and only two days after he had seen the couple in the alley, Antonio requested that Diego be jailed and his property seized and called for his wife to be sent to the harsh confines of the Santa Clara convent. The alcalde granted his request, arresting them both and issuing the formal request to the vicar general for Manuela's confinement.[104]

In the coming weeks, two processes appear to have unfolded. As was the norm, clergy urged the husband and wife to reconcile, which apparently they did.[105] Antonio also negotiated with Diego and his family and agreed to Diego's perpetual banishment from La Plata under bond. This was arranged through Diego's mother, who had come from the region of Mizque, promising that he would live in "quietude and calmness." Despite this, after about three months of exile Diego was back in La Plata trying to persuade his erstwhile lover to return to him. As Antonio explained,

> he had been gone scarcely three months when he returned to this city . . . with the odious objective of repeating the . . . abominable crime he committed in . . . November, and shamelessly he proceeded to seduce my wife again, stalking her through every street which she transited. . . . He has had the audacity to hang around my corner . . . at night, with his little guitar. And what is more . . . I am about to commit an act which I could not retract, possessed as I am by the sheer suffering caused by his arrogance in insisting on perverting my wife.[106]

By mid-August 1783, nine months after the affair was exposed, Diego was back in jail, having been captured, whipped, and marched to jail by Antonio. He denied any illicit relationship, asserting that Manuela could be his mother and that she and Antonio were his sworn enemies. Antonio noted that Diego's return to town, and his behavior, had made a mockery of the court's order and called for him to be sent to the mines of Potosí. From behind bars, Diego indicated that he would gladly marry in order to be released, a tactic more frequently used by women to be freed from depósito. He was not, however, sent to the mines of Potosí; after he had spent about nine days in jail the alcalde ordered him released back to exile when and if the bond was paid.[107]

Banishment, like the enforcement of moral codes generally, could also reflect elite rivalries, in the middle of which Petronila Caseres de Ulloa found herself caught in late 1758. In September, Potosí's corregidor had banished her from the city for hosting scandalous parties, and she and her elderly mother withdrew to their hacienda. Her advocate, Sebastián de Malavia, insisted that there was no basis for the order, as people came only to hear her sing. Moreover, he averred that the corregidor had failed to follow proper procedure by neglecting to gather testimony and warn Petronila prior to banishing her.[108]

In responding to the audiencia's inquiry concerning these procedural irregularities, the corregidor's representative explained how

> it is public knowledge, and even notoriously so, that the fandango hosted by Petrona Cáceres . . . was attended by the Count of Casa Real de Moneda, the Treasurer don Antonio Asín, don Manuel Mozo, don Juan Joseph Navarro and by Bartolomé Gil de la Madrid; and that it lasted two days with the sole object of disobeying the orders of said gentleman, don Ventura Santelices, who with great zeal and in the fear of God had banned said fandangos, due to their pernicious nature, since only women inclined toward prostitution attend them. . . . Nothing else is talked of in the city but that these three men, so publicly and with such notoriety, had gotten together in order to challenge the Corregidor [Santelices], which is even more obvious because these same gentlemen frequent this woman's house every afternoon to partake of ice cream and other refreshments, more to defy said gentleman than for any other purpose. It is widely rumored . . . in the city that they are the sworn enemies of said Mister Santelices.[109]

As the statement indicates, some of those in attendance were there more to protest the corregidor's supposed moral zeal and other policies than to hear Petronila's enchanting voice, and it appears that he targeted Petronila because she was the mistress of the Conde de la Moneda, Juan José de Lizarazu y Beaumont de Navarra y Centeno. At the behest of the audiencia, the corregidor reluctantly summoned people to testify, including Joseph Antonio Mendibelzua. He stated that Petronila had had a years-long affair with Manuel de Aballa, from Salta, before he was ordered to live with his wife after getting another woman pregnant around 1753. Petronila had her first experience with banishment around this time, not so much as a result of her affair with Manuel as due to her other lovers, who included Pedro Yribarren, an architect who had been working on the construction of the mint, as well as an unnamed but "honored priest."[110] Despite her banishment in 1753, Petronila returned to the city and later began the affair with the Conde de la Moneda.[111]

By January 1758, Petronila had left her hacienda for La Plata and hired a new attorney, Juan de Cabrera Urrioa. He belittled the accusations, insisting that "it was not a scandal, but rather only amusement" with "distinguished personages," and portrayed her as a pawn in the corregidor's effort to extract vengeance from his political enemies. The audiencia's prosecutor was unconvinced and supported the corregidor's decision because Petronila's "dissolute lifestyle has provoked so much scandal."[112] Her attorney challenged this, and Petronila also prevailed upon the priest of Puno, Francisco de Poso, and an attorney, Carlos Montoya, to testify on her behalf. Montoya affirmed Father Poso's view that the whole issue concerned the enemies of the corregidor and that he had "neither seen nor heard" that she had ever caused scandal in Potosí.[113] Although the prosecutor was far from convinced, the testimony was sufficient to persuade the audiencia to lift the banishment order in February 1758 with the proviso that she abstain from having parties in her house that would give rise to scandalous accusations. Although the corregidor appealed the decision, it appears that it stood.[114]

Despite its apparent severity, exile does not appear to have been an effective means of social control. Its imposition could be delayed by legal challenges, and when imposed it was often only briefly adhered to. At another level, however, it had value, as it provided a face-saving solution that restored the honor of the offended party and could provide a cooling off period to both antagonists and lovers.

Above the Law

Priests and military personnel were subject to the laws of their respective fueros and hence exempt from civil law.[115] This gave them considerable protection when accused of moral, or any other, transgressions and may have discouraged people from reporting them in the first place. Among priests, illicit affairs and concubinage were common, as Viceroy Castelfuerte noted in 1725 when he described how many clerics "have . . . many different women with sons, and families, going to their houses, as a father of a family to his own."[116] Three years later, the bishop of Quito noted that many regular clergy "keep their mistresses and the many children they have," while those sent to investigate such accusations often examined the parish accounts instead.[117]

Writing of their time in what is today Ecuador and Peru between 1735 and 1746, Jorge Juan and Antonio Ulloa noted that both regular and secular clergy "live very licentiously, scandalously, and frivolously" and that a cleric's concubine "causes no surprise in the village. . . . It is not even considered noteworthy."[118] They averred that many concubines lived with their lovers in monasteries, coming and going "without restraint" while other regulars would live in their own homes "acting like married men in every way."[119] They affirmed that the "regular clergy," given their wealth, "have greater advantages in getting the best quality women."[120] Excepting the Jesuits, they asserted that even those who appeared virtuous were not and that "those who make up the main body of the orders are simply not religious men."[121] The children of such unions, known as *sacrilegios*, were often proud of their parentage, sometimes adopting as a nickname their father's position in the religious hierarchy. Such was the scope of the problem, they asserted, that "monasteries have become public brothels . . . [with] vices of a kind that stagger the imagination" and that to describe all the cases they had seen "a large volume would be necessary."[122] Things had not changed by the 1780s, when a civil official in Cuzco accused Bishop Moscoso of having a mistress and observed that "the majority of ecclesiastics in these parts, both secular and regular, maintain public concubines."[123]

Things were no different in Charcas, where some clergy lived openly with their mistresses. In the case of Luis Belsu, the assistant priest of San Miguel de Achila, in Chichas Province, in 1770, it was common knowledge that he lived with his lover, Narcisa, who "governs his house with a temperament well suited for the task."[124] His personal lifestyle was the least of his parishioners' complaints, however, as they accused him of coercing them to participate in, and pay for, various religious festivities, conducting forced marriages, doubling the collection of first fruits, not paying for transport services, kidnapping children to ensure funeral debts were paid, and spitting in the face of at least one prominent parishioner.[125]

The Mercedarian Ramón Rejas not only had a mistress but also a family. In late December 1775, Melchora Mendoza, a single mother, filed a complaint with the vicar general over Father Rejas's affair with her daughter, Sebastiana, which had produced a child. After living in Santa Ana Mataca, in Porco Province, the family briefly lived in Potosí in the home of a fellow priest before moving to Tinquipaya, also in Porco Province, where Father Rejas was sent as an assistant priest. In March 1776, he acknowledged the relationship, although he claimed Sebastiana had disappeared. Despite this, she was ultimately apprehended and sent to Potosí's girls' orphanage. By this time she was pregnant again, and although she was cloistered, Rejas was able to communicate with her. By November 1777, she had been released from recogimiento to give birth to her son and subsequently disappeared, while her mother sought to have Father Rejas banished and made to pay child support.[126]

Such cases suggest that vicars general spent considerable time contending with, and warning, wayward priests and their lovers. This was the case in 1777, when Vicar General Juan de la Cruz Paredes warned Father Miguel Zorruto, assistant priest of Siporo, in Porco Province, concerning his lack of adherence to his vow of celibacy. His admonitions unheeded, Cruz ordered an investigation that revealed that Father Zorutto lived with his mestiza lover, María, their two daughters, and his mother. This was common knowledge in the parish, as the priest and his lover would attend social functions together. This, along with testimony concerning his drinking and neglecting to hold mass or personally conduct burials, resulted in his confinement in the Real Colegio de La Plata, where after initial denials he confessed to the relationship.[127]

The exemption from civil jurisdiction that military personnel also enjoyed made it difficult for civil officials to intervene in illicit relationships, as the Indian Pascual Rodríguez experienced in Cinti. In early 1805, his mestiza wife, María Valdivieso, abandoned him and took up residence in the home of militia captain Pasqual Olivera, ostensibly serving as his cook. Left with their children to support, Rodríguez found work as a peon on a nearby hacienda, where he soon became indebted and bound to the estate. He filed a complaint with the local alcalde pedaneo, Antonio Rosales, seeking to have his wife returned to him. Rosales and an armed escort went to Olivera's home to intervene but were flatly told by him that he was not subject to civil jurisdiction. Not entirely dissuaded, Rosales returned one evening during night rounds and searched the house, yet he did not find María. The next day, an enraged Olivera mustered the soldiers who had participated in the ronda before upbraiding them and "vomiting all of the venom of his resentment against the magistrate, and strutting about the patio with his sword unsheathed."[128]

The subdelegado, Gregorio Barrón, then became involved, not as a civil, but military, official. He ordered the alguacil to search the house again, return María to her husband, jail Olivera, and embargo his goods. Olivera was by now playing a shell game with his mistress, sending her to a hacienda he owned while the alguacil searched his house and bringing her back just before a search party arrived at his hacienda. Finally, the authorities captured her in Olivera's house and briefly imprisoned her before she escaped to La Plata. Subdelegado Barrón requested that authorities there arrest her and send her back to Cinti, where he would judge María under civil jurisdiction and Olivera under military jurisdiction. Meanwhile, Olivera arrived in La Plata seeking an order for the Cinti authorities to desist, insisting that María was his cook and accusing the husband of abusing her and of committing incest.[129] As with many cases, this one appears to have been resolved extrajudicially.

As these cases illustrate, the high rates of illegitimacy in Charcas were a reflection of forced and failed marriages, adulterous affairs, and concubinage. The near-impossibility of divorce, which even if granted prohibited remarriage while the other spouse was alive, also figured in the equation and will be treated separately. Despite the official sanctions against illicit liaisons, they were commonplace, socially accepted, generally known about by those around them, and often based on a couple's genuine affinity. Such relationships frequently endured for years, until a spousal complaint or personal, political, or economic rivalry precipitated action. This often occurred during night rounds and could lead to confinement or banishment. Women generally suffered the greater punishment, often cloistered indefinitely in a religious institution and left without support, while the man could be jailed, usually briefly, and fined. For their part, wives were not powerless and could and did utilize the civil courts to pressure their wayward husbands by having them jailed and essentially holding the key to their release. Despite its apparent severity, banishment was generally a temporary and often ineffective means of ending relationships. Exacerbating the situation was the protection offered to clergy and military men by their respective fueros, which facilitated such relationships by exempting them from civil law. Also contributing to the prevalence of adulterous relationships and abandoned wives was the power, both formal and informal, that a father exercised over the marriage choice of his son or daughter, which is the focus of the next chapter.

CHAPTER 2

The "Owner of Her Will"

Pragmática and Patriarchy

Among the goals of the Bourbon monarchs, especially of Charles III (1759–1788), was the centralization of political power, the erosion of the power and wealth of the Catholic Church, the preservation of social hierarchies through the assertion of morality and patriarchy, and the assertion of law over custom. Regulating marriage was one means of achieving these aims because it transferred power from couples and the church to the father and the state. With roots in Roman and precedent in Spanish law, the Pragmática Sanción of 1776 was a watershed in this regard. It allowed fathers or other guardians in Spain to disinherit minor offspring (those under twenty-five years old) if they opposed their marriage choice on the basis of racial inequality. If the son or daughter believed that the opposition was without merit, he or she could file a civil suit in which the proceedings were to remain secret and the decision could be appealed by either party.[1]

This and subsequent measures conflicted with canon law, which in theory required the free will of both parties for a marriage to be valid. Parental efforts to influence marriage choice, whether through threats or inducements, were contrary to this doctrine, and a priest could separate potential spouses from their parents to determine whether the proposed union was voluntary. The fact that parents could engage their children when they were seven years old and marry them at twelve underscores the fact that the doctrine of free will had long been compromised. Earlier, under the Siete Partidas (1251), a man and woman could become engaged, have intercourse, cohabitate, and later marry themselves, all without the intervention of a parent or priest. Although the Council of Trent (1545–1563) mandated a wedding ceremony officiated by a priest, it did not require parental permission. The Pragmática of 1776 changed this, and in essence it formalized coercion in marriage choice in Spain. While the church favored a marriage between social or racial unequals over concubinage, the crown sought to restrict marriage to social equals, even if concubinage or illegitimate births were the result.[2]

While the Pragmática of 1776 concerned racial inequality, and especially whether someone was of African descent, in application it often subsumed issues of social status, birth, and public reputation. As a result, parents often sought to prove that a suitor was of illegitimate birth, and they would bundle accusations of inequality in terms of origins, status, and moral rectitude. Beyond seeking to maintain the integrity of social hierarchy and affirm regal and patriarchal power, there were more mundane reasons why Charles III issued the 1776 Pragmática. The decision of his younger brother, Luís Antonio de Bourbón, to marry a person of lower social standing had implications for the Bourbon bloodline and hence royal honor.[3]

In 1778, the law was modified and extended to the Americas. However, the lack of a clear definition as to what constituted "unequal," combined with widespread racial heterogeneity and often distant parents, made its application problematic and more subject to interpretation. Spaniards legally in the Americas whose parents were back home, and others who could not easily solicit parental approval, could obtain permission to marry from a local judge and appeal to the audiencia it they disagreed with his ruling. In cases of parental opposition, the alcalde served as the magistrate in the first instance. He was to gather testimony and render a decision within one month, although cases could drag on for much longer. Seeking to maintain the focus on white marriages, the Pragmática exempted blacks, mulatos, and mestizos while requiring Indians of questionable parentage to obtain the permission of their parish priest.[4]

In 1783, three edicts further enhanced a father's power over his offspring's marriage choice in the Americas. One, on May 26, decreed that if a court upheld a father's opposition to a marriage, his decision to disinherit his son or daughter was total and extended to his wife's property as well. Five days later, the crown extended to the Americas the law requiring adults to seek the counsel of their fathers or guardians, or a court's favorable decision, prior to the issuance of a marriage license.[5] A third edict of 1783 affected the military fuero by decreeing that if the father of a soldier opposed his marriage, the case was to be handled in civil, as opposed to military, court. Rank and file soldiers separated by great distance from their fathers were required to obtain the permission of their commanding officers in place of their fathers, while officers could not marry without both parental and royal approval.[6]

In 1787, Charles III yet again tightened marriage laws by prohibiting priests from conducting marriages of racially distinct people, even if they accepted disinheritance, thereby making the parental veto almost absolute. There was a loophole, however, that allowed a clergyman to override parental objection if a parishioner, for reasons of conscience, sought to marry a woman after having sex with her. In addition, civil courts gained jurisdiction over cases of broken engagements that had been made without parental consent.[7]

On June 1, 1803, Charles IV (1788–1808) mandated parental consent for all women under twenty-three years old, and for all men under twenty-five, irrespective of their race. Worse for those minors seeking to marry, fathers and guardians were no longer required to offer a rationale for their opposition. This effectively ended the ability of minor offspring to challenge parental decisions, although if they chose to do so the audiencia now had exclusive jurisdiction. The only bright spot for those who had reached majority was that they no longer had to seek the counsel of their fathers or guardians prior to marrying.[8] In 1805, Charles IV issued two additional edicts concerning marriage, one of which banned marriage between nobles and anyone of African descent, although the viceroy, or audiencia, could issue a dispensation, while the other prohibited Spaniards from marrying anyone descended from a slave, irrespective of her or his age.[9]

The Marital Protocol

The marriage process had four distinct steps. The first was engagement, which may or may not have been in writing, set a date for the ceremony, and involved the exchange of the arras. Subsequent to engagement, the couple would meet with their parish priest and provide the *información de libertad*, in which they provided documents and witnesses to verify that they faced no impediments, such as being otherwise engaged, having had sex with a relative of their fiancée, or being closer than third-degree relatives. Once the priest had verified the couple's eligibility to marry, he would announce the planned nuptials in the banns. This was usually during three consecutive Sunday services, during which anyone who had reason to object to the union was morally bound to voice their concern. The final step was the marriage ceremony itself.[10]

There was a distinction in canon law between an engagement for proximate marriage and for one in the future. For example, in June 1796, Mariano Arce had impregnated Mauricia Uriona in Tarata, in Cochabamba Province, who herself was illegitimate and wanted to spare her child the same stigma. As a result, they agreed to marry within two years, that Mariano would recognize the child, and that if for any reason the marriage did not occur, he would pay her dowry and child support.[11]

This distinction between present and future engagements emerged in the fourteenth century, as prior to that it was widely held that if a verbal promise to marry was followed by intercourse, then the couple were married, irrespective of when the ceremony was intended to take place. By the sixteenth century, the canonical view was that any engagement established an unbreakable union and hence precluded those so bound from marrying anyone else. There were circumstances that could break the engagement, however, such as if either party entered religious life, contracted a serious illness, left the area for three years, had sex with another person, or changed her or his mind upon reaching the age of majority. As the eighteenth century progressed, however, the breaking of an engagement was increasingly viewed as indicating an absence of desire, and hence free will, in forming a union.[12]

Responding to an increase in suits over broken engagements, in 1803 a new law required that such agreements be notarized with the signatures of the parties, or their guardians if they were not adults, and could be terminated by mutual consent. While the breaking of a marriage contract was of little consequence for a man's honor, this was not the case for women, especially in cases of pregnancy. Indeed, premarital sex, following a verbal or written engagement that often involved an exchange of rings or other symbolic articles, was common.[13] In practice, many "engagements" were a thin veil for an open-ended affair, and the man was often pressed to honor it only if he was about to leave the region, marry someone else, or got his fiancée pregnant. Then, to escape the commitment, men would commonly impugn the honor of the women, even if it meant the loss of the arras and a payment of a fine or dowry for lost virginity.[14]

This time-tested method of casting doubt on a woman's virtue was what Manuel Aguirre used to break his verbal engagement to Rudicinda Mogro in Pampa Quemada, in the Cinti region, in 1795. When she learned that he was preparing to marry another woman, she complained to the parish priest, Evaristo Salamanca. She explained that "a few months ago, deceived by his promise . . . I consented for him to make use of my body, persuaded by his deceitful words, the result of which is that I am pregnant."[15] Because of this, she wanted the marriage to occur, despite describing Manuel as a "a badly brought up young man, even inattentive in venerating his own mother . . . who lives the life of a wastrel, keeping company with likeminded boys and deceiving more than one poor woman with their habitual illicit friendships."[16]

Manuel acknowledged having sex with her but averred "that there was absolutely no troth pledged, which would have been conditioned on her being virgin, and since she misrepresented her situation, having already been corrupted . . . no further promise or pact was forthcoming."[17] Rudicinda offered several witnesses who attested to her "good name, modesty and reputation" and insisted "that if the suit I had filed were not true, it would be of no avail for a modest woman to reveal the insults and infamy to which she had been subjected, or to undertake an action so unflattering to herself."[18] Father Salamanca decided not to make any decision on the validity of the engagement and sent the file to the vicar general for a decision.[19]

Engagements formalized in writing were much more difficult to break, as the eighteen-year-old Spaniard Joaquín de la Sota discovered in La Paz, in 1760. His passion exceeding his prudence, Joaquín had signed a document that stated "under the promise of marriage, I deflowered doña Bartolina González de la Fuente."[20] Despite this, he was reluctant to proceed, and his fiancée went to court to pressure him to move forward with the union. She did so because of "the loss of my virginity that, with the promise of marriage . . . [left] me dishonored."[21] Faced with his own words and signature, as well as the involvement of the vicar general in the case, he acknowledged that he signed the letter, and, on October 29, 1760, indicated his willingness to "freely and spontaneously" formalize the vows.[22]

His deeds, however, belied his words, and he soon left town in a supposed search for witnesses to testify concerning his eligibility to marry. This precipitated a filing by María's mother, who had her ill husband's permission to seek the court's assistance. She explained that that they were a poor family and that "she had placed her hopes for betterment on her virginity," underscoring the honor and economic value associated with maidenhood.[23] She also called for an arrest warrant to be issued for Joaquín and for his goods to be seized, seeking thereby to induce him to honor his word and to have his case serve as an example to other men. Although the audiencia acceded to her request, Joaquín remained a fugitive.[24]

Rather than an expression of a couple's free will and affect, marriages frequently were the result of familial accords, with honor and economic interests in the balance. As a result, there was a fine line between coercion, inducement, and free will. This was especially the case for the eldest male, because an unequal marriage would have a negative impact on the marriageability of other siblings. Beyond parental pressures, many couples experienced clerical coercion, as priests pressured them through incarceration, reclusion, fines, and spiritual sanctions.[25]

That free will was often more a concept than a practice was especially apparent among Indians in the Andes, where forced marriages by priests were common. Part of the reason for this was the prevalence of *sirvinacuy*, or a trial marriage, which could turn out to be an informal marriage. To the church, this was nothing more than concubinage, the tolerance of which would only encourage emulation. This had not only moral implications but financial ones as well, as clergy derived income from marriages, both in terms of fees for the service and through the *viucho*, or "gifts," such as food and animals.[26] Incarceration, whether of women in depósito or men in jail, was the standard means of persuading a reluctant Indian couple to marry. The use of a priest's home as depósito also often reflected "other indecent ends" of the priest for the girl.[27] The *cabildo*, or city council, of Cuzco noted the frequency of forced marriage in their jurisdiction in 1768, relating how clergy routinely married girls as young as fourteen years old to people not of their choosing as a means of generating a steady revenue flow.[28] One clergyman in Azángaro demonstrated just how profitable such an arrangement could be by performing three hundred marriages in two months, or an average of five a day. As one would expect, such unions were often unstable, and many couples soon separated to continue previous, or establish new, relationships.[29]

Deeds and Dispensations

As noted, once a couple was engaged, they were required to provide the información de libertad. This would, in theory, reveal whether there were any impediments to the marriage, which could be either minor or major.[30] The former usually concerned issues of process, did not prevent a marriage, and could easily be dispensed with by the local priest or vicar following acts of atonement or financial sanctions. Major, or diriment, impediments could prevent or even annul a marriage and included dual engagements, coerced and prepubescent unions, consanguinity at the second degree or closer, infertility, taking religious vows, and incest.[31]

Dispensations reflected a choice by the church between doctrine and deviance, with marriage, honor, reputation, and even legitimacy at stake. Just as a daughter's pregnancy could persuade a reluctant father to cease his opposition to a marriage, it could also facilitate a dispensation so that the child would not be born out of wedlock. Dispensations could even be retroactive, thereby eliminating a potential basis for an annulment. They were common in cases of consanguinity, especially in rural areas, if one could demonstrate that there were no other suitable candidates, or a gender imbalance, in the region. The need for dispensations was increased by the definition of incest, which included intercourse with the brother, sister, parent, other relatives of the proposed spouse through the second degree of consanguinity, or god-parental relatives. This, combined with the fact that relatives often had better access to a household than a stranger, led to many requests for dispensation. Incest had its risks, however, as certain forms were punishable by between four and ten years of prison and subsequent exile.[32]

Social upheaval, such as the war for independence, presented challenges in obtaining dispensations, or at least could serve as a pretext for inaction. In San Lucas, in the region of Cinti, Pedro Manuel Polo had married Josefa Araneivia in February 1816 in a ceremony officiated by Father Alejo Cuyza. Although Pedro had not told his wife, he had confessed to Father Cuyza that he and his sister-in-law, Josefa Pimentel, had intercourse prior to his marriage, thus creating a need for a dispensation for incest. Pedro claimed that he and Father Cuyza had decided not to tell Josefa and instead planned to go to La Plata to seek a dispensation, however they were prevented from doing so because the roads had been closed by insurgents. Father Cuyza decided to officiate the marriage, and when Josefa learned of the relationship she indicated that she did not want an annulment. Rather, she sought a dispensation and revalidation of the marriage. In the end, the prosecutor agreed, as to do otherwise would cause scandal and dishonor Josefa.[33]

The degree to which the church would investigate the need for a dispensation was demonstrated in Corquemarca, Carangas Province, in 1819.[34] Andrés Choque, an Indian, explained that in 1809 he had married Mónica Mamani at the insistence of one of the village leaders. About two months later, just before departing to serve the dreaded *mita*, or forced labor draft, in Potosí, Andrés was shocked when his priest told him that he had married his own mother. Despite the efforts of the priest to separate them, she accompanied him to Potosí. Upon his return to Corquemarca, he became an outcast and related how people looked at him "with those evil eyes."[35] As a result, he left his wife and moved to the village of Toledo, where he had been for the previous nine years, and sought an annulment. The ensuing ecclesiastical investigation revealed that Andrés was not married to his mother but rather to his aunt who had raised him. The investigating clergyman accused Andrés of wanting to annul the union because Mónica was of a "mature age" and remitted the file to the prosecutor in La Plata for his opinion.[36]

The prosecutor, however, was unsatisfied with the extent and detail of the testimony. He ordered Mónica to be placed in depósito and for the cleric who had performed the marriage to testify. Mónica stated that she and Andrés's mother, Augustina, were cousins, and as a result her husband was her "nephew once removed." She further confessed that she not only had premarital sex with Andrés but knew of their blood relationship the entire time. In his testimony, Andrés confessed that his mother had died when he was young and "has had and has always known as his . . . mother . . . his wife Mónica Mamani." Efforts to contact the priest who performed the marriage were unsuccessful, and the file was then sent back to the prosecutor for his opinion. He indicated that the extra effort was worth it, as technically they were not aunt and nephew but rather related in "in the third degree of transversal and unequal consanguinity." Furthermore, Pope Paul III had issued a bull allowing Indians to marry "in third and fourth degree of consanguinity, and in third and fourth degree of affinity," a fact that had also been discussed in legal guides. The result was that no dispensation was necessary. So, despite his being separated from his wife for nine years and being married to the woman who had raised him, Andrés marriage was, to his chagrin, valid.[37]

In some cases, marriage could transform an adulterous relationship into an incestuous one.[38] In 1812, in Poopó, the Indians Manuel Hidalgo and Martina Gonzales married, they claimed, under pressure from Martina's mother, Magdalena Flores. Although Magdalena was married, she and Manuel had a long-standing relationship, which Martina indicated she knew about prior to, and that continued after, their marriage. She explained how Manuel would slip out of bed at night, spend the night with Magdalena, and return to her bed in the morning. Manuel testified that he married Martina only when her mother threatened him in some way and insisted that he had confessed the relationship to the priest who had married them. His suggestion of coercion was belied, however, by the fact that he and Magdalena had run off together and lived on a hacienda for two and a half months before they were caught and Magdalena was placed in depósito. From her confinement, Magdalena claimed to have no recollection of any intimate relationship with Manuel and that if Manuel had had sex with her it was when she was "in a perfect state of inebriation."[39] Ultimately, the marriage was annulled after a year passed during which Martina steadfastly refused to rejoin her husband. While she was free to remarry, Manuel was sentenced to sweep the floors of the Poopó church for two months and to "attend . . . mass on bended knees holding in the right hand an extinguished candle."[40]

Banns and Rites

Like the información de libertad, the reading of the banns could bring skeletons tumbling from the closet, such as a prior engagement or incestuous relationship.[41] Even if the accusations were false or regarded acts for which one could receive a dispensation, they could delay or derail a marriage and cause considerable embarrassment. Isidro Ferrufino may have been concerned about this as the banns were read in Tarata in anticipation of his marriage to Gregoria Terceros in 1814. About five years earlier he had seduced Nicolasa Cabrera, allegedly with promises of marriage, and as a result they had a daughter whom Isidro had never supported.[42]

The banns provided an opportune time for Nicolasa's mother, Manuela, to seek redress. As a result of writing to the archbishop, she was able to suspend the process and demanded that if Isidro refused to marry Nicolasa he be made to pay her dowry or be exiled. Isidro confessed to the relationship but denied ever promising to marry her and insisted that "her behavior was not that of" a virgin.[43] Moreover, he pointed out that neither Nicolasa nor he were of age to legally make an engagement without parental approval, and it would have had to have been in writing in order to be binding. Consequently, he asked that his planned marriage be allowed to go forward. It appears that the issue was settled locally, probably with a financial settlement, as there is no further record of it.[44]

Once a couple had provided the información de libertad and the banns had been read, the parish priest of the bride was to officiate the rites. Given that marriages were an important source of revenue for clergy, conflicts over jurisdiction could arise in which the couple, such as Faustino Ampuero and Ignacia Urquizu, were caught in the middle of a sacred squabble. In May 1816, during the war for independence, Faustino was a captain in the royalist forces stationed in La Plata. As a result, he worshipped with, and was married by, the military chaplain, Father Mariano Huerta. Ignacia, however, lived in the parish of San Roque and was a parishioner of Father Augustín Risco. Unless he or his superiors granted permission to the contrary, Father Risco should have conducted the ceremony. Father Risco angrily demanded that the union be annulled on the basis that Ignacia was not Father Huerta's parishioner and that he had not properly gathered the información de libertad. In mid-June, the prosecutor noted that Father Huerta had recently been named military chaplain due to his "extremely reliable conduct," making it a "delicate issue." Nevertheless, he did demand to know whether Father Huerta had gathered the información de libertad.[45]

Father Huerta responded that he had conducted "infinite" marriages in his nine years as a priest and lamented that Father Risco "has gravely injured my reputation and honor."[46] He also provided the información de libertad, signed by other military officers, and claimed that the vicar general had dispensed with the banns. Moreover, he insisted that Father Risco had declined to officiate in the ceremony, claiming that he was busy with celebrations for the day of San Fernando and thus had given him "a tacit license" to officiate.[47] Despite this, Father Risco continued to push for an annulment on the basis that he had not officiated and continued to call for Father Huerta's punishment. In late January 1817, the vicar general agreed that Father Huerta had the authority to conduct the marriage and that Father Risco had chosen not to do so and as a result should pay court costs. He did, however, find Father Huerta guilty of an unspecified omission and ordered him to fast for the next seven Fridays.[48]

The Parental Prerogative: Opposition to Marriage Choice

Beginning in 1778, the cascade of increasingly restrictive laws concerning marriage in the Americas led to a host of lawsuits between offspring and their parents.[49] Many occurred after the couple had become privately engaged and consummated their union. This was often an effective means of overcoming parental opposition given the difficulties and loss of honor associated with marrying off a non-virgin daughter or having an hijo natural in the family. Fathers who were adamantly opposed to a union often accused a male suitor of civil crimes such as abduction, rape, vagrancy, or concubinage, all of which could send him to jail. Similarly, accusations of immoral behavior were effective in having women placed in recogimiento, while other fathers effectively exiled or held their offspring against their will in an effort to prevent their marriage.[50]

Many of these elements were intertwined in the case of Felipa Gallardo y Lora and Manuel Barrientos, who faced vehement objections to their marriage by Manuel's father, Francisco Barrientos. On the evening of November 16, 1779, Felipa and her mother were at home when the alguacil suddenly appeared, arrested Felipa on the charge of maintaining an illicit relationship with Manuel, and placed her in the Convent of the Virgin of Los Remedios in La Plata. Felipa's advocate, Simon Narciso de Valenzuela, called for Manuela to be released and for Manuel's father to pay a fine as a result of having made a false accusation that affected her honor. Narciso contended that the father and alcalde had "trampled the entire judicial order" as not only had there been no written complaint against Felipa but, furthermore, the couple had not been caught in the act of sexual relations.[51] In December, Felipa complained that she was suffering and ill in reclusion because she lacked money to support herself and purchase medicine. The audiencia subsequently ordered her release, dispatching a scribe to the recogimiento, who read the order to the abbess on Christmas Day. While the abbess acknowledged the order, she explained that she could only act upon the direct order of the archbishop, which delayed her release. By January 3, however, Felipa was back home, and at around 4:30 p.m., a messenger delivered a letter to her from Manuel, written at his father's hacienda in Mojocoya, Tomina Province.[52] It read:

> Most esteemed and dearest wife of my highest regard and veneration:
>
> I shall be happy if, on receiving this note, it finds you in good health along with all those of your household; in mine all are well and eager to serve you . . .
>
> The news of your imprisonment has put me beside myself with worry, since there is no one who can inform me of all of this, and especially of your release. I have only learned . . . that someone else will inherit . . . which I tell you is fine by me,

> as long as they do not interfere in my life. In the end I say let them disinherit me, but let them take my life before I would believe what they have said about you.
>
> My soul is strong, and as for me, it is impossible to undo what has been said. I assure you that we shall prevail, and that, when they take you before the Crown Attorney, he will give us the license to wed. To that end I have learned that my brother has done a thousand things out of his desire to spare me, but all is in vain, since it may be years before I see you again. Nevertheless, I am determined, and I pray to our Lord God that he keep you safe for many years.
>
> Mojocoya, December 26, 1779
>
> Your devoted husband, for the world to know, sooner or later or within a year,
>
> *Manuel Luis Barrientos*[53]

In submitting this letter directly to the court, Felipa emphasized that Manuel had referred to her as his wife and also that he had indicated that he was ready to be disinherited in order to marry her. The court endeavored to present this and other documents to the father via the translado, however this was impossible as he was away at his hacienda, busy persuading a captive Manuel to change his mind. His efforts soon bore fruit, as Manuel wrote directly to the alcalde, Joseph Eustachio Ponce de Leon, expressing that he had reconciled with his father and that his original intention had emerged "from mere caprice and with no reflection . . . [but] this effort has presently ceased." He added that he now recognized the "just repugnance" that his father had of the marriage and did not want to be disinherited. He went on to insist that he never was formally engaged to Felipa and that he was making his decision without "the least violence nor extortion," and he requested that the court order Felipa "to keep perpetually silent on this issue."[54]

This must have come as a surprise to Felipa after having received

Manuel's previous letter. In her response, she insisted that Manuel had not written his statement freely and successfully petitioned the court to order him to testify concerning his true intentions. Now released from his father's captivity, Manuel was back in La Plata with his brother Francisco. There he testified that he and his brother had presented the letter desisting from the marriage to the alcalde, who questioned him repeatedly in order to determine his true intentions. But no sooner did the brothers arrive back at their house in La Plata than Manuel slipped out of a window to meet Felipa and her aunt on a plaza where he told them what had just happened. After some discussion, at around 10:30 p.m. the three then went back to the home of the alcalde, who expressed surprise at their late visit. He asked to speak privately with Manuel, who now indicated that he did indeed want to marry Felipa and had only presented the letter "to avoid displeasing his brother, and other relatives." By this time, the alcalde was quite perplexed and "remained for a while suspended, and not talking."[55]

After some reflection, the alcalde suggested that Felipa and her aunt return home and that Manuel be placed in depósito to shield him from his father's influence and determine his true intentions. The next day, January 11, Manuel informed the alcalde that after thinking more on the issue, he did not want to go forward with the marriage. By this point the alcalde was exasperated, writing, "It is understood that when don Manuel Barrientos is with doña Felipa Lora, and relates to her, [his ardor] is inflamed and he ratifies their marriage, but when he is separated from her, and no longer sees her, he thinks differently, calms down and his enthusiasm wanes."[56]

Manuel's indecision had confused all those around him, including Felipa, who asked that, yet again, he "categorically [and] without any ambiguity" indicate his desire under oath.[57] He did so on January 13, insisting that he did not want to go ahead with the marriage. In his ensuing testimony he admitted writing the letter in which he desisted from the marriage and expressed his desire not to be alienated from his father. Yet no sooner had he testified to this effect than he yet again changed his mind and claimed that he wanted to go forward with the wedding. And at this point a new, undated letter surfaced that read:

> My dearest Felipa:
>
> I know not how I manage, not knowing what has happened in our matter. It seems that my declarations may have provoked some kind of reaction or pressure on me to suspend the marriage out of fear, or because my father is upset upon learning of my spirit and determination. I have no choice but to remain firm and faithful to my vow to you, and to pledge that if you are not to be my wife, none other will be. So that in order to remove all doubts and confusion I again say to you . . . that I will not retract my troth, nor will I not marry you, unless you repent of your decision, since before God and for the tranquility of our consciences we are already married, and the sooner the better. I send you these lines so that you may show them to the Lord Mayor, to assure him that under no circumstances will I weaken in my resolve and determination. He in turn can show it to my father so that, once and for all, as I have said, he may give us his blessing. I am your beloved,
>
> *Manuel Luis Barrientos*[58]

Meanwhile, Manuel's father went back on the attack, invoking the 1776 Real Pragmática, as opposed to that of 1778 which applied to the Americas. He argued that marriages without a father's consent only led to "grave harm" and that there was an "unimaginable inequality" in both origins and reputation between his son and Felipa. Were the union to go forward, he insisted, it would dishonor his family, which "has been and still is illustrious and outstanding, with honors, distinctions and noble occupations."[59] He then launched a vitriolic attack against Felipa, characterizing her and her family as "a mixture and mishmash of all the races . . . dedicated to the business of the flesh with all kinds of men, and made vile by her public prostitution and scandal, through which she . . . corrupts the sons of [decent] families . . . distracting them from their studies and occupations, as she has done with my . . . son."[60] On this basis, on January 22, 1780, the first alcalde ruled in favor of the father, prohibiting the issuance of a marriage license. This was a remarkable ruling, as both the 1776 and 1778 Pragmáticas only allowed fathers to disinherit only their minor offspring.[61]

Reeling from this setback, Felipa obtained a new advocate, Manuel Robles, who appealed the decision to the audiencia in March while resisting an effort by Manuel's father to have her returned to reclusion.[62] Robles pointed out to the court that the issue was not parental consent but rather whether Manuel was willing to be disinherited. He insisted that Felipa had been the victim of the "most atrocious and grave calumnies" and that as her family were "well-known Spaniards and of clean blood" there was no racial inequality. In demonstrating her lineage, he also revealed that Felipa's father was Jacinto Gallardo, an "ecclesiastic of well-known nobility."[63] Robles revealed the crux of the case: Felipa was a sacrilegious child. Despite this, he insisted that since Manuel had indicated that he was prepared to be disinherited, the marriage license should be granted, according to both the 1776 and 1778 Pragmáticas.[64]

In his response, Francisco Barrientos's new attorney, Gregorio Nuñez, insisted that it was plain to see that Felipa was a mestiza. He also reminded the court she was the daughter of a priest and claimed that, as a prostitute, her mother had no equal.[65] As a result, the court upheld the alcalde's decision not to grant the license on May 29, 1780. While ensuing events are unclear, in the end, Manuel overcame his indecision and his father's opposition. The couple married, had children, and owned a bakery before Manuel died a widower in 1836.[66]

Francisco Barrientos's decision to hold his son captive was not that unusual. In 1787, Juan Buenaventura Salinas had not only reached the age of majority but supported himself for many years as an attorney and professor at the University of San Francisco Xavier in La Plata. Having established himself professionally, he was ready to marry Bernabela

Ángeles y Paniagua, to whom he had been engaged for over three years. Back in his hometown of Tarata, however, his father, Juan Salinas, disapproved of the proposed union on the basis of the dishonor that Bernabela's supposed illegitimacy would bring to his family. To stop the wedding, he sent a group of at least five people, including one of Juan's brothers, to kidnap him and bring him back to Tarata. After several months of captivity, Juan escaped and made his way back to La Plata, where he submitted a petition to the audiencia seeking a license to marry and an order to prevent his father from harassing him. In April 1787, the audiencia demanded that the father present his case to the audiencia, either in person or through an attorney, an order that he did not obey.[67] Meanwhile, although Bernabela admitted that she was a natural child, the prosecutor supported her, observing that she had "decent birth and honorable conduct." As a result of this and the father's disobedience, the court granted the couple a license to marry.[68] Generally, a failure to respond to the court or substantiate one's objections in a prompt manner was a tacit acceptance of the union, and a license would likely be granted.[69]

Other fathers opposed their sons' marriages because they would derail the careers in which they had invested family resources. This was the situation in which José Manuel de Miranda found himself in 1793. Having financed the education of his son, Juan Manuel Gutiérrez, in La Plata, he was dismayed to learn that Juan was planning to marry Agueda Lora. Although José Manuel opposed more the timing of the marriage than his son's choice of mate, he feared he would abandon his studies and threatened to disinherit him over the matter. In seeking to obtain a marriage license, Juan submitted as evidence the following letter from his father:

> My dear Juan Manuel, the son of my heart:
>
> Just when I thought that you were honoring your promise to me to get an education, and when everyone here in the valley

believed that you had changed, and just when we all had hopes that you would become the man of your household and that you might redeem your father's good name, you inform me that you are going to marry, that there is no way to prevent it, and that if I do not give you my permission it would only occasion greater expense, for in the end you are determined to marry.

To this I respond, do what you wish, marry or do not marry, and since it is none of my concern I will not get involved. I only warn you that, as far as I am concerned, from now on you can be assured that I will no longer look upon you, or ask about you, since I now realize that you are not the same Juan Manuel who gave me so much proof of his good conduct here, who is now someone else, and who has forgotten his promise to study and become a good person.

If you think that, after you marry, you can bring a wife here to Cinti, and that here you will be in the land of milk and honey for your sustenance, you are mistaken, because with regard to your inheritance, it is clear to me that what is coming to you is a pittance, and is burdened with so many liens that when the time comes for you to receive [your legacy], you will need to borrow in order to work what little [land] is coming to you. . . . If you are capable of maintaining a wife in these circumstances, just do as you please, but I will not get involved by writing to the vicar or authorizing my brother to give you any of the money that is destined to support Toribio, who I hope will also soon get over the idea of marrying, since the university is for studying.

No one waits for you here, nor will any of your sisters answer you, because such letters do not merit a reply. I respond because I am obliged to, since all of them, and all of your other relatives say that if you and your woman are thinking of living with any of them, you are mistaken, since they all work until

> they burst in order to support themselves in this afflicted Cinti [valley]. Don Juan Cabero says that, if you marry, do not expect to cross his threshold as long as he is executor of your estate, and others say the same thing . . .
>
> Farewell, do as you will, and may God give you his holy grace, bring you to a true reasoning, and guide you for many years, in order that you may command me, your wretched father.
>
> *José Manuel de Miranda*
> *San Pedro, August 8, 1793*[70]

Although the outcome of the case is unclear, the father indicated that he would not oppose the marriage in court, and it appears that there was no other legal basis to prevent it.[71]

Like sons, daughters also had to contend with their fathers' opposition to their marriage, a task made especially difficult when they were legal minors. In La Paz in 1785, Benito Oquendo and the city councilman Juan de Dios Mauje were friends, and Benito was a frequent visitor to Juan's house. As a result of this access, Benito and Mauje's eighteen-year-old daughter, Eustaquia Monje, became enamored and secretly engaged. On October 28, she feared their plans were about to go awry when she overheard a conversation between her parents and a visitor, who proposed a candidate to marry Eustaquia. Her fear turned to panic when she heard her father agree to the proposal and indicate that he would force her to accept it. Hearing this, she resolved to elope with Benito that evening and soon escaped the house and went in search of him. When they met, Benito urged calm, and they sought the counsel of the precentor of their church. He in turn directed Benito to confer with the bishop, who ordered Eustaquia to be placed in depósito in the home of the *alférez real*, or royal standard-bearer, Tadeo Foronda.[72]

Meanwhile, Juan had discovered his daughter was missing and had no doubt that Benito had kidnapped her. At around 10:30 that evening the alguacil, the prison warden, and two soldiers began to search for Benito, arresting him the next day. He was clearly well educated and from the upper echelon of society, and as a result he was segregated in the jail. From his cell he penned a vigorous and articulate letter laced with Latin phrases in which he insisted that "not even in his imagination" did he kidnap Eustaquia.[73] It was on the basis of Eustaquia's exculpatory testimony, however, that Benito was released the next day.[74]

Juan, however, was unrelenting and complained that Benito had offended his "honor, house, [and] reputation" and that as a result his health had suffered. He denied arranging Eustaquia's marriage, insisted any engagement without his permission was invalid, and complained that "with gifts, or with tender affection, or with the promise of a better life in the future . . . the temptations of the flesh prompted by caresses lead to seductions like the present one."[75] On this basis, on November 9, 1785, he requested that Eustaquia's statement be ruled inadmissible, that she be put in a monastery, and that Benito be sent back to jail. The alcalde declined to rearrest Benito, however, while the intendant, Sebastian de Segurola, instructed Juan to present any future motions through an attorney. Although Juan averred that he would appeal to the audiencia, it appears that the case was resolved without further legal action.[76]

A father's opposition to a marriage was less tenable if he had been absent for a long period and had not contributed financially to the child's upbringing, as Juan José Martínez learned in 1805. He had separated from his wife, Manuela Ruíz, eleven years earlier after they had begun a divorce proceeding. Martínez's objection was not entirely unreasonable, as their daughter was only thirteen years old. Nevertheless, Manuela argued that he had squandered her dowry and not supported their daughter and that as a result he had lost his paternal prerogatives. Martínez ignored this line of reasoning, noting that according to the 1803 Pragmática, he was not required to give a reason for his opposition. He indicated, however, that if he had to, it would be on the basis of inequality, which he insisted was obvious to the eye, and because the proposed groom was unemployed. His opposition revolved more around economic than racial issues, as the groom was a creole but worked as a painter. Martínez in essence abandoned the case when he failed to present any witnesses to substantiate his assertions. As a result, the court decided in favor of the mother on the basis that the father had been physically and economically absent for over a decade and had in effect lost his paternal rights.[77] Like the cases of Felipa Gallardo and Lorenzo Farfán de los Godos above, the decision of this case appears to have gone against the letter of the law.

The Pragmática of 1778 and associated edicts were intended to serve elite fathers, but women and the poor also sought recourse in it. Among them was the widow María Miranda, who strongly rejected the planned marriage of her eighteen-year-old daughter, Micaela Ponce de Leon, to Evaristo Tadeo Flores Porcel.[78] María was hardly of La Plata's social elite, operating a chicha bar in 1801 that Evaristo, the city council's chief scribe, frequented. Represented by an indigent defender, she claimed that she had never been consulted on, much less approved of, the proposed union and that Evaristo, "with guitar in hand late at night," had seduced her daughter.[79] She irately insisted that while her family were descended from "old Spanish Christians free of the race of Moors and Indians," Evaristo was a "mulato, drunk by profession, of malignant habits, illegitimate by birth [and] famous as a knifer."[80]

Evaristo insisted not only that he and Micaela had become engaged in the presence of a priest but also that the mother had approved of the union until others convinced her she could find a better match for her daughter. Witnesses attesting to his character stated that Evaristo was not prone to excessive drinking and that, while he could play the guitar, he did so poorly. In recogimiento in the Beaterio de Santa Catalina, Micaela initially testified that she wanted to marry Evaristo and that her mother had given her blessing to the union. She began to have second thoughts as she was giving her testimony, however, expressing fear of alienating her mother. Meanwhile, her mother had considerable difficulty finding witnesses to testify on her behalf, although one affirmed that Evaristo's father had been a tailor but knew nothing of his racial origins or alleged drinking. He did, however, describe how at a party he hosted Evaristo had hit a woman and then stabbed the man who stepped in to defend her. Evaristo later explained that he had been cleared of the stabbing charge, although the decision had been appealed.[81]

By mid-January 1802, Evaristo complained about the mother's recurrent tardiness in responding to traslados. While the court denied her an extension to gather more witnesses, they did grant her request for Micaela to testify again concerning what her mother characterized as a "mistaken, ill-considered, poorly thought out and even more ill-advised marriage."[82] To give testimony, Micaela was then moved to the home of Rosa Ricón, where she was held in depósito. In her statement, at which Evaristo was present, she indicated that she was ready to go forward with the marriage, perhaps because she was pregnant. While she was there, Evaristo gave her the following letter, written on faded blue paper that was folded many times in the shape of a triangle:

> My Micaela, my love:
>
> Yesterday I received the latest papers regarding our matter, with the assurances that on your part there was no faltering and that when you gave your statement to Marín you said again that, once and for all, this matter must be settled. This spat among women or the plebes which has been so roundly criticized; this law suit which cast doubts on my honor, has me all tied up in knots, since I am a man of good faith in your regard. All of this has befallen me because I love you.
>
> I have received reliable news from the mouths of those visitors who have called at your house that people have even gone to you with gossip about my cousin, and that all of Chuquisaca is creaking with the news that you have said that you do not wish to marry. That you may well do, it is your decision in God's eyes and not mine. But it is not for this reason that I bring up this matter, but rather so that my lady

María and the whole world may know that I am not as she says I am, but rather very different, and that if I, with my own money, was drinking and sharing with others it was not because of any vice, but rather just to have an enjoyable time there without letting you out of my sight for an instant, since I really loved you, I still love you and I will ever love you, even though your fickleness wounds me. I expected this all along. . . . All you have to do is pull yourself together, haul anchor, and hoist sails to the first favorable wind.

If my discretion seems cruel to you, if my fidelity and conscience have altered my luck, I too could do the same, but no! It is unreasonable! I offer you my heart and my pain, even though I know they will be the target of your cruelty. I see you laugh, and I remember that afternoon when, on bidding you farewell, your beautiful face bathed in tears, you took me into your arms. How can I forget you when I remember everything? Oh dear darkie, would that my pen were a paint brush to paint for you, to remind you of our past. But it might fatigue you, because when one's will flags, even words become irritating.

So I tell you that this is the appropriate case for my legitimate defense, but even if the whole world is angry and you should decide not to marry, I shall subpoena you, I shall call on you and challenge you, so that when my suit comes before the Divine Tribunal and before your mother and your defenders you may know of my love. For my part, I will affirm that as far as I am concerned, I am your husband until death do us part and even beyond the grave.

Yours, Evaristo Thadeo

[P.S.] The handkerchief that I sent you, I bought for you and has your name on the corners, and in one, my last name, which you can have removed.[83]

The audiencia ultimately declared the mother's opposition to be without merit and ordered that a license to marry be granted. Her low social status, disorganization, and lack of witnesses, combined with Micaela's stated intentions and, perhaps most importantly, her pregnancy, informed their decision. In the meantime, Micaela was to remain in depósito, and her mother was ordered to send her clothes and her bed. While she grudgingly sent some clothes, she refused to send the bed. Even when the alguacil came to demand it, she "refused to obey the order, and with insolence and shamelessness became upset, causing a fuss in the neighborhood."[84]

Beyond resisting the alguacil, the mother appealed the court's ruling, still trying to gather testimony concerning Evaristo's racial origins. Her plan backfired, as witnesses described the "honor and Christianity" of his parents, who were a tailor and a washerwoman.[85] Evaristo had a very capable advocate, José Manuel Malavia, who called for the original decision to be upheld, noting that the mother had never indicated her own racial origins and ignored the "torrent of reason" that upheld the proposed marriage.[86] The prosecutor then offered his view of the case, noting procedural irregularities and suggesting that the office of the alcalde may have been sympathetic to Evaristo because he worked in there. Further, he was critical of the fact that that Micaela had not been sequestered while in depósito, as the love letter demonstrated. He called for her to testify again, and in late March 1802, Micaela stated that her earlier misgivings were a product of her fear of her mother and that she wanted to marry as soon as possible as she was pregnant and very ill. As a result, in mid-May, the prosecutor urged the court to uphold its earlier decision to grant the marriage license. Not only had Evaristo triumphed in court, he also had demonstrated, at least officially, his non-African origins through the witnesses, and he asked for those documents to be returned to him "for other affairs."[87] Ironically, in 1808, Evaristo served as the representative of a purchaser of a house that was sold at auction, and among those involved in the sale was none other than Manuel Luis

Barrientos, who also had faced vehement opposition to his marriage and was listed as the "interim alguacil."[88]

As these cases demonstrate, the Pragmática of 1778 and subsequent edicts were not legal tools of elite fathers alone. Instead, mestizos, the poor, and single mothers utilized them in often unsuccessful efforts to prevent marriages, especially of daughters. While the law provided racial, social, and economic elites a tool to prevent sons and daughters from "marrying down," commoners saw it as a means to thwart a marriage that would prevent their offspring from contracting with another and improving her or his, and her or his family's, social and economic status.

Seduction and Eloping

The term *estupro* refers to the taking of a female's virginity and has several connotations. They range from forcible intercourse to intercourse involving a degree of pressure or deceit to voluntary sex. It could also involve seduction, which could be entirely voluntary or involve deception, such as an insincere engagement.[89] While a seduced woman was usually confined for some time, the punishment for seduction for men evolved during the colonial period and could, in theory, result in the loss of one-half of their property, marriage to the victim, flogging, imprisonment, or five years of exile. The possible punishment for a household servant convicted of seduction was worse: they could be burned alive. In practice, however, if there was any punishment at all, the man was made to pay either a "virginity debt" or the woman's dowry.[90] As with seduction, the penalty for rape varied considerably depending on whether the woman was a virgin, her overall reputation, and the social status and resources of the man. If the victim was under twelve, or a virgin, nun, or widow, the crime was, technically, punishable by death and the forfeiture of all of the rapist's property to the victim.[91]

Overall, the colonial period saw a lessening of the punishments for seduction, which from the 1670s no longer included exile, although one could be sentenced to three years in jail. By 1796, an edict essentially limited punishment for seduction to probation, and in 1801, the crown decreed that in cases of estupro a suspect could post bond or, if unable to do so, should be confined to his city of residence. With the issuance of the Novísima Recopilación de las Leyes de España in 1805, estupro and rape were more clearly differentiated, with the former limited to seduction of a virgin. Rape was defined as forcible intercourse and was no longer punishable by death but only by incarceration.[92]

When the twenty-five-year-old Irish merchant Ricardo Reynolds set his eye on thirteen-year-old Margarita Echeverría in 1753, he did not know he would soon be entangled in such laws. His shop was adjacent to that of Margarita's mother, Josefa Arias de Velasco, the wife of the itinerant Field Marshall Francisco de Echeverría. Not long after Josefa, Margarita, and her younger brother Francisco arrived in La Plata, Ricardo encountered Margarita on the main plaza while she was running an errand for her mother and flattered, propositioned, and seduced her on the same day. Margarita confessed the relationship to her mother's slave, María Antonia, who later testified that the couple soon began to surreptitiously spend time together both in Josefa's store and kitchen.[93] While the slave knew about the relationship, others had their suspicions, such as Bartolomé Rodríguez. He testified that he once saw Margarita returning home from Ricardo's house and became even more suspicious when he saw the couple "exchanging certain signals, and with that one of them left by the door of the store and the other by that of the room behind the store." His curiosity piqued, he went to the patio and found Margarita hugging a man, whom he could not, or declined to, identify.[94] Another witness, Francisco Vidal, testified that on July 11, 1751, he stopped by Josefa's store at around 9:00 p.m. on his way to mass. The slave María Antonia answered the door, telling him that Josefa had gone to mass. Peering inside, Vidal discerned Margarita and an unidentified man behind the counter "and according to the movement they appeared to . . . be lying down." He quickly left to find Josefa, cryptically urging her to be careful in the management of her household.[95]

The next evening, Josefa left on an errand, ordering young Francisco to lock the door. Instead, he left it open and Margarita slipped out to

Ricardo's house and the two then spent the night together. The next morning Ricardo and his friend Juan Morris brought her to the home of attorney Claudio Rospillori, whom they persuaded to broker her return and conceal the previous evening's activities. Rospillori, in turn, brought Margarita to the house of an audiencia judge, who returned her to her mother. Apparently Margarita was unwilling to go home due to the "roughness of her [mother's] character and the treatment she inflicted on her" and insisted that "she would let the Devil take her" before she would return to her mother.[96]

Josefa described how she had done her best to properly raise and educate Margarita and asserted that Ricardo had a history of seducing young girls with "flattery, persuasion and presents."[97] While seeking to have Margarita placed in recogimiento, she demanded an exemplary punishment for Ricardo, the same, she insisted, as if she were a person of "distinguished quality."[98] On August 17, 1751, Ricardo was arrested in the patio of the audiencia, and his property was seized, while Margarita was placed in recogimiento. Three weeks later, Ricardo testified that Margarita had told him she was not a virgin and that he had never promised to marry her. On this basis, he petitioned to be released on bond. Josefa's attorney argued that even if the relationship was consensual, Ricardo had harmed the family's reputation and demanded, at the least, a fine.[99]

Relying on a well-worn strategy, Ricardo's attorney presented various witnesses who impugned Margarita's reputation and hence the validity of the case. Among them was a fifteen-year-old boy who stated that Margarita was "reputed to be a woman of the world" and that she had confessed to him that she had had affairs with an unnamed Augustinian priest as well as Claudio Rospillosi, who brokered her return to her mother, and Francisco Varela, whom she would meet in the corral of her house.[100] Another witness chastised Josefa for allowing Margarita to move about unescorted and described how he had once entered a room where the unnamed Augustinian priest had just stated that Margarita was not a virgin. This would have come as no surprise to Varela, Morris, and Reynolds, all of whom were present and supposedly had sex with her. Additional witnesses suggested that she had had relationships with other unnamed priests, and one testified that in the entryway to their house he saw Margarita and a man "both covered in dust, from which one can infer her perdition."[101] Juan Morris testified that she had told him that her uncle had deflowered her on the road to Potosí and that many people had told him that she had been involved with three people "whom it is not advisable to mention as they are . . . ecclesiastics."[102] This testimony led to Ricardo's exoneration in November 1752, although he was fined two hundred pesos for court costs and had suffered the ignominy and hardship of imprisonment.[103]

Ricardo Reynolds did not disappear from the documentary record after this affair and went from being a seducer to a cuckold. By the early 1760s, he had married Catalina de Miranda and had two daughters, Isabel and Isadora, and a son, Mariano. Catalina was a prosperous and independent woman, owning at least two haciendas, additional lands, and a silver mill. She also laid claim to a dowry her mother had never delivered to her. Their marriage, however, was not a happy one. Around 1764 she became romantically involved with Diego de Torres, a merchant from Lima, whose own wife was in the Convent of the Virgin of Los Remedios as a result of his physical abuse. Upon discovering the affair, and the children it produced, Ricardo moved to Tomave, where he operated the family's silver mine, and by 1770 he and Catalina were in the process of divorce. Although it was ultimately granted by 1771, the archbishop ordered a secret investigation into Catalina's character. During it, one witness testified that he had heard of her liaison with Diego Torres "innumerable times from many people" and that the couple spent considerable time on his hacienda in Potolo.[104] When presented with the testimony, Diego denied the charges but indicated he would soon be departing to Cochabamba.[105]

Because of the frequency of arranged marriages, many couples eloped in an effort to force their parents to accept their choices of mate. This not only demonstrated their resolve but often resulted in pregnancy.

Parents, however, often portrayed this as kidnapping and rape, with the assumption that force was used. Not only was this a civil crime, but the use of force violated the concept of free will, creating an impediment, and thus requiring a dispensation.[106] Nevertheless, elopement was an effective means of turning the tables on the parents, and even on the church. By consummating the union the potential groom was in a better position to negotiate to "restore" the woman's, and her family's, honor through marriage. Such a strategy was fraught with risks, however, as the man was liable to be jailed and face criminal charges for kidnapping or rape, while the woman was usually put into reclusion.[107]

Accusations of force were, however, difficult to prove when the couple clearly wanted to be together and there was no incriminating testimony from the supposed victim. Despite this, Estefa Ovando challenged the odds in La Plata in 1748 when she sought to break up her daughter's romance. Although poor, Estefa insisted that she had tried to raise her daughter Manuela Berasaín as an honorable girl and was outraged to learn that she had run off to Potosí with a Spanish merchant, Manuel Robledo. Determined to separate the couple, and reclaim her daughter, she pursued them, as she explained, "leaving behind my home and giving up my health."[108] After considerable effort, she found them in a home in Potosí. When Estefa knocked at the door, Manuela appeared and her mother tried grab her, to which Manuela responded by crying out for help. Manuel quickly appeared with his slave, who "dragged [the mother] along the ground . . . [while] Robledo abused my body and head, tore the white outfit I was wearing, cursing me and saying that he had the financial means to defend himself and that no judge could touch him."[109] Her efforts violently rebuffed, the mother appealed to the corregidor, who went to Manuel's home, secured her daughter's release, and placed her in recogimiento in the girl's orphanage. Although Manuela was released when she promised not to return to Manuel, she nevertheless went right back to him and was soon sent back to reclusion. Despite the subsequent orders of the audiencia and corregidor, neither the abbess nor the vicar would release Manuela to her mother.[110]

It was at this point that the case became entangled in bitter jurisdictional rivalries between the civil and religious authorities. Viewing the vicar's refusal to release Manuela as an ecclesiastical challenge to his authority, the corregidor sent the alguacil to the orphanage to take custody of Manuela. Encountering the resistance of the abbess upon his arrival, he entered the patio to apprehend the girl, thus physically violating the ecclesiastical fuero. His entry caused consternation and chaos, with Manuela being whisked to and locked in a cell and the church bells violently ringing to signal alarm. Hearing them, the corregidor rushed to the orphanage, arriving as the chaplain and alguacil were in the middle of a heated argument that was about to come to blows. The vicar also arrived around this time and persuaded the corregidor and alguacil to leave. He walked the corregidor home, acknowledging that it was a very complicated issue, and urged him to show greater restraint.[111]

This turn of events was only the latest episode of a festering rivalry between the corregidor and the vicar, and, more broadly, between the civil and ecclesiastical fueros in Potosí. In a subsequent exchange of letters, the corregidor insisted there was ample precedent for alguacils entering a place of recogimiento to take custody of people and criticized the vicar for his practice of sentencing people to bakeries, which, he insisted, was strictly the purview of civil authorities. In a polite and measured response, the vicar offered legal arguments to uphold the immunity of recogimiento from civil authority and the right of ecclesiastical authorities to order people to work in bakeries as a form of punishment. Despite its respectful tone, the letter foreshadowed what would happen next by noting that the corregidor, alguacil, and scribe were subject to excommunication for violating the sanctity of the recogimiento, a penalty that would be imposed by the vicar general in La Plata on July 28, 1749. In a violation of protocol, the excommunicates were not informed of their punishment prior to the posting of the notices on the church door, and a week later the cabildo of Potosí called for the order to be lifted. The vicar ignored the request and again refused when the councilmen appeared at his door contending that they had not made the request "with the humility corresponding to the offense." The excommunicates then went to La Plata to request that the order to be lifted, which it ultimately was.[112]

As this played out, Manuela's mother Estefa had returned home to La Plata and prevailed upon the audiencia to demand that the archbishop release Manuela from recogimiento in Potosí. Instead of returning her to her mother, however, the archbishop ordered her into depósito and warned Manuel not to see her or else face exile. Despite these admonitions, Manuel helped her escape from depósito in late December 1748, and the two went into hiding for the next six months.[113] By early July 1749, the mother had obtained an order from the audiencia for Manuela to be placed in the Convent of the Virgin of Los Remedios and for Manuel to release her or else suffer imprisonment, a five-hundred-peso fine, and the seizure of his property. Facing this, Manuel secretly gave his lover up to two priests, who conducted her to the recogimiento in Potosí, not La Plata as the audiencia had ordered. This only complicated the jurisdictional issue, as Manuela was taken into custody by clergy, as opposed to civil authorities, provoking yet another angry response by the corregidor.[114]

By August 13, 1749, the excommunicated corregidor was seeking an exemplary punishment for Manuel, not so much because of his relationship with Manuela but because he was "the cause of all of these disturbances" that had resulted in his own excommunication.[115] The audiencia also offered their perspective that even if the recogimiento was immune to civil authority, if the religious authorities accede to their request to place someone in recogimiento, then they should do the same concerning their release. The waters had become even more roiled in late September when Manuela claimed before the vicar, "I am resolved to remain the rest of my life in this Holy House, in order to protect my soul and to serve the Lord our God, shunning the temptations of the world . . . to achieve peace in my conscience."[116] The punishment, if any, for Manuel, is not indicated.

As with Miguel Caldevilla's illicit relationship in Asunción discussed above, this case also spun out of control and became the vortex of much larger jurisdictional rivalries that involved not only the audiencia but also the archbishop. It is also interesting how Manuela is variously referred to in the case, going from a *mujer soltera*, or a single woman disparagingly referred to as a non-virgin, to being respectfully referred to as "Doña" by a witness when she indicated she wanted to lead a religious life.[117]

Clandestine Marriages

The increasingly restrictive edicts concerning parental power over marriage choice led some couples to resort to desperate measures that challenged not only parental, but also civil and ecclesiastical, authority.[118] Ironically, in so doing, they invoked canon law, which held that, barring diriment impediments, if a couple verbally accepted each other as husband and wife in the presence of the bride's parish priest and two witnesses, they were, in the eyes of the church, married. As with elopement, such a course carried the risk of incarceration and public humiliation in addition to disinheritance and annulment. It is ironic that in a society characterized by arranged, broken, and informal unions, those who actually sought to be formally married in some cases were left with no alternative but to violate social norms and civil law. In the face of such obstacles, many couples engineered clandestine marriages in which they surprised their parish priest and exchanged vows in the company of at least two witnesses, dispensing with the información de libertad, banns, and marriage license.

This was clearly not what twenty-nine-year-old Martín Medrano, a colonial official in Buenos Aires, desired in 1794 when he informed his father that he intended to marry twenty-two-year-old María Pasquala Yraola y Sustaeta. Despite the fact that Martín was legally an adult, his father, Pedro Medrano, vehemently opposed the union. Initially, Martín prevailed in court when the alcalde ruled that his father's objections were without legal basis because Martín was a legal adult. His victory was short-lived, however, as his father had him jailed on unspecified charges and appealed to the audiencia of Buenos Aires, which, despite the law, overturned the ruling. When the news reached Martín on the afternoon of February 21, 1794, he had been transferred to the Bethlehem Hospital. There he arranged to meet Pasquala and her mother, Juana, and told them of the court's decision. Despite the bad news, Martín was resolute, telling María that he had anticipated this and that "no matter what prison they put me in . . . I will escape in order to marry."[119]

Martín's confidence reflected the research he had done on the topic, having learned of a clandestine marriage in Potosí during a visit to the home of the ecclesiastical prosecutor, Dr. Juan José de Suero Andrade. There, and in his studies in Córdoba and readings in another person's home, he had also learned that Pope Benedict XIV had issued a bull on November 17, 1741, that facilitated such unions. The day after the audiencia ruling, Martín was transferred to the jail known as the Oruro prison, which he described as a "cruel dungeon."[120] Creole prisoners from the 1781 Oruro rebellion were held there, and among them was Clemente Menacho, who advised Martín on the matter.[121] Meanwhile, Martín was planning a bold move.

On February 23, 1794, he unexpectedly appeared at María's house at around 9:00 p.m., having just escaped from prison. He urged her mother to ask a carpenter they knew, José María de León, to be a witness to their wedding, which he planned to effectuate immediately. Juana told José that they had finally obtained the marriage license, and he readily agreed to be a witness. Walking down the darkened street toward their priest's house, they encountered Gerardo Borda, who also agreed to serve as a witness, without asking what for. Meanwhile, Martín instructed María on what she should say in front of the priest. At around 9:30 p.m. Martín and María, accompanied by her mother, Juana, and the two witnesses, knocked at the door and entered the home of their parish priest, Father Alonzo de los Ríos, and informed him that they wanted to be married.

Upset over the hour of their visit, he angrily asked whether the archbishop had issued them the marriage license, to which Martín responded he had not. Father Ríos would later write that Martín suddenly "said to her 'do you receive me as your spouse and husband,' to which doña María Pascuala replied, 'yes I do, sir' . . . but in view of this action I immediately removed myself from their presence, saying that I had never heard or witnessed such evil and wickedness."[122] In a loud voice, Martín then told everyone that they were witnesses to the marriage. Like the priest, the witness Gerardo Borda was also upset to learn what he had been brought into, as he and Martín's father had been, until then, on good terms. Later, he told Martín's father what had happened.[123] José Maria de León would later relate how the priest refused to bless the marriage, and when Martín stated that they were all witnesses, the priest "covered his ears with his hands and left the room saying 'witnesses? what witnesses?' . . . so hurriedly that he even tripped over this testifier."[124]

Meanwhile, the group left Father de los Ríos's home and went directly to that of Martín's lawyer, Dr. Domingo Antonio Ezquerrenea. He was getting ready for bed and was quite surprised to see Martín, whom he thought was in jail. To his question of how he had escaped, Martín replied cryptically, "Who knows?" and indicated that he was going to return to his confinement.[125] After reluctantly receiving them, Ezquerrenea asked the witnesses whether they had heard each party give consent, and on that basis he confirmed that, according to canon law, the two were married. José Maria de León would later testify that María accepted Martín as her husband, although she did so in a low voice. After verifying the legality of the marriage, Martín and María consummated their union at the home of her mother, and the next morning Martín returned to prison.[126]

While the newlyweds were at the home of Martín's attorney, a very upset Father de los Ríos reported the night's events to the vicar general, Juan Josef Yolis, who was well aware of the couple's intentions and called for testimony to be gathered. As a result, on March 1 he called for the arrest of Martín and María and the seizure of their goods. While it appears that Martín was already in jail, María was apprehended several days later and held in a cell in the city hall. The vicar general rejected her request to be placed in depósito in her mother's home or in recogimiento, despite her protestation that her imprisonment was "grievous to my honor, to my gender and to my social position, and even in violation of the Sacred Canons and Civil Laws."[127] In her testimony, María stated that in response to Martín's question as to whether she accepted him as her husband, she responded "yes, sir."[128] In his confession, Martín left no doubt that he knew he had not adhered to the proper procedures and fully expected to be exiled as a result. In his defense, he insisted that there was no serious inequality between him and María and that he had married to restore her honor.[129]

The ecclesiastical prosecutor pressed for an exemplary punishment to deter others from such acts, and perhaps to protect his own reputation. Ironically, Martín had learned of the similar case in Potosí during a visit to Suero's home. In his response, the couple's attorney stated that there was no question that the marriage was valid, as it occurred in the presence of their parish priest with at least two witnesses. He further argued that canon law did not require a formal ceremony with the priest's blessing, parental consent, or a marriage license. Nor did it require the banns, and if their absence made a marriage clandestine, then he averred "there would be very many clandestine marriages."[130] While he admitted it was wrong to have surprised the priest, deceived the witnesses, and ignored the audiencia's decision, he insisted that it was all in the name of María's honor. Moreover, Martín had acted precipitously in order to preempt his father's plan to exile him to the Malvinas Islands.[131]

On June 5, 1794, the ecclesiastical court rendered its decision, in which the vicar general noted that many youth are

> carried along solely by the flood of their passions . . . [and I] condemn . . . don Martín Medrano to six years of banishment from this Capital and from 100 leagues around it, and said doña María Pascuala to six years of confinement in the Women's Hospital of this city, subject to legal expenses . . . and with regard to the suit against

> doña Juana Josefa de Sustaeta, who facilitated this illicit marriage by seducing the witnesses and falsely claiming that it was licensed . . . she is sentenced to two months' prison in the House of Spiritual Exercises.[132]

Pending their appeal to the archbishop in La Plata, María began to serve her sentence in the hospital, while Martín indicated he was ready to begin his exile and thus be released from prison. He soon journeyed to Potosí, where in a document giving power of attorney to Manuel Miranda, he described himself as María's "legitimate husband."[133]

In May 1795, Miranda initiated the appeal to the vicar general in La Plata on behalf of the couple and noted that despite their honorable origins they had suffered "all of the ignominy imaginable."[134] Meanwhile, the tide had further turned against them when the ecclesiastical court in Buenos Aires declared their marriage null on April 5, 1795, at least in part as a result of doubts over whether witnesses actually heard María give her consent as opposed to simply the sound of her voice. Things only got worse for Martín, as by late 1796 he had been sent to the island prison of Martín García, perhaps for having returned to Buenos Aires and violating his exile. On Christmas Eve, sustained by little other than his hope and resolve, he signed a power of attorney for Silvestre Orgáz, an act witnessed by the colony's commandant. Orgáz, who practiced in La Plata and had experience in marriage cases, argued that it was irrelevant whether or not all witnesses heard María voice her consent, as the circumstances unequivocally demonstrated that it existed. Not only had the couple appeared at Father de los Ríos's home and held hands, but in her confession María explicitly indicated that she had given her consent. Orgáz did not dispute that the couple had made major transgressions but noted that they were of civil, not canon, law and that the case as a result was a "purely profane . . . issue."[135]

On March 2, 1797, the ecclesiastical prosecutor offered his perspective of the case. He determined that the mother was a valid witness and that consent could reasonably be inferred on the basis of the totality of the events, which reflected "the fervent desires they had to unite . . . in complying with their engagement."[136] While critical of the fact that the marriage had lacked the customary "prior solemnities," he declared that Martin's actions were "allowable in such circumstances" as previous marriages of this nature had been considered valid.[137] On April 19, 1797, over three years after they exchanged vows, Archbishop Joseph Antonio de San Alberto upheld the marriage.[138]

As Martín and María's case shows, clandestine marriages required careful planning, strong wills, surprise, and usually the deceit of witnesses. These elements came together in La Plata on the evening of December 14, 1819. There, the regidor Toribio Cabiedes, his wife, Augustina Berdeja, and daughter, Manuela Cabiedes, were at home entertaining the vicar general, José de Oliveros. Manuela's husband, Captain Isidro Arbos, had decided to forgo staid conversation for the more lively company of his friends at a bar on La Plata's main plaza. An acquaintance of Isidro came inside and told him there was a young lady outside who would like to speak with him. Leaving his hat on the table, he came to meet her near the door. She introduced herself as Melchora Estrada and asked whether he would accompany her on an important errand. He agreed, returned to get his hat, gave her his arm, and they departed. Nineteen-year-old Melchora had just come from the home of a friend, the construction foreman Feliciano Martín, having told him that she urgently needed him to be a witness to a legal act so that she could enter conventual life. He agreed, and they planned to meet at 7:30 that evening at a cockfighting establishment. Between the two meetings, Melchora had changed from a white dress to a rumpled black one, to better resist the cold, she said. Isidro, Melchora, and Feliciano then met and walked to the home of Isidro's parents-in-law and knocked on the door. A servant let them in and Isidro led them to the room where the people were gathered. He greeted those present, who initially thought Melchora was a priest due to the black garb she wore. Isidro then heard whispering behind him and suddenly a man in a cloak and large white hat appeared.[139]

It was Mariano Zilvetti, a twenty-two-year-old attorney, who exclaimed as suddenly as he appeared, "Mr. Provisor, I present to you my legitimate wife doña Melchora Estrada" to which Manuela responded by saying, "This gentleman is my husband." As they exchanged vows, an astonished vicar general shouted that he was not her parish priest and therefore could not marry them. Ignoring this, Mariano continued, stating that "gentlemen, you are my witnesses," adding, "Mr. Provisor, Your Grace will forgive me for having proceeded in this fashion, since I have been unable to do this in any other way."[140] Mariano, Melchora, and Feliciano then immediately fled, leaving the hosts bewildered and a furious vicar general demanding that Isidro pursue and capture the group.[141]

Mariano was the only one apprehended that evening and was placed in the public jail. Melchora would soon also be captured and placed in depósito. Only days before, Mariano had been released from Potosí's jail, where he had spent the previous two months on undetermined charges levied by Melchora's mother, who was "tenaciously" opposed to the marriage.[142] He appears to have developed his plan in jail, begun his trip back to La Plata the day he was released, and put it into action the day after he arrived. Somehow, he knew where the vicar general would be that evening and that Isidro was a regular at the plaza bar. In his confession, Mariano left no doubt that his "intent in the depths of his heart was to marry" Melchora.[143] Melchora testified that the two had been verbally engaged for two and one-half years yet her mother objected through "the most terrible and indecorous means."[144] She insisted that none of the witnesses had any idea what they were getting involved in. Like Mariano, she was also adamant that "it was with such spirit of all of her heart because she believed that that way she would be really married" and that "it was mutual the love that they professed."[145]

The ecclesiastical prosecutor referred to the couple's actions as "criminal sacrilege" and urged that priests in the couple's respective parishes read the banns.[146] They did so, and no impediments emerged.[147] Although their act was especially outrageous as it involved the vicar general, the prosecutor had no doubts that the marriage was valid. Suggesting that such marriages were not unusual, he noted that there was ample precedent in the diocese and that "the marriage took place between two eligible adult persons, by mutual consent, and with a formal expression of their wish to wed, free from all intimidation . . . [and that] Your Excellency . . . [is] the true parish priest of one of the contracting parties."[148] Although the marriage was valid, the manner in which it was conducted would not go unpunished. The prosecutor went on to note the "grave insult" made to the vicar general and his hosts, that the event happened at night with the couple wearing disguises, and that the witnesses were duped. Further, he argued that previous cases had been treated too leniently, and, like his colleague in Buenos Aires, he believed that a lack of serious punishment only encouraged people to do the same thing. On February 24, 1820, the ecclesiastical court upheld the validity of their marriage but ordered the couple to do

> a month of spiritual exercises from the day on which they are released, the male in the Franciscan convent of the Recoleta of this city, and the woman in the Female Orphanage where she is presently confined. . . . In addition, they are to pay a fine between them of 100 pesos. Once this is done and the fine is collected, Dr. Zilveti and his wife shall present themselves, in humble attire and with their heads covered with ashes, at the doors of the parish church of Saint Michael on their knees, where they will be ushered inside by the vicar or his lieutenant, to receive a Holy Blessing during the mass, kneeling on the top step of the presbytery so that they may be seen by all the faithful attending mass. And once this scandal has thusly been resolved . . . they will pay the parish priest to declare them betrothed . . . according to the established tariff, and will also pay the Prosecutor and the Actuary the procedural costs.[149]

Although they had already been in jail for over two months, by the end of March their penance was completed, and, despite their humiliation and punishment, they had triumphed.[150]

The element of surprise, in what amounted to a verbal ambush, was central to a clandestine marriage. This is what Father Francisco Alvarado, an assistant priest of Cotagaita, Chichas Province, explained had happened to him in September 1821. He acknowledged that two months previously, he had met with Ángel Borda and Juana Manuela Villegas in the nearby town of Anejo de Vichala, where they stated that they wished to marry over the objections of Juana's parents. Rather than viewing it as a formal engagement, he characterized it as a consultation. He went on to explain how on the morning of September 7, he paid a visit to the home of Juana's uncle, José Gabriel Villegas. There he encountered Juana and her brother-in-law, Francisco Esquivel. They had been enjoying a pleasant conversation and beverages for about two hours when Ángel arrived and joined the conversation. Later, as Father Alvarado was preparing to leave, his hosts invited him to stay a bit longer and partake in some soup, but he declined so as not to break his diet. Just as he was about to collect his hat, Ángel and Juana suddenly exchanged vows, an act that infuriated him.[151]

Father Alvarado quickly reported this to his parish superior, Father José Julián Arreta, who was unable to apprehend Ángel before he escaped to Potosí. By mid-October, Father Arreta believed that a solution was possible, as an impediment concerning incest could be dispensed and Juana's father had written to tell him that he no longer opposed the marriage. Ángel was also ready to accept the consequences of his actions and indicated this in a letter to the vicar general, Father José de Oliveros, who as we have just seen had personal experience in, and probably very little sympathy for, such marriages. Ángel was unaware that Oliveros had died, and the letter was opened by the new vicar general, Toribio Urquiza. Describing the event as "abominable and scandalous," he called for the arrest of the couple.[152]

Ángel was soon apprehended, and he testified that the marriage was anything but a surprise to Father Alvarado. Not only had he been present during their engagement, but, he insisted, he had paid the priest over fifty pesos to officiate. He further argued that the union was legally valid, as there were three witnesses, including one of Ángel's servants, named Manuel Sánchez, as well as Juana's uncle, José Gabriel Villegas, and Juana's brother-in-law, Francisco Esquivel. The latter was the only one who had no idea of the plan, as he had been asked to be a witness to a financial document. Juana testified that, in Father Alvarado's presence, Ángel had asked her, "'Do you receive me as your husband, Doña Juana Manuela?' And she answered yes, [and] likewise she asked Borda if he accepted her as his wife, and he said yes, and they both held hands."[153] Francisco would later testify that Father Alvarado was engaged in casual conversation when he arrived at the house and that after the vows were exchanged the clergyman stayed there to continue the conversation and eat, his diet notwithstanding.[154]

On December 10, Ángel wrote to the vicar, arguing that his arrest was unjust. He dismissed the notion that a crime had been committed, as Father Alvarado had come to the house voluntarily and was paid for his services. Further, he argued, under the new constitution of Bolivia, he had not committed a jailable civil offense.[155] By Christmas Eve, Ángel was again a free man and on his way to La Plata to plead his case before the vicar general, while Juana had been returned to her parents. On January 8, 1822, Ángel prepared his brief, arguing that there was no inequality between the couple and noting that they both consented to the union, which occurred before a priest and had a sufficient number of witnesses, and that, moreover, she was over twenty-five years old and hence the "owner of her will."[156] Like the ecclesiastical prosecutor in the case of Mariano Zilvetti and Melchora Estrada above, Ángel suggested their approach was not unusual, noting that "this is done every day in this, and other, capitals, and many have given me very many examples."[157] He added that had he known he was breaking any laws "I would not have been able to put myself in this labyrinth."[158]

In his opinion of the case in late January, the ecclesiastical prosecutor was highly critical of the investigation. He not only declared that Father Urreta should have gathered testimony after his investigation, but he also noted that Juana's brother-in-law, Francisco Esquivel, never testified, that the couple's ages were not included in the record, and, importantly, that Father Alvarado's testimony was not given under oath. The result, he averred, was that the investigation "had not moved a step," and he ordered a new priest, José Ignacio Roso of Toropalca, to conduct the investigation properly.[159]

Father Roso was in no rush to gather testimony, and, noting that the rivers were high, instructed witnesses to come to him. While Father Alvarado declined to do so, claiming illness, Juana's uncle testified that she was a legal adult. Juana also ratified her earlier statement concerning mutual consent. By March 22, 1822, Father Roso had wrapped up his minimal efforts, removed Juana from her parents' custody, and placed her in depósito in her uncle's house to spare her parental pressures and reprisals.[160]

Reviewing the file in April 1822, the ecclesiastical prosecutor had no doubts that the couple "violated the Holy Sacrament" but viewed the primary issue as a previous incident of incest. He also noted that there were "several examples [of clandestine marriages] that have occurred in this diocese."[161] He recognized that Juana's father had desisted from his opposition and declared that the impediment could be dispensed. Despite this, he called for a "rigorous penance" for them both, to be followed by a new, properly conducted ceremony. Concerning Father Alvarado's prevarication, he noted that "such weaknesses are typical of this class of individual, who are motivated by ignorance or by self-interest" and called for him to be sent to a monastery and prohibited from serving as an assistant priest anywhere.[162]

As was generally the practice, the vicar general accepted the prosecutor's suggestion and, on April 20, 1822, sentenced Ángel to do spiritual exercises in a monastery in La Plata of his choosing for ten days and Juana to do the same in her uncle's house. Subsequently, they were to confess and collectively pay a fine of sixty pesos, which the priest of Santiago de Cotagaita was to distribute equally between the town's fifteen poorest people on a fiesta day. After this, they could apply for a dispensation. If it was granted, Ángel and Juana were to suffer the identical public humiliation as Mariano Zilvetti and Melchora Estrada.[163] Father Alvarado's punishment mirrored the prosecutor's recommendation, although it may not have been as bad as it sounded, as he was still eligible to serve as a priest. Ángel lost little time serving his sentence, going to the San Augustín monastery from April 22 to May 2, confessing, paying his fine, and immediately asking the vicar general for a dispensation, which was granted. Juana also completed her penance and paid her fine, and both suffered the standard public humiliation called for in the sentence.[164]

Unlike parental consent, witnesses were essential to any marriage, clandestine or conventional. In the village of Pala Chica, in the region of Cinti, Father Lorenzo Melean was enjoying the quietude of his home on the night of August 7, 1806, when Juan de Dios Cavero, accompanied by Petrona Meriles,

> surprised me by saying that he wished to receive said Meriles as his wife, and she answered to my surprise that she too wished to receive him as her husband. Both were from Cinti and were my parishioners. Shocked by this, I . . . went into my bedroom, closed the door and tried to lock it, but Cabero did not give me time to do so, pushing hard on the door. I came out angrily, took him by the chest to restrain him and told him that a marriage could not be contracted with just one witness.[165]

At the time it was dark, and as the only witness was his servant, he informed them that the marriage was invalid not only due to insufficient witnesses but also because they both lacked parental consent. Afterward, he requested the subdelegado, Gregorio Barrón, to arrest the couple. Although the authorities soon apprehended Petrona and placed her in depósito, Juan had fled. The ecclesiastical prosecutor agreed that the marriage was invalid and ordered the couple to report, personally or through representatives, to the ecclesiastical court in La Plata. When they did so, they insisted that there had indeed been a second witness, Ramón Torres, although under oath he had denied being present.[166] In a later letter to the viceroy, Father Melean revealed that he had learned that there had in fact been four witnesses, two of whom Barrón knew, and he had also informed the vicar general of this.[167]

The couple had decided on this course of action due to the opposition of Juan's father, Pedro Cavero, who was the feared military commander of Cinti. When he learned what had happened, Cavero was outraged, and Father Melean explained, "He disrespected me, face to face and with threats, in the presence of several honorable persons, without doffing his hat, even though I am curate and judge commissioned by His Excellency the Prosecutor."[168] Soon after the wedding, Cavero captured and shackled his son in an effort to persuade him to tell Father Melean that he wanted to desist. In his letter to the viceroy, Father Melean expressed his desire to be removed from the parish due to Cavero's harsh temperament, as he expressed it, "because the commander was even capable of saying that I had whipped Jesus Christ."[169]

When Father Melean dispatched his file indicating the validity of the marriage to the vicar general, Barrón intercepted the messenger, brought him to his house, seized the file, removed any documents that suggested the marriage was valid, and then sent the messenger and the dossier on their way to La Plata. Meanwhile, instead of sending Juan to La Plata as the vicar general had ordered, Cavero sent him to Córdoba and then to Buenos Aires. Juan ultimately returned to Cinti, however, and consummated the marriage. Barrón had also imprisoned Petrona, who was terrified of him, while Juan sought to have the vicar general order her brought to La Plata. While Father Melean was a reluctant officiator of the marriage, he had an intense dislike for Cavero and diligently sought to defend the couple, stating, "As the pastor who was of this flock of Jesus Christ, I must defend them from the infernal dragon even with the blood of my veins."[170] Although in January 1808 the viceroy demanded that the issue be resolved after learning that Juan was in Buenos Aires and interested in marrying another woman, it is unclear whether the clandestine marriage was ratified.[171]

These cases illustrate how regal efforts to enhance paternal and patriarchal power in marriage choice, and regal power more broadly, played out on the ground in Charcas. The Pragmática and subsequent edicts exacerbated a growing divide between, on one side, canonical views of marriage based on the free will and mutual consent of a couple and, on the other, civil laws that progressively eroded that doctrine in the name of patriarchy and regal prerogative. The church long had powers of dispensation in order to facilitate unions and viewed marriage not only as a lifelong and indissoluble union but as a bulwark against the tide of illegitimacy. The 1778 Pragmática and related edicts, however, left many couples with no alternative but eloping or conducting a clandestine marriage. On the whole, and despite formal repugnance for the practice, the church accepted clandestine marriages as an expression of free will—and as a means of overriding regal edicts. In many cases, civil courts also sided with the couple who wanted to wed, especially among the lower class and less politically connected. Indeed, many people of low social and ethnic standing, including single mothers, utilized the courts to resolve such disputes, ironically often impugning the race and social status of the potential spouse. Often, a woman's pregnancy could not only force the hand of a reluctant parent but also that of civil and ecclesiastical officials. Regal efforts to enhance parental power in marriage choice only exacerbated the prevalence of forced marriages, informal separations, and, as we shall see, women's agency.

CHAPTER 3

"Without Excuse nor Reply"

Moral Imperatives

Bourbon initiatives regarding marriage and morality included a series of measures introduced in the 1760s that compelled absent husbands to return to live with their wives. Such efforts had the goal of reinforcing the marital bond, ensuring that women were not economically abandoned by their husbands—and were directly subject to male control.[1] In many respects, such efforts to promote a *vida maridable*, or moral, marital life, were far from new, as similar edicts had been issued in 1544, 1549, 1555, 1565, and 1619. The primary innovation concerned enforcement, although it was inconsistent and largely ineffective.[2]

As applied in eighteenth-century Charcas, enforcement, although sporadic, did lead to a host of complications for both men and women. Many couples had been separated for years and had little affinity for, if not outright hostility toward, each other. Much like prosecutions for concubinage, the measures presented local officials and their allies with opportunities for political or economic gain, or vengeance, based on selective enforcement. Many absent husbands were merchants, itinerant or otherwise, and claimed the application of the law would ruin them financially, expose them to debtor's prison, and tarnish their honor. Others argued that their separation was with their wives' permission and was necessary in order to support their family, or that their skills were needed and served the royal interest in the place in which they lived. Whatever the case, the result was thousands of people dreading the prospect of an unhappy reunion.

Local Lethargy

In Charcas, the enforcement of spousal reunification laws began on June 3, 1767, when the audiencia directed corregidors and alcaldes to enforce the order. It directed authorities to "watch with special care those married men who live in districts separate from their wives, continually inquiring into their activities and taking the necessary measures aimed at expelling them and sending them to the places where said wives reside, in order that they observe married life with them."[3] The edict was customarily posted on the door of a public building, such as the cabildo, and announced in the plaza by a crier. On July 14, 1768, the audiencia noted that in the "long time" that had passed, only the authorities in Oruro, Chayanta, and Porco Provinces had sent their annual enforcement reports. They demanded that those corregidors who had not done so submit them promptly or suffer a five-hundred-peso fine.[4]

The threat of fines did at least get the attention of some local officials in late 1768, such as the corregidor of Mizque, Jacinto de Iriate. He explained that the order had been misplaced in the voluminous papers of his predecessor, Andrés Fernández de Trujillo, and, after considerable searching, he had only just found and officially received it. The audiencia then called on Iriate to implement the order and for Trujillo to explain why he had not already done so. In La Paz, the corregidor asserted that he had been unable to implement the law because he had been focused on issues relating to the expulsion of the Jesuits. This, in addition to his quotidian responsibilities, had generated such a volume of paperwork that the order had also been lost, or, more likely, ignored.[5] As a result of the audiencia's prodding, by October 1768, he reported that although he had identified several people subject to the law, one had perished and the others had moved elsewhere.

Civil lassitude in enforcement was mirrored by the clergy, who despite royal directives were on the whole uninterested in assisting in identifying those subject to the law. This was noted in January 1769 by the audiencia's prosecutor, who also criticized the court's functionaries for their carelessness in cataloguing the various orders and responses. In the same month, the audiencia yet again directed corregidors and other officials to enforce the law. Meanwhile, Charles III was preparing a similar edict that would be issued on February 19, 1769, followed by another in 1771.[6]

The cabildo of La Rioja, in the province of Tucumán, responded to the 1771 order in February 1772, reporting that several merchants had departed to reunite with their wives and only one man had to be forcibly returned to his spouse. Similarly, in July 1772, officials in Poopó indicated that those subject to the law had been sent on their way. Beyond this, the order was met with silence, prompting the audiencia to reissue the circular in October 1773, "indicating the court's unhappiness over the delays and carelessness in compliance."[7] The fact that it took this long for the audiencia to follow up indicates their own lack of enthusiasm in enforcing the measure.

In January 1775, the audiencia reiterated the order along with the request that clergy assist in its enforcement, and in April, Charles III ordered an accounting of the actions taken in response to the 1771 edict. In a subsequent decree issued on November 3, 1776, he directed authorities to continue to demand adherence to the law. Despite royal insistence, enforcement and reporting remained lax, with the corregidor of Atacama tersely, and improbably, reporting that there had "not . . . been before nor now during my employment" any men subject to the law.[8]

In a candid appraisal in April 1777, the audiencia's prosecutor noted the practical difficulties of enforcement. He noted that it was nearly impossible to enforce against those with wives in the Americas "due to the well-known laxness of many of the lower judges, who only notify the married men of their obligation, without forcing their compliance."[9] Not only were corregidors habitually remiss in enforcement and sending their annual reports, there were problems verifying whether a person had actually returned to his wife if he did indeed depart a town. In some cases, people were married but managed to keep it secret, while others simply moved to another town and started anew. The prosecutor suggested mandating that men subject to the law pay a bond, from which they were to be released only when they had been certified as having reunited with their wives. Likewise, those sent to Spain via Buenos Aires would obtain certifications upon arrival and embarkation in Buenos Aires, both of which would be sent to the audiencia. Barring such measures, and based on the experience to date, he had no doubt that the edicts and related orders would remain without effect. His proposal was adopted by the audiencia on July 7, 1777.[10]

On February 9, 1784, Charles III issued yet another edict seeking to tighten what was obviously a widely ignored law, calling for all men not in royal service who had wives in Spain to return home without exception or extension. Responding to the edict, on October 26, 1784, Viceroy Nicolás del Campo, Marques de Loreto, sought to reinvigorate enforcement by reaffirming the ban on extensions for those with wives in Spain and ordered that those who had been absent from their wives in the Americas for "quite some time" should either go to them or have their wives come to them within eight days.[11] This did suggest some flexibility in terms of defining what length of time was acceptable and also left open the possibility that the husband could enjoin his wife to come to him. In the city of La Plata, enforcement revealed that over 140 people, including Indians and mestizos, were subject to the various edicts. Some, however, had died; others were widowed, in the process of divorce, imprisoned, or fugitives or, supposedly, had already left to rejoin their wives.[12]

Political/Personal Rivalries

The inconsistent nature of enforcement highlights that it was often applied selectively, in response to opportunities for political or economic advancement or as a means of ending scandalous relationships.[13] It could also be effective in settling personal scores, as the corregidor of Oruro, Miguel de Landaeta, demonstrated in 1753. The early date suggests that

Landaeta was not responding to pressures from superiors in La Plata but rather was utilizing a long-standing law to his advantage. In a letter to the viceroy, Landaeta accused Juan José Herrera of being the cause of discord in the city and intended to make him return to live with his wife, Francisca Xaviera Espinosa de los Monteros, in Arequipa. The viceroy had in turn sent the case to the audiencia of La Plata, where José's representative argued that it was all a result of the enmity between his client and the corregidor. Moreover, he insisted that Juan supported his wife economically and was in "friendship and good company" with her.[14] He went on to argue that Francisca had given Juan permission to go to Oruro alone, as her health had prevented her from accompanying him, despite his entreaties. Finally, he contended that Juan had come to the region in the service of the king as the corregidor of Paria. Although he no longer held this official position, he insisted that he was legally prohibited from leaving because his *residencia*, or mandatory investigation of his administration, had not been completed.[15]

Corregidor Landaeta had a very different view of the matter. He asserted that Juan and his brother Nicolás, whose wife lived in Cochabamba, had been away from their spouses for the previous seven years, during which time instead of supporting them they had been "living . . . with the liberty of single men."[16] Further, Nicolás, Juan, and his son Melchor de Herrera, who was a regidor in Oruro, had all abused their power in official positions to "harass and oppress the poor subjects with countless vexations, venting in this manner their passions."[17] There appears to have been at least some truth to this assertion, as Melchor had recently been jailed and fined for using false weights in an official capacity. Upon reviewing the case, the prosecutor also concluded that all three were living "licentiously and scandalously" and urged that Juan and Nicolás be ordered to reunite with their wives in Arequipa and Cochabamba, respectively. On the basis of the prosecutor's recommendation, the audiencia ordered them to depart Oruro and rejoin their wives within one month or face jail, the seizure of their property, and a two-thousand-peso fine.[18]

In August, Juan appealed the audiencia's ruling, insisting that he supported his wife economically and that she had a morbid fear of Oruro because one of Juan's brothers had died there. He also insisted that the case was entirely motivated by the "blind passion" of Corregidor Landaeta and that he had no means of supporting himself or his wife in Arequipa, while in Oruro his family owned silver mines. The prosecutor noted that the primary issue was Juan's scandalous lifestyle in Oruro and that, because he was no longer corregidor of Paria, he was no longer in the service of the king and hence exempt from the measure. On August 14, the audiencia gave him three months to reunite with his wife, either in Arequipa or Oruro. Juan soon claimed to be "gravely ill" and at the end of October requested an extension due to the rains and high rivers that had impeded his efforts to bring his wife to Oruro and because he was busy with his mines and residencia.[19] The prosecutor lost no time in dismissing his reasons and called for his immediate departure. He also was concerned that Juan would simply go to Poopó, where his family's mines were, or to Paria, where one of his brothers was corregidor. Although what Juan finally did is unclear, the audiencia upheld the prosecutor's view and gave him eight days to depart or else face a two-thousand-peso fine, the seizure of his property, and transport to Arequipa as a prisoner.[20]

Like Juan José Herrera, Juan de Herrero, a physician in Potosí, was also facing the imminent possibility that he would have to return to live with his wife, although she was in Spain. To avoid this, he had enlisted the support of the city's cabildo, which in March 1771 petitioned the audiencia on his behalf for an exemption. They averred that he was not only a man of the highest moral caliber but also the only professionally trained physician in Potosí. As a result, his departure would provoke "the most fatal, sad and melancholy consequences for the many unfortunate ones to whom he lends his support."[21] They reasoned that if the employees of the royal mint were exempt, then so should he be. Juan also was able to obtain the support of the friars who operated the Bethlehem Hospital, which served the indigent. They argued that he should be allowed to remain at least until they could replace him, because without his care the *mitayos*, or forced mine and mill workers, would perish and the crown's interests would consequently suffer.[22]

The audiencia's prosecutor was sympathetic to the request, and as a result the court allowed Potosí's governor, Miguel Martínez de Escobar, to grant him an extension. The cabildo's acknowledgment of the order was written by the scribe Tadeo Chacón, who three years later would be facing his own, very similar, problems. Despite Governor Martínez granting Juan two months to depart, he failed to leave in the time specified. Consequently, on May 28, the governor ordered his arrest, his property seized, and for him to be brought as a prisoner to Buenos Aires. However, when the alguacil went to his house to read him the order, Juan had fled, prompting the governor to issue a circular from Lima to Buenos Aires to be on the lookout for the physician.[23]

Just as Juan de Herrero framed his case in terms of royal interests, Antonio Portuondo followed a similar approach three years later, also in Potosí. He had left his wife, Ana Josefa Ramos, in Chile and in 1774 was serving as an administrator of confiscated Jesuit properties. During his time in Potosí he had also acquired an unnamed mistress, something that might not have been problematic had she been single. Instead, the affair had led to divorce proceedings between her and her husband, Damian Falcony, who perhaps had denounced Antonio. After gathering testimony in mid-July, the audiencia ordered him to depart within eight days and to rejoin his wife. He ignored the order for three months before appealing it in November, contending that the accusation of an affair was "harming my honor, good reputation and better conduct."[24] In the end, the court allowed Antonio to remain in Potosí but ordered him not to have any direct or indirect contact with his lover. As was often the case, the woman was more severely punished: she was placed in a convent as a result of the affair and ensuing divorce proceedings.[25]

While the authorities of Potosí were pressing their case against Antonio Portuondo, Tadeo Chacón, a scribe in the city's cabildo since at least 1758, was also facing the prospect of having to move to La Plata to live with his wife, Mauricia Delgadillo. She petitioned the audiencia to exempt him from the requirement, asserting that far from abandoning her, it was only through his work in Potosí that they were able to have a "vida maridable," and the city's harsh climate made it impossible for her to live there.[26] Perhaps because he worked in the cabildo and had well-connected political allies, and because Mauricia stated that he was there with her blessing, the prosecutor supported her request. Despite the law, he noted that it was common in the region for men to be absent from their homes and families for long periods in order to support them and that there was no suggestion of abandonment. Tadeo may have been ill, or concocted a scheme to put the whole issue to rest, as a short time later the prosecutor noted that he had died and that his wife was dressed in mourning clothes. For whatever reason, the authorities abandoned the case, and he continued to work in the cabildo for many years.[27]

Potosí appears to have had more than its fair share of men who were away from their wives, or perhaps officials there were more aggressive in enforcing the spousal reunification laws, or both. The spike in enforcement in Potosí in the mid-1770s was mirrored in Buenos Aires, where in 1776 authorities ordered all married men who were apart from their wives to give an account of themselves. Scores of men appeared before the alcaldes, offering a variety of reasons why they were away from their spouses. These ranged from serving a term of exile and asserting that their wives were coming to join them or had given them license to be absent to claiming that they had been granted extensions or were protected under the military fuero. Despite their efforts, the next year authorities in Buenos Aires noted that many people subject to the law had failed to present themselves "without fear of God and with less love for their familes."[28]

Some men, like Juan Antonio Rodríguez, would go to extraordinary lengths to avoid reuniting with their spouses. In April 1785, the alcaldes of La Plata ordered him to return to his wife, Valentina Cáceres y Rodríguez, in Arequipa. He indicated that he "would embrace the order with the blindest obedience" and would have left that very day had he not received some devastating news.[29] Eleven months earlier, on May 13, 1784, an earthquake devastated much of Arequipa. A month later, he claimed to have received a letter from a friend there with the tragic news that his wife had perished in the disaster. The alcaldes doubted his word and rejected his request for eight months to prove his widowhood. When he did not depart in three days, they arrested him.[30] Juan was back in a familiar place, as he had only just been released from having been in jail about a month earlier for debts. In April, he successfully petitioned from behind bars to be released on bond and to be given two weeks to leave, an order he promptly disobeyed.[31]

Unfortunately for Juan, in late June 1785, the prosecutor learned that he had been "mocking the judicial system." He had come into possession of two letters from Cipriano Valdés, Arequipa's administrator of tobaccos, indicating that Juan had fled Arequipa due to debts and that Valdés had conversed with Juan Antonio's wife only a few days before he wrote one of the missives. In their conversation, she related how Juan had urged her to come to La Plata but that she had refused because "she knows so many things about her husband," adding that he "never has had the best reputation."[32] In addition to his debts, he had presented himself as a Spaniard, when in fact he was from Genoa. On June 27, 1785, the prosecutor called for him to leave within two days, although by July 14 he had not and was rearrested.[33]

Despite Valentina's dislike for her husband, she wrote the following letter to him that appears to have arrived when he was imprisoned the second time:

> Husband of mine:
>
> I received your short note, but instead of receiving notes all I ever get is greater sorrows. I would be better off if I never received a letter from you, since all you ever do is injure me instead of succoring me, even though you may have been in a

position to, since I have heard from others there that you are not as poor as you portray yourself. . . .

Your behavior and mistreatment towards me are apparent, since whenever someone arrives here from Potosí and is asked about you, he responds how well off you are, and how much you drink, and wonders why you do not provide for your household. . . .

Today I have only God as my good husband and man, who gives me [the courage] to ask you for all that you owe me, which is, as you know, so much I cannot even imagine it. So you can do whatever suits you best, since as your wife I will make my appeal in the court of reason.

[You say] that you cannot send me money because you do not have the wherewithal to pay the postage and you cannot leave because, as you say, you owe so much. I know not why you went to Chuquisaca, you must have something that draws you there. I enclose a draft for you to collect the two pesos, so you can at least wear a shirt, since I know the laws of God, which call upon us to pardon our enemies to be in turn pardoned. I cannot go on since I am somewhat indisposed, so God keep you many years more.

She who wishes to ban herself from your concerns.
Arequipa, June 29, 1785[34]

Juan responded as if the fact that his wife was alive was momentous news, and on August 6 he petitioned the court for his release so that he could rejoin her.[35]

Among those most affected by the spousal reunification measures were merchants, who both received and extended credit in the operation of their businesses.[36] In their ranks, and targeted by the corregidor of Cochabamba in 1777, was the shopkeeper Diego Espinosa, also from Arequipa. Given fifteen days to leave to rejoin his wife, Antonia Muñoz, he petitioned for an extension. As was common, he asserted that his distance from his wife was only a "material separation" because they maintained contact and "good relations" and that he should be exempt because the law was intended for "those who were separated and on bad terms."[37] Like many merchants, his situation was complicated by debt: he owed 2,777 pesos to creditors in town and was awaiting payment of over 5,000 pesos from debtors. Despite the economic consequences and fire sale opportunities it presented for others, Diego was granted only eight additional days to settle his affairs.[38]

In the same year, in Santiago de Estero, the interim governor, Josef Miguel Silveti, noted that although he had ordered married men to depart to rejoin their wives, the directive had been widely ignored due to the "well known disobedience" of the residents.[39] Despite this, he had identified the people subject to the law and posted a letter with their names on it on the cabildo door, giving them three days to leave or else face jail and the seizure of their property. This precipitated a series of appeals, primarily from merchants from Buenos Aires, who usually claimed that they had been away from their wives only a short time, that they supported them economically, and that such a hasty departure would ruin them financially.[40]

Stemming Scandal and Wavering Wives

Although the law demanded that the husband return to his wife, some men sought to convince, or force, their wives to come to them.[41] In other cases, married women of ill repute were sent to their husbands, as happened to Dominga Montero y Bersaín in Potosí in late 1782. Dominga had been banished from the city on the orders of the alcalde Manuel Pérez Fariñas, however her attorney, Gregorio Nuñez, appealed the decision to the audiencia. He explained how in December she and several others had been in the home of a priest at around 9:00 p.m., a gathering that was a regular occurrence. On this occasion, however, the alcalde raided the house, discovered the guests engaged in "forbidden games," arrested them, and ordered Dominga into depósito.[42] Nuñez argued that "despite the suspicion, or reality," of gambling, the others were released the next day but Dominga was not. He complained that the alcalde then began to investigate "all of the passages of her life," the result of which was that she was given eight days to return to her husband and hometown in Oruro. Nuñez went on to contend that not only was Dominga the victim of false testimony but she also never had the opportunity to offer her defense.[43]

In contrast, the alcalde referred to her "incorrigibility" and described her as "among the many prostitutes . . . of this neighborhood" who had ignored his warnings and were apparently immune to the effects of incarceration.[44] One witness characterized her as "the most audacious and daring woman. . . . For many years she has sought carnal satisfaction and has been known as a scandalously public prostitute. At the present time she lives as the public concubine with an individual of strange origins," referring to the unnamed priest in whose home the gambling occurred. He went on to relate how as a result of insulting the alcalde the previous year she had been sent to a bakery as opposed to reclusion "since they will not receive her in any place of reflection or religious house, due to her temerity."[45] Although Dominga denied the accusations, she indicated that she preferred banishment to reclusion, and in August 1783 the audiencia allowed her to serve her exile anywhere as long as she resumed a "vida maridable" with her husband.[46]

In other cases, men, such as Lorenzo Antonio Díaz Caballero, sought to force their wives to join them in their cities of residence. In May 1771, Lorenzo served as a collector of treasury revenue in La Plata while his wife, Sabina Pezoa, lived in Buenos Aires. The fact that he had been appointed to his position by the audiencia, and hence was in royal service, gave him grounds to contest the order for him to rejoin her in Buenos Aires. Instead, he insisted that it was she who should come to La Plata so that she could "enjoy the sociable and sweet company of her legitimate husband."[47] Despite Sabina's reluctance, the second alcalde in Buenos Aires granted Lorenzo's request and on September 2, 1771, ordered her to go to La Plata. She appealed and was able to get the order suspended, insisting through her lawyer that her illness made it "absolutely impossible for now" for her to make the journey upland.[48] Meanwhile, in late October 1772 Lorenzo petitioned the audiencia to suspend their order, but instead they directed officials in Buenos Aires to give her a two-month extension. The order was received in the port city on July 1, 1773, over two years after proceedings began.[49]

In an effort to further delay her departure, Sabina insisted that her health continued to impede her from taking such a "long and difficult journey" and requested a certification of her illness.[50] The court-appointed doctor subsequently testified that she suffered from arthritis, especially in the cold and damp months, and his report arrived in La Plata in mid-February 1774. By this time, Lorenzo was also feeling the pressure, as the audiencia had given him eight months to reunite with his wife in either La Plata or Buenos Aires, and he demanded that she join him "without excuse nor reply."[51] Meanwhile, Sabina continued to challenge the order, but now on the basis that the edict concerned men who did not support their wives and families. This did not include Lorenzo, and she contended that he would be unable to do so in Buenos Aires and indicated she had no objection to her husband staying in La Plata.[52]

Back in La Plata, Lorenzo also pointed out that he had diligently supported his wife, which is what the law sought to achieve, and insisted that it was the wife who was obligated to accompany her husband. On October 22, 1774, almost three and a half years after the case began, the prosecutor noted Lorenzo's efforts to persuade his wife to come to La Plata, that he had supported her economically, and that she was ill. He straddled the fence, however, noting that extensions, not exemptions, could be issued by the audiencia, and only for a limited period of time and for "urgent necessity."[53] The outcome is unclear, although the audiencia did accede to Lorenzo's request to order the alcaldes to cease processes against him, suggesting that the case was then largely abandoned.[54]

Authorities, spouses, and even parents also utilized the reunification laws to put an end to affairs. This is what María Mercedes de León y Osio had in mind when in late 1780 she petitioned to have her husband, Julián Velarde, return to her in Toracari, in Chayanta Province. Hers is one of the very few in which a wife petitioned for her husband's return, although it appears the primary objective was to end Julián's "licentious life, and indecent pastimes," which he had been enjoying in La Plata with his mistress, Francisca Estupiñan. María had petitioned the governor of Potosí, Jorge Escobedo, for assistance, and he in turn requested that the second alcalde of La Plata quietly investigate this "delicate issue."[55] Perhaps Julián was tipped off, as by January 1781, the investigation revealed that he had recently left to rejoin his wife.[56]

While neighbors may have often been willing to turn a blind eye to illicit liaisons, they could also provide damning testimony.[57] In Aiquile, Ramón Lazarte and Paula Moreira had been having an affair, which was facilitated by the frequent absences of Paula's husband as he traveled to gather saltpeter in the Clisa Valley and sell soap in La Plata. Witnesses, almost all neighbors of Paula, testified that the relationship was common knowledge in the neighborhood because the couple frequented *chicherias*, or chicha bars, and organized frequent boisterous gatherings in Paula's house when her husband was away. Many also noted that not only was this setting a poor example for Ramón's two daughters and son but it had also created considerable discord in the neighborhood. Although Ramón was said to have told his mother that "first he would go to the devil than leave that woman," he was given three days to pack up and return to his wife in Cochabamba.[58] In an effort to spare the husband shame, and the wife abuse, the case was ordered to be placed in the cabildo's "secret archive."[59]

Divorce Delayed

The dread of reunification was perhaps most acute among those who were in the often interminable process of a divorce, such as Pastora Torres. She was divorcing her husband, Feliciano Zuazo, as a result of his affections for a woman of African descent and because "he was a tyrannical man, full of vices, lazy and greedy, and as such had tried to kill her."[60] In 1785, she challenged an order in La Plata to reunite by obtaining a certification from the ecclesiastical court that a divorce was underway. The process had, however, stalled as Feliciano had resorted to the common tactic of not responding to a translado. While ecclesiastical officials were usually the ones to urge reconciliation, in this case the lieutenant governor urged them to "put aside past resentment, in a Christian manner, renew your married life, pardoning each other any and all offenses that you may have committed."[61] Although they were told to report back in four months to update the court, the case does not appear to have been resolved.[62]

The tobacco seller Simón de Aldunate y Rada was in a similar situation in Potosí in late June 1776. He had been given three days to start on his way to Oruro, where he was to rejoin his wife, María Martina Bengoa, although they were in the midst of a stalled divorce process. Simón appealed the order, asserting that the archbishop had decreed that they could live apart pending the outcome of their proceedings. Simón had petitioned for divorce twelve years earlier after allegedly twice catching his wife in the act of adultery with a man named Antonio from Guamanga, today's Ayacucho, Peru. The audiencia's prosecutor indicated that the court could not render a decision without substantiating documents. Ramón, however, explained that his efforts to obtain them from the ecclesiastical authorities had been unsuccessful as the case had been "suspended a long time ago."[63]

In his pleading, Simón related how, four months into their marriage, he had traveled from Oruro to purchase coca in the Yungas and "upon returning I found her such another person."[64] In late June 1756, María ran off with her lover, and the two lived together in Poopó for the next six years before they were both arrested and brought as prisoners back to Oruro. Seeking a new start, Simón secured her release and departed for Salta, but after four days on the road she begged him "with a thousand tricks, oaths and tears, promising to completely reform and that she would live henceforth like a saint" if they would return to Oruro.

He relented, and they returned to the city in November 1762.[65] By September 1763, she petitioned the vicar of Oruro to be placed in depósito, where she stayed until August 2, 1764, and Simón decided to file for divorce, no longer able to demonstrate the restraint that had required him to be "as strong as Hercules, and as discrete as Homer."[66] Part of the reason for his decision was because of the very liberal terms of her depósito in the home of Rafaela Subieta, which he insisted included "receiving many letters and behaving scandalously until all hours of the night, as well as attending public invitations and banquets." The case ended with a request by the audiencia to the archbishop on the status of the divorce, as it was clear that Simón had no intention of reuniting with María.[67]

While it appears that Simón de Aldunate y Rada avoided reunification with an adulterous wife, Francisco Velásquez was not so fortunate in La Plata. His wife, Gertrudis Pimentel, had run off with an unnamed priest to Poroma, Yamparáez Province, before being placed in depósito there. This did little to end the affair, as the house in which she was kept became the "theater of her scandalous life."[68] She was then transferred to depósito in Moscari and subsequently, as she put it, placed in "violent reclusion" in the Santa Catalina convent in La Plata before reuniting with her husband in 1785.[69]

While widowed, single, and separated women had more agency than their married counterparts, their situations were always tenuous. In 1796, Augustina Bracho y Caviedes found how quickly an independent life could be upended. She had ceased to be under her parents' authority when she married Manuel Valverde, from whom she later informally separated due to his infidelity. She then lived independently and comfortably for many years in and around Cuzco before moving to La Paz with her maids, property, "and everything needed to demonstrate the decency of a woman of my standing."[70] About a year after her arrival, the governor of La Paz placed her in reclusion, eventually sending her to the Santa Clara Monastery in La Plata. This was in response to a request by her mother, who in letters to the governor and viceroy had accused her of illicit affairs. The mother later withdrew her complaint, but not before the viceroy had also ordered Augustina incarcerated.

She vigorously challenged the accusations and was determined to clear her name, emphasizing in her direct petitions to the viceroy and audiencia her high birth and "irreprehensible conduct."[71] Seeking to be released on bond, she noted that the crimes for which she was accused did not require her imprisonment, nor was there any testimony or evidence against her. She also pointed out that her husband had not filed any complaint against her and that her mother had no legal authority over her. While relationships may have been the cause of her troubles, in the end, it was a relationship that saved her. Between her time in Cuzco and La Paz, she lived for four years on a hacienda with the wife of an alcalde of Cuzco, Antonio Paredes. The wife journeyed with her to La Plata in April 1796 to escort her back to their home, in which she was to reside.[72] Interestingly, she did not indicate that she was in the process of divorce, nor was she forced to return to her husband. Rather, the events demonstrate the continuing power of parents, in this case a mother, over an adult daughter. The fact that higher levels of government became involved, as well as how the case was resolved, highlights the political dimension such cases could assume.

Regal efforts to promote morality were intertwined with a broader effort to reinforce patriarchy and constrain women's autonomy.[73] Charles III's concern that many women had been economically abandoned by their husbands masked the fact that many of these women were also often free of a man dominating their household or life. The crown's repeated efforts, especially in the 1770s and 1780s, to enforce spousal reunification found little resonance not only among husbands and wives but also colonial officials, from the audiencia to corregidors and alcaldes. Very few wives demanded their husbands' return, and husbands often appealed orders to return to their spouses, a process that some were able to prolong for years. Others, when finally forced to leave, simply went elsewhere. While all married men were subject to the law, enforcement appears to have focused on the middle and upper strata of society as opposed to the poor and the indigenous. The former were not only more itinerant but were also seen as setting an example for the rest of society.

Despite this, sporadic enforcement turned many lives upside down, creating expense, anxiety, and possible financial ruin, especially in the case of merchants. When local officials did enforce the laws, it was often a means of ending a public and scandalous relationship. In other cases, far from being motivated by moral urgency, officials appear to have viewed the law as yet another tool in ongoing political and personal rivalries or as a means of creating economic opportunity by leaving merchants with few options other than selling their wares and collecting their debts quickly and at a discount. The cases also underscore the prevalence of both informal separations and legal separations in the context of ongoing divorce proceedings.[74] Even then, some couples, such as Francisco Velásquez and Gertrudis Pimentel, were forced to reunite, notwithstanding the fact that Gertrudis had run off with a priest. Overall, the spousal separations that characterized colonial society created a little-recognized yet important sphere of female agency, as many married women effectively ran their own affairs. Another consequence of coerced marriages, and cause of informal separations and divorce petitions, was spousal abuse, to which we now turn.

CHAPTER 4

The "Executioner of My Innocence"

Domestic Violence and Rape

Life in Charcas was circumscribed by violence, and domestic abuse was both common and socially accepted.[1] A husband was permitted to "correct" his wife if she failed to fulfill her marital obligations, which, among other things, included the "matrimonial duty" of sex, as well as fidelity and obedience. Carlos de Vargas, who was accused of spousal abuse, expressed a common colonial view of a wife's responsibilities when he stated that "it is a . . . wife's responsibility to attend, serve and please her husband in everything."[2]

Within this context, the issue was not so much physical abuse but more what had provoked it and its severity.[3] Because there was nothing unusual about a man "correcting" his spouse, abuse was generally only reported when it had repeatedly crossed the ambiguous threshold of *sevicia*, or extreme cruelty, which usually required convalescence or hospitalization.[4] As the ecclesiastical prosecutor explained in 1820, claims of abuse were only acceptable "when the punishment and ill-treatment of the husband exceeds the limits of permissible, moderate and discrete correction."[5] While sevicia was an oft-stated basis for divorce petitions, an effort of reconciliation at the behest of clergy—and usually more abuse—were in practice necessary steps for such a request to be accepted by the ecclesiastical court.

The consequences of clerical pressure to return to an abusive husband,

and the few alternatives that women had, were put in high relief in Potosí in the mid-afternoon of February 5, 1803. There was commotion in the streets as a severely beaten Feliciana Vásquez was carried to the Convent of the Virgin of Los Remedios "in a sedan chair . . . covered with a rug." She was escorted by a notary in the company of the vicar, Joaquín José del Valle, and her brothers Tomás, Mariano, and Eusebio, a priest. Her husband, the councilman and royal standard-bearer of the cabildo Joaquín de la Quintana, was livid, claiming that during the procession her brothers were "shouting that I had stabbed my wife and pushed her to the brink of death."[6] In an irate letter to the vicar, he accused him of coming to his home without warning and essentially kidnapping his wife of twenty-five years. He went on to contend that Feliciana wanted to remain with him and had only signed a power of attorney to her brother Mariano, a lawyer, under duress.[7]

In a letter to the archbishop, he described being immersed in an "ocean of confusion, calumny, and pain" and how the episode had been at the expense of his and his family's honor.[8] Further, he accused the vicar of using his position as Feliciana's confessor to manipulate her. He then requested that the archbishop order that his wife be returned to his custody, that the vicar be removed from the case, and that she be isolated from him and her brothers. Joaquín did, however, admit, "with the economic and managerial authority that the law gives me over her and my family, and with all moderation and measure . . . [I hit] her ten or twelve times on the arms with the broad side of my sword, in order punish her for several things."[9] As a result of his letter, the archbishop directed the vicar to reunite the couple.[10]

This was the last thing Feliciana wanted, and in a letter to the vicar she recounted how she had endured abuse "many times" in order to preserve her marriage and to ensure the education of her children. On this most recent occasion, she explained that her "robust" husband gave her "an infinity of hits."[11] This was substantiated during her medical examination by the convent's physician, who described patches of hair that had been ripped out, three puncture wounds on her hands, a bruise on her right knee, and so many bruises on her back that one melded into the other. He predicted that recovery would take some time not only due to the severity of the wounds but also because she was "chronically ill, as can be seen in her face and in her weak constitution."[12]

Feliciana would later testify how her brother, Father Eusebio, had previously urged her to "carry her cross with patience." A few days before this latest episode, she confided in him her desire to leave her husband, which prompted him to ask why "she wanted to cast off the cross that God had given her, to save her soul."[13] Her brother Mariano had earlier shared this view, noting that the ensuing scandal would damage the family's name and that, worse, to leave her husband would be an offense against God. She added that while she initially had her doubts about signing the power of attorney to him, they were dispelled by the thought of returning to her husband. Not only did she consider her own previous violent experiences of reconciliation but also those of others, including her sister-in-law.[14]

Armed with the power of attorney, Mariano soon initiated divorce proceedings on her behalf on the basis of sevicia. In so doing, he requested testimony from the residents, including servants, who lived in the neighboring home in which Feliciana had sought refuge that afternoon. The lady of the house, Melchora Yribarren, related how her maids alerted her to the sounds coming from Feliciana's house, with which their house shared a wall. They initially thought Joaquín was punishing all of his servants, as the cries lasted about two and a half hours, during which time she heard a woman scream, "Enough for God's sake!"[15] She believed, as did her servants, that whatever punishment was being meted out was excessive, as it went on for so long. Despite the cries from next door, Melchora went to take a rest but soon heard banging on the front door. The servants opened it to find Feliciana, who was in such shock that she was unable to speak. After a warm drink, she composed herself, explained what had happened, and expressed her fear that her husband would come to attack here there. She then requested that Melchora call the vicar so she could be placed in recogimiento. Upon his arrival, she begged him "not to turn her over to her husband as the other vicars had done on other occasions."[16] When the vicar acceded to her request, Melchora produced an old and dusty sedan chair, they put a rug over it, and she was carried through the streets to the convent.[17]

Mariano indicated that there were additional reasons for divorce beyond sevicia but that in order to avoid further injuring Joaquín's honor, Feliciana was leveling only that specific charge. He added that any "correction" should not have lasted more than fifteen minutes and would not leave wounds that caused "horror . . . to those who see" them. Worse, he insisted, Joaquín's sadistic behavior "is not new but rather an inveterate custom."[18] Like Feliciana, he noted that other vicars had sent her back to her husband after similar incidents and said that to believe Joaquín's version of events would be to believe that that "the sun does not give light . . . that good is bad and bitter is sweet."[19]

Manuel Malavia, representing Joaquín, endeavored to have all testimony dismissed on the basis that Feliciana had been illegally taken from her husband, while Joaquín complained of "litigation that I should not have to endure."[20]

By May 10, Feliciana had been in Potosí's Convent of the Virgin of Los Remedios for three months and was physically, emotionally, and financially worn down. In a letter to the archbishop, she noted the frequency of her husband's abuse and complained of the costs of the divorce, saying, "My husband, surrounding me with penury, only barely contributes to the food I need."[21] She explained that a future lack of response to translados was not due to negligence or disrespect for the court but rather lack of funds. Although the outcome is unclear, she had been abandoned by her brothers and left destitute by her husband and had few alternatives but to return to him.

The frequency, prevalence, and nature of spousal abuse was appalling, and given its social acceptance and legality, underreported.[22] Among its victims was María Josefa Peres de la Reynaga, who in 1805 was seeking a divorce from Melchor Nuñez, also in Potosí. When she met him, she was attracted by his apparent "affability . . . [and] leniency." Soon after their marriage, however, the beatings began and continued to the point that she had become "the object of general compassion in that town."[23] When she informed her priest of the abuse, he admonished Melchor to mend his ways, which he agreed to do, she averred, "only so that his prey would not escape."[24]

Her effort at reconciliation led to her being held captive on his hacienda, where he would beat her five or six times a day. On one occasion he gave her "such a ferocious beating that she no longer had the figure of a woman," despite the fact that a visitor to the hacienda had dropped to his knees and begged him to stop.[25] On other occasions, he had kicked and beat her in public, once doing so in front of the assistant priest and Indians as they went to mass. Recognizing the inefficacy of priestly intervention, María appealed for help from Potosí's intendant, who dispatched the alguacil to convey her to Potosí. He also ordered Melchor's arrest but soon released him on the basis of his "promises . . . to amend his ways."[26]

The couple reunited yet again, and Melchor soon resumed his abuse. On one occasion he brought María behind the house of the priest Santiago Costas and "with a palm stick gave her a deadly beating" amid shouts that he was going to kill her.[27] The beating only ended when a girl ran to tell the priest what was happening. No longer able to ignore the screams behind his home, he and other people encountered a bloodied María with missing teeth and cuts to her chest and face. A doctor certified that "no part of her body remained unbeaten." She complained, "The priest was witness to it all, but only admonished him, because his only interest was in silencing such a formidable event."[28] Recognizing Melchor's intractability, the intendant placed María in depósito and sent the alguacil to order him to stay away from her. María then filed for divorce, and given her "advanced age" and Melchor's indigence, she was allowed to remain in depósito as opposed to recogimiento. The ecclesiastical authorities also ordered Melchor to leave her alone, yet the case apparently stalled after Melchor refused to respond to the translado.[29]

Things were worse for the Indian Melchora Flora, who also sought a divorce, from her husband, Manuel Salazar, as a result of sevicia and his affair with a widow in Mizque. In her petition in 1757, she explained how her husband was "not much of a worker and only has an ability to mistreat me." She took his threats to kill her seriously, as he "was not content with whipping and beating me, but began to chew on my body and my ears, eating them like a dog."[30] As a result, she had been living with their single daughter for the last year and a half, with no financial support from Manuel, despite the fact that he owned over one hundred head of livestock.[31]

The alcalde ordered Manuel imprisoned and both the lover and wife placed in separate depósitos. Meanwhile, the protector deplored "that he ate almost half her ear and face, as only a dog would do."[32] Subsequent testimony revealed that Manuel had abused her for at least the previous six years. Despite this, Melchora did not object to Manuel's release on bond after he had spent a month in jail. Although the alcalde urged her parish priest to promote a divorce, the town's senior priest was unconvinced. Instead, he insisted that they settle the issue in civil court, saying, "Since the litigants are Indians and by nature inconstant, today they may be at odds with one another, and tomorrow they may have made up . . . making a legal admonition more appropriate than a formal divorce."[33] As a result, it appears that Melchora would have had to reunite with her husband in order to be released from depósito, and to petition the vicar general if she was going to pursue the divorce.

Another Indian, Bárbara Cuiza, had also long suffered at the hands of her husband, the mestizo Fermín Sandi, in Potosí. In their eight years of marriage, she explained, "I have done nothing more than sacrifice all of my love and respect."[34] She herself was almost sacrificed to his wrath when on different occasions he tried to cast her off a cliff and beat her while she was pregnant. Worse, one day, when he did not like what she had cooked, he took a foundling that was perhaps her baby and threw the infant to the ground in the patio, causing fatal injuries. As a result of this abuse, and his heavy drinking, she sought a divorce in

1805. Like many men, in his response Fermín relied on an ad hominem attack, accusing her of being a rebellious Indian who led a "licentious life," describing her accusations as "imaginary," and insisting, "I have never thought of mistreating her with cruelty."[35]

Not only were wives abused, but so were domestic servants when they intervened on a woman's behalf. In 1766, María Jacinta de Melo filed for divorce from the corregidor of Yamparáez, Juan Antonio de Silva y Acuña, due to the "intolerable sevicia" that she suffered. This included "hits, kicks, punches and even dragging her on the floor." She claimed that on one occasion she might have perished had her female slave not put herself in between them, injuring herself in the process.[36] María tried to flee Yamparáez to nearby La Plata, however her husband was waiting for her as she approached the city and marched her to the Santa Clara convent. Once she was there, a court-appointed doctor certified that she was bruised in various parts of her body and noted that she had been spitting blood. Ironically, years later, in January 1780, Corregidor Acuña would be conducting a different captive to La Plata, the rebel Tomás Catari. On this occasion, he and his escort were ambushed and Acuña was stoned to death before having his eyes poked out.[37]

The limits of legal and clerical intervention and punishment were underscored in the case of Polonia Salazar in La Plata. In 1786, her mother explained how Polonia's husband, Josef Chalar, viewed "her not as a consort but rather as a slave" and was given to "abusing her with furious hits."[38] In January, Josef had been arrested and sent to a bakery, from which he was soon released under bond after "promising to mend his ways and treat his wife well. This promise, which was only made in order to escape from confinement, has not been kept in any way, since after just a few days he increased his abuses," including hitting her with a rock on the head.[39]

A surgeon and scribe inspected the wounds, which were not life-threatening, and the court ordered testimony to be gathered. One neighbor, the mestiza Rufina Velásques, testified how on February 1 she was passing by Polonia's house on the way to visit a friend and heard screams from the building. Entering, she found Josef "in the patio . . . [where] he grabbed . . . Polonia, by the hair, and dragging her on all fours he cruelly abused her."[40] She intervened and was able to make him stop, but shortly after leaving she heard Josefa screaming again. Returning with another neighbor, they "realized that the man had a baby in his hands, which said Polonia asked him to give to her, but the man, in a total rage, abused her with denigrating words until finally he took a water jar and threw it at her hip, knocking her to the ground, despite the pleading and begging of the witness."[41] He then shoved the witnesses out, and "taking up his poncho and hat, he escaped into the street."[42]

The women went back in and "finding her half dead, speechless and unconscious to the point that, on the ground, a pool of blood had formed."[43] She and her friend then called Polonia's relatives and helped transport her to her mother's house. The mother petitioned for the arrest of Joseph and the seizure of his goods, and while they managed the latter, Josef had disappeared.[44] While Polonia's mother interceded on her daughter's behalf, the fact that many relatives of victims of domestic violence did not, or did so only after years of abuse, underscore the degree to which it was socially accepted.

These cases also show not only the severity and consistency of abuse but also how it reached all levels of society, from urban wives of colonial officials to rural Indian women. Overall, intervention had little effect other than enraging the husband, who viewed his wife as his property and insisted that his actions were a legitimate exercise of his authority as head of the household. Recogimiento and depósito did offer at least temporary protection in cases of spousal abuse, and abused women, such as Gertrudis Mercado de la Huerta, often requested reclusion. Born illegitimate and having lived as an independent, single woman, Gertrudis married José de Arisa when she was around twenty-five years old. Her belief that he was an honorable man from Lima was soon shattered when she discovered that he was a violent gambler. When she refused to sell her few jewels or give him money to support his vice, he began to beat her, such that "there has not been a night or day in which he has not laid hands on me" or threatened her with a "a broad strip of leather . . . swords, blunderbusses and offensive weapons, swearing that he would kill me and steal my meager possessions."[45]

With scars and bruises on her face and body, in mid-May 1796, Gertrudis and her husband came to live with her sisters in La Plata. Far from being moderated, his abuse continued, and it came to include Gertrudia's sisters. This, combined with his threats to kill them all, led her to seek an annulment, and she was placed in recogimiento in the Convent of the Virgin of Los Remedios in late August 1795. Once she was inside, as was the norm, her priest urged her to reconcile. Her brother, Antonio de la Huerta, shared this view, telling her that "I should suffer for my sins, everything came from the hand of God."[46]

She followed their advice, but things only got worse. She related how "from the night of our reunion he began with more force to mortify me" and went on to describe how he locked her in the house, threatened her life, and held pistols to her chest and how she was often bound or dragged through their home by her hair.[47] She could no longer flee to her sister's home, as they were also fearful of José's fury, so she returned to recogimiento. In a letter to the archbishop, she explained how her neighbors, although well aware of the abuse, were powerless to intervene, as "on hearing my cries, they only appeared at the door, without being able to do anything."[48] Two priests had intervened and tried to assist her, but even they were afraid to return to her residence. She went on to explain how she had "suffered not only in my person, body, reputation and honor, but also in my limited property" and insisted that "the saintly sacrament of marriage was not instituted for my martyrdom."[49]

Even while she was in reclusion, José's threats did not stop. On one occasion he entered "until the first arch of the convent," while on another he stood outside with "dagger in hand verbally abusing the doorkeepers."[50] Although he was not apprehended on either occasion, because he claimed to be protected by the military fuero, the vicar general requested that either the audiencia or the military court take action, because the ecclesiastical fuero, and sanctity of the convent, had been violated. As a result, in May 1796, the audiencia granted her request to be moved to the Santa Clara convent and ordered José to cease wearing a military uniform, because he was not entitled to do so, and to send Gertrudis her bed and clothes.[51]

José insisted, "from my part there has not been the lightest persecution" against his wife, while complaining of her "incorrigibility and her pride." He went on to describe, improbably, how "when she gets mad I kneel before her, begging her to calm down, but she does not back off as a result of my submission, which . . . only enhances her fury. . . . Everyone here admires my patience, and I am the object of general pity . . . so that being in her company is hell for me."[52] As with many such cases, the outcome is unclear, yet it is interesting that José managed to avoid jail given both his abuse of his wife and his violation of the sanctity of the recogimiento. By 1812, Gertrudis was widowed, and again an independent woman.[53]

Alcohol commonly exacerbated abusive relationships, and contributed to the attack on the Indian Melchora Olmos by her husband, mestizo Toribio Terrasas. In late 1798, Melchora and her female friend Tomasa Torre had gone to purchase a block of salt in their La Plata neighborhood. They were apparently trailed by Toribio, and as they were about to agree on a price, he suddenly appeared in a poncho, asked her what she was doing there, and stabbed her in the buttocks before fleeing. Toribio was soon arrested, and his property seized. He denied any memory of the episode, insisting that the alcohol he had been drinking "went to his head" and had left him unconscious until he awoke in jail and his father explained to him what had happened.[54] By December 15, Melchora had recovered, and Toribio sought to be released from jail on bond, despite his wife's insistence that this was not the first time he had stabbed her. Instead of pardoning him, she called for him to be sentenced for attempted murder, claiming that was his intent. Toribio portrayed the issue as a consequence of his wife's disobedience, denied that he had threatened to kill her, and insisted that the wound was minor and would have healed more quickly had his wife not been given to chewing coca. By March 27, 1800, after he had spent sixteen months in jail, the court found him guilty of the assault, ordered him to pay her medical and court costs, and sentenced him to time served.[55]

Melchora's case was unusual in both that she did not petition for her husband's release and that he was jailed for so long. More frequently abuse victims, such as twenty-six-year-old Rafaela Camacho in Mizque, requested the release of their abusers from jail, even when they were habitual offenders. Rafaela had few illusions about her husband, Antonio Beisaga, contending in November 1803 that he "serves no other purpose than to abuse my body." He did, however, "have an ability to dissipate that which is from my work" to support his drinking and gambling habits.[56] In a letter to the second alcalde, she explained that the abuse had started with their marriage, and despite warnings from the vicar, it had reached such a degree that "there is neither tongue nor pen which can explain." Her wounds spoke for themselves, as she had a black eye, scratches on her face, bruises on her back and neck consistent with strangulation, and injuries in "other hidden parts which I will not show out of shame."[57] Antonio was no stranger to the local authorities, with the first alcalde characterizing him as "incorrigible," while the second alcalde warned him of the severe punishment he would experience if he did not mend his ways.[58]

The regidor Blas Méndez also noted how Rafaela had come running to his home many times at night after suffering abuse, despite Antonio's multiple arrests. Similarly, a neighbor, Mariano Vargas, testified how Antonio had the "custom" of abusing his wife. He related how once he was awakened by her screams but did not intervene, as he did not want to get involved, but noticed her head injury the next day.[59] Another person in the neighborhood explained how Rafaela had come to her house to iron clothes, and Antonio arrived in a rage, as she had not prepared a fire in his forge. He then proceeded to drag her by her hair and beat her to the point where she was spitting blood. In his testimony, twenty-eight-year-old Antonio claimed he had no idea why he was in jail, although he did admit that it was his fourth time behind bars. While he would ultimately concede that he was usually drunk when he beat Rafaela, he denied throwing pepper in her eyes and admitted, and then denied, that he had "covered [her] body with ants."[60]

The prosecutor had no doubt that alcohol was the "godfather" of his actions and lamented that he had not yet felt "the weight of justice." To make him change his ways, he called for the rather mild punishment of twenty-five days of work in the San Francisco Church on tasks assigned to him by the vicar "so that with this weight he will amend his continuous vices, injuries and abuse."[61] Antonio's attorney had little to go on and suggested that Rafaela's nocturnal absences were to see a lover as opposed to fleeing her husband's abuse. After about a month in jail, and perhaps at the urging of her priest, Rafaela called for his release. She expressed her belief that his crimes had been "purged with prison" and said that because "he is my legitimate husband with whom I should be . . . I pardon him for all of his injuries and abuse."[62] Perhaps because of his recidivist ways, the prosecutor objected, and in early December the second alcalde imposed the tepid sentence he had requested, allowing him to return home at night and warning him against further abuse.[63]

Alcohol also played a role in the years of abuse suffered by Tomasa Mariscal in Arani at the hands of her husband, Lorenzo Méndez, prompting her to petition for divorce in September 1812. She characterized him as not only a drunkard but also "a lazy, slothful man without a trade or means of earning a living." She was determined to put an end to his "continuous extreme cruelty, stabbings and blows with a sword."[64] She related how on one occasion she was so severely abused that she confessed to her priest in preparation for death and described the gashes on the wall where he customarily beat her with a sword. Her priest, Diego Felipe Llanos, attested to the many times she had complained of the abuse and described one incident in which she was left "completely bathed in blood due to several wounds and contusions."[65]

Similarly, the alcalde pedaneo stated that two years previously Tomasa had filed a complaint against her husband after he beat her with "the rein of the bit and the harness of his saddle." Despite this, the alcalde refused to certify her wounds because he was busy with "things of greater importance."[66] The previous year, however, he did order a formal record of her injuries and the damage on the wall that resulted from another beating, which led to Lorenzo's arrest. Tomasa remitted these depositions to the archbishop, who assigned a prosecutor in Cochabamba, who then ordered them to separate "provisionally." He also ordered the husband to cease abusing her and for Tomasa to formalize her charges within one month or be placed in depósito.[67] It is, however, unclear whether she proceeded with the case.

The isolation of country life could exacerbate a spiral of abuse, as María Carion learned during her time on the hacienda of Chilcani, near Poroma. She had married Carlos de Parraga, whom she described as having a "rude and rustic nature," around 1751. On a previous occasion she had fled to La Plata and been placed in the Convent of the Virgin of Los Remedios as a result of his abuse.[68] As was the norm, she soon reconciled, but whatever hope she had soon turned to desperation as he soon began to subject her to "the most severe cruelties that one cannot reduce them to writing."[69] Instead, she described how she had been kept isolated from her father and stepmother, how he had squandered her dowry, and how he once put a knife to her throat while threatening to cut off her head before being dissuaded by her "pleas, persuasions and tears."[70] This type of abuse was a bit of a deviation from his custom, as "in order for my . . . husband to satiate his cruelty and the extreme loathing with which he regards me . . . with no provocation he would take me to the hills, where he would tie me to a tree and proffer blows and lashes to my bloody body."[71]

By late October 1756, she was back in recogimiento in La Plata, and a notary arrived to inspect her wounds and reported that "in her intimate areas I found that, on both sides of her buttocks, as well as around her eyes and her left arm" there were numerous bruises.[72] On this basis, in early December 1756, she petitioned for divorce from her husband and for him to cover her living and court costs. Meanwhile,

Carlos had fled La Plata despite being ordered to remain there under threat of excommunication. By late January 1757, he had been notified of the order to provide four pesos a week to support María, who in the meantime had been sustaining herself in recogimiento by selling her jewelry. She was clearly miserable there, lacking clothes, "sleeping on the ground," and afflicted by "tumors . . . all over the body."[73] She had also been forsaken by her father after he reluctantly contributed twenty pesos for her upkeep and then refused any future support. In late April, with María having sold her possessions, abandoned by her father, and faced with Carlos's refusal to support her, her attorney, Juan de Cabrera y Urriola, sought to have her placed in depósito in her aunt's home. He argued that if neither her husband nor father would support her, she was no longer obligated to remain in reclusion. As a result, on May 7, 1757, she was released to her aunt, with the admonition to live chastely. Although the case was left unresolved, she had obtained a separation.[74]

In some cases, a forced marriage was a prelude to years of abuse, or worse, as Melchora Michel de Zárate related in November 1807. She sought an end to the thirty-one years of marriage to, and beatings by, Toribio Daza. She claimed that she had married at a "young age, forced and obligated by my parents."[75] Toribio soon revealed his "devilish nature" through his violence, heavy drinking, laziness, and lascivious ways. She summarized only her most recent experiences of abuse in her petition, she said, "so as not to tire your . . . attention with a long account of my suffering, which would [also] not only reawaken my pain, but take up much paper."[76]

Melchora related how nine months earlier she had been at a fiesta with reputable people in their building in La Plata when her husband erupted into the room. Enraged, he dragged her away, shouting that he was going to kill her for not having prepared a meal. Once inside their room, he threw her to the ground and began to beat her. Those at the party clearly heard how "the hits were . . . excessive and inhumane."[77] Melchora's daughter soon came running to her aid, crying and begging her father to stop, only to be shoved to the floor and injured. A neighbor who was a carpenter then intervened, bringing the daughter to a safe place and helping Melchora to escape to the street, where she spent the night. She took her husband's death threats seriously, explaining that "he made it known that he was willing and even determined to finish me off once and for all, due to the great hatred and ill will he professed toward me, and that for this reason he was already in mourning for me, having donned his mourning clothes several days ago, as if to announce my imminent demise."[78] The vicar general accepted her divorce petition, although it appears that Melchora abandoned her case and either reconciled or informally separated, as she did not respond to the translado.[79]

In Oruro, the Indian Margarita Nina also had good reason to fear for her life in 1807 when she petitioned for divorce from her Indian husband, José Gutiérrez. During the course of their twenty-year marriage, she averred, her husband had had six lovers and three illegitimate children. She went on to explain how he would abuse her while she was "hanging from a beam in my house, where he left me for half dead, something that he did several times, so that instead of the clothing, food and sustenance that he should have provided, he gave me beatings, whippings and ill-treatment."[80] She related how on another occasion he waited until everyone was asleep in the house then dragged her to their well and held her upside down in an effort to drown her. In so doing, however, he lost his grip and "I fell standing up and my skirts kept me afloat on top of the water, allowing me to scream for help, and since there were some Indians lodged in the house, they soon got me out."[81] After civil officials in Oruro ignored her complaints, she petitioned the vicar general for divorce, although it is unclear whether the case was accepted.[82]

Melchora's fears of being killed were not without merit, especially in the climate of abuse that characterized a pre-forensic society.[83] Moreover, given the apparent frequency of female infidelity, it is surprising that there are not more cases of men killing their wives or their lovers, as they were legally entitled to do if they caught them in flagrante. The absence of prosecution does not indicate the absence of the crime, and it is possible that many such deaths were concealed or simply not investigated. Despite the paucity of cases, such events did occur, such as when Nicolás Calderón arrived at his home in Juli at around 2:00 a.m. in mid-October 1788. There, he found his wife, Catalina Mariaca, in bed with a priest, who, as usual, was not identified. Through his attorney, Gregorio Nuñez, Nicolás explained how "in the throes of his most justified passion he could do no less that accidentally stab his unfaithful wife." Although she later perished, supposedly from a fever "and other assorted reasons" that likely included the stabbing, Nuñez argued that Calderón's actions were "more worthy of compassion than punishment." Despite the fact that he had broken no law, the subdelegado had placed him in a "dark cell, deprived of all contact, with two pairs of irons and a clanking chain." Further, he complained, "the whole process moves so slowly that, for the miserable prisoners, their confinement is worse than the very sentence they face with fear." Nuñez requested that the file, much of which the subdelegado claimed had been lost, to be sent to La Plata, along with the prisoner, to resolve the case.[84]

Like Catalina Mariaca, Tomasa Ortíz perished as a consequence of being caught in flagrante with her lover in La Plata. She had long endured the abuse of her husband, the thirty-year-old mestizo Fermín Zambrana, and had come close to death on previous occasions. At around 10:00 p.m. on New Year's Eve 1807, Fermín arrived home from tending his wheat field only to find Tomasa locked inside her room. When she responded to his demands to open the door, she and her lover named Gregorio scuffled with Fermín. The lovers were beaten with a stick and a rock before Gregorio escaped and Tomasa was left without a "healthy bone."[85] She was then taken to the Santa Barbara Hospital for treatment of "six wounds that cover almost all of the head, made, it would appear, with a blunt instrument, stick [or] rock. Said wounds were deemed by the surgeon to be mortal, not only due to their location, [but also because] . . . the . . . skull [is] exposed."[86] By late January, the doctors reported that she was recuperating and, oddly, noted that if she died, it would not be as a result of the wound.[87]

In his declaration, Fermín admitted that he had punched his wife the previous December during an argument over her affair with the guitar-playing Gregorio and was briefly jailed as a result. While he was in jail, the alcaldes ordered Tomasa to end the affair and attend to her husband.[88] With Fermín in jail, Tomasa admitted to the affair and asked the authorities to have mercy on him. By February 12, however, she had died, according to the doctor as a result of diarrhea brought on by something she had eaten. As a result, on March 7, 1807, the prosecutor called for the arrest of her lover Gregorio who, in his view, was the cause of her death.

Two months later, he had not been captured, so the prosecutor called for him to be tried in absentia and agreed to release Fermín on bail. By mid-June, the prosecutor was essentially serving as Fermín's advocate, arguing that since he caught them in flagrante then he had committed no crime and that, as a result, he should be "absolved of all blame and responsibility."[89] Further, he noted, she did not die from her wounds but rather from "from a subsequent cholera and from overeating," which could have been caused by poison.[90] Likewise, Fermín's advocate for the indigent also called for his release, insisting that "this innocent . . . should not suffer," and on July 17, 1807, he was freed.[91] The authorities concluded that "Gregorio Guitarrero" was probably dead but left open the possibility of his prosecution if he was found.[92]

In another case, in September 1799, a group of muleteers were on their way to La Plata from Potosí when they discovered the body of a woman, identified only as María, who had been beaten to death on the banks of the Chicapilcomayo river. Surrounded by bloody rocks, she was wearing only a shirt and had at least three wounds to her head and "a sash that was said to belong to her aggressor, the end of which the deceased had torn off with her teeth while defending herself."[93] The woman and her missing husband, Ascencio, were Indians who had arrived from Turuchipa a few weeks earlier and found work on a nearby hacienda. Just prior to María's death and Ascencio's disappearance, the couple had attended a friend's saint's day celebration that had lasted well into the night. Although authorities issued an arrest warrant for Ascencio, there was a notable lack of urgency in investigating the murder, as by December no one had given testimony nor had authorities seized Ascencio's goods.[94]

Rape

Rape was yet another frequently underestimated manifestation of violence against women that often crossed caste lines and elicited little interest from colonial authorities.[95] As one alcalde put it, "We are in a country in which the frequency of these crimes appears to have caused the loss of the horror that they inspire in a truly Christian spirit."[96] In such a context, it is not surprising that many people were unwilling to report the crime, which would make a private humiliation public and damage their, and their family's, honor.

The lack of punishment for such a crime was demonstrated in an early afternoon in November 1772, in San Sebastian Parish, Yamparáez Province. Micaela Estrada had sent her ten-year-old daughter, Manuela, on an errand to the shop and home of the mulato barber Tadeo Andrade to see whether he was interested in purchasing some plates. Tadeo feigned interest and invited the girl into the shop. Hardly had she entered when, "locking the door from the inside, he took her violently to the bed and raped her without any resistance from her, due to her little or no strength, covering her mouth so that she would not scream."[97] Manuela could barely walk afterward, and two weeks later still had not recovered. She did testify, which was unusual, and related how when Tadeo invited her into the store "he told her to lie down in his bed, that it was a nice bed, but she refused to" before he covered her mouth and "did with her as he pleased."[98] Afterward, he told her not to tell her mother and gave her two reales that she insisted were for some of the plates, not the sex. Tadeo negotiated a settlement in which he was to pay the mother twenty-four pesos within fifteen days, essentially as a virginity debt. Although he made a down payment of six pesos, he was arrested when he failed to pay remainder.[99]

A person who had been raped could also find herself under pressure to marry the attacker, as was the case with fifteen-year-old Manuela Casimira Pacheco. She and her mother, Tomasa Rica, were renters in the house of Vicente Flores in Limapampa, in Yamparaéz Province, in May 1797. Tomasa often left Manuela in the elderly Vicente's care when she had work to do outside of the house. On one afternoon, however, when another tenant was also away, "behind a closed door [Vicente] . . . chased her around, hitting her with rocks, until her scant resistance failed, and thus tired out and covering her mouth with a handkerchief . . . he carried out a lascivious, impudent and diabolic plan" which was "the execrable, scandalous and delinquent act of raping her, with force and terrible violence."[100]

He then gave her one-half real and a tin pitcher and told her not to tell anyone or else she would be punished. Manuela initially kept her silence, although Tomasa noticed that Vicente became angry when she sent Manuela out on an errand, yet attributed it to a protective instinct because "as an old man he wanted to take care of her."[101] For her part, Manuela would cry and shudder at the prospect of being alone with Vicente and then confessed to her mother what had happened. Tomasa confronted Vicente, who admitted to the rape and suggested that the best solution would be for him to marry Manuela. As a "rustic, poor woman" Tomasa did not know what to do, and she consulted with her priest, who agreed with Vicente and began preparations to marry the couple.[102]

Having gathered the información de libertad and issued the banns, the clergyman came to their house one day and placed Manuela in depósito in his own house prior to the ceremony. Tomasa protested and was able to have her daughter released, as it was clear neither the girl nor the mother approved of the union. She also filed criminal charges against Vicente, resulting in his arrest. In his testimony, Vicente stated that he was prepared to marry Manuela and attributed Tomasa's reluctance to his age. The second alcalde wrote that he had arrested Vicente on the basis of Manuela's tearful testimony but noted that it was difficult to convict Vicente on her testimony alone. As a result, "the court has seen fit not to prosecute the case, but rather to incarcerate said Florez in order to moderate his lasciviousness and so that, in some manner, it serve as a lesson."[103] He then sent the case to the audiencia for guidance, the outcome of which is not indicated.[104]

People could also be coerced into sex by the hope of gaining their freedom, as the slave Margarita Campero experienced. In 1794, she claimed that when she was very young her deceased former master, Manuel Velásquez, had promised to liberate her "under the . . . condition that he make use of my body, and . . . this had happened in a manner satisfactory to him, since he took my virginity. In addition to this, he made me pregnant with a girl, who has since died."[105] Manuel did not honor his word even on his deathbed, and his widow had since remarried Lorenzo Cuevas. Margarita asserted that Lorenzo had made the same promise, and as a result they had a daughter. Lorenzo was now about to sell her to a third man, which Margarita was resisting. In responding to the accusation, Lorenzo indicated that Margarita had originally been owned by the corregidor and mine-owner Francisco Guemes and denied making any promises to Margarita. He went on to accuse her of being a loose woman and requested that "perpetual silence" be imposed on the issue. It appears it was, as there is no further record on the case.[106]

Rape, incest, and adultery could converge, such as in 1784 when Simón Revollo confessed that, "carried away by my weakness," he had raped his prepubescent sister-in-law, Hilaria Padilla, whom he and his wife Manuela had reared since infancy.[107] Manuela left him as a result of the rape, while Simón sought a dispensation for incest. Church authorities ordered him to do spiritual penance and, once it was complete, on March 26, 1784, ordered his wife to return to him. Although Manuela petitioned for divorce, there is no indication that Simón was ever charged with a criminal offense.[108]

Civil authorities were even less interested in Indian rape victims. This was the case in Totora in 1771, after the Indian Felipe Roque's wife was raped by Juan de Dios Sacama, also an Indian. The corregidor did not act on Felipe's complaint, leading him to complain that he had been deprived of "satisfaction of my injury," and, one might add, that of his wife. When Felipe appealed to the audiencia, the prosecutor called for Juan's arrest—not, however, for rape but rather for adultery. The case is revealing in its male bias, as the wife's name is never mentioned, the focus was on Felipe's "injury," and the rape was never prosecuted.[109]

Similarly, in the village of Chalguani, in the region of Mizque, the alcalde pedaneo, Manuel Aguilar, largely turned a blind eye to a series of rapes in his jurisdiction. In October 1807, nine-year-old Luisa Montaño had been tending her family's sheep just outside of town when Mariano Rojas "followed her into the countryside, whereupon he forced her." When her father went to report the crime, the alcalde pedaneo refused to meet with him or his daughter "since he was occupied with other matters."[110] He did, however, order Mariano to pay a fine of ten pesos, only three of which were given to the father, who accepted them "totally against my will."[111] Gerónimo appealed to the subdelegado, who, in February 1808, ordered Alcalde Aguilar to prosecute Mariano. In mid-August, ten months after the attack, the alcalde reported that only one witness had appeared, and the case was subsequently abandoned due to lack of testimony. This was not the only rape in the area, and it is noteworthy that when Alcalde Aguilar acknowledged the subdelegado's order, a serial rapist, Gregorio Agudo, signed as a witness.[112]

Gregorio's close relationship with the alcalde would serve him well. The cantor of the village church, Gregorio was drinking chicha with friends at the home of Eugenio Ríos on the evening of June 8, 1808, when the preceding case was playing out. After he left the party, he was accused of entering a home and raping an intellectually disabled girl, Ignacia Cobarrubia. Ignacia was the servant of Juan Terrazas and his wife, Nicolasa Villarroel. Nicolasa had directed her to sleep in, and keep watch over, a neighbor's vacant house, as someone had recently stolen chickens from it. With the permission of her husband, Nicolasa testified that she heard Ignacia screaming and ran to intervene when she found Gregorio in the house and scuffled with him.[113]

Beyond the rape of Ignacia, Nicolasa also accused Gregorio of raping her mother-in-law, Manuela Terrazas. The ensuing testimony revealed that Manuel Nogales, a resident of the town, had caught Gregorio just after he had raped and impregnated Manuela. Nogales also accused him of raping another servant of Juan and Nicolasa, twenty-two-year-old Nicolasa Merida. This victim testified that Gregorio had raped her once and tried a second time. Although she had reported it to the alcalde, nothing was done. As a result, Juan Terrazas, whose mother and two servants had been raped by Gregorio, appealed for action from the subdelegado. The official, however, did nothing more than instruct the alcalde, who was also Gregorio's protector, to "notify the defendant Gregorio Agudo that, in the future, if he causes even the most minimal complaint due to his atrocious and iniquitous behavior, after being severely punished he will be banished to the wilds, which sentence is not being handed down now due to the court's clemency, only obliging him to pay court costs."[114] The response of the subdelegado, the alcalde's complicity, and the fact that a serial rapist was let off with a warning and signed as a witness to a document concerning a rape investigation illustrate the challenges victims faced in obtaining justice.

The challenges were even greater for domestic servants, such as those in the employ of Joseph Gregorio Pérez de Guzmán, in Poroma. In 1777, his wife, Esperanza Escobar, described his "scandalous life . . . and bold and daring personality," which included spousal abuse, multiple lovers, and a predilection to settle arguments with a knife. She also accused him of being a serial rapist, contending, "I cannot keep a maid that he doesn't try to rape, taking her out into the countryside."[115] Esperanza had long kept quiet about it all to protect the family name, and also in the hope that her husband would change. Now she had given up and petitioned for divorce on the basis that she had married against her will, as well as due to sevicia and economic abandonment. Ultimately, Joseph was never charged with rape, and Esperanza desisted from the divorce and returned to him when he promised to not abuse her again and abandon his "licentious life."[116]

This case is unusual in that it concerns the sexual abuse of domestic servants. Although such court cases are rare, the abuse such people suffered was probably not. They were in a position of economic dependency and physical vulnerability in a society where male predation was common. Instead of punishment for the attacker, taking one's master to court would probably result in more physical abuse and preclude other employment options. This explains the paucity of such complaints from servants, and even this case was not filed by the victims but by the wife of the rapist, who was seeking a divorce in ecclesiastical court.

Beyond the protection offered by the accompanying political connections, the enforcement of morality and public safety through night rounds provided rapists with abundant opportunities. Such was the case with José Cabrera, who participated in night rounds in Poopó, Paria Province, as an advisor to his friend the *justicia mayor*, or chief magistrate, Sancho Bracho, on the night of July 3, 1749. Illuminating their way with a lantern, they stopped at the home of Josefa Villa and Juan de Dios Pazza, whose daughter had rebuffed José's marriage proposal. They then arrested the parents for concubinage, and José soon returned, brought the unnamed girl to his house, and raped her.[117]

The parents appealed for help from their parish priest, Friar Bacilio Remusgo, who in a letter to the audiencia related that Cabrera was "well known . . . for his bad behavior (with Your Excellency's forgiveness for my boldness) as an addict of Venus, as I have become aware . . . unable to quench the fire of his sensuality with the virginal integrity of a young woman." After relating the capture of the parents and the rape of the girl, he wrote, "Here I should pause my pen, but my impatience will not allow it, since . . . Cabrera is more violent than Amnón was with Tamar, in taking his pleasure, riding roughshod over the sacred image of the Virgin of the Rosary, in whose name the girl pleaded with him, amid crying and screaming that he stop."[118]

Perhaps hoping to further engage the civil authorities, he also accused Sancho of defrauding the crown of tribute and sowing discord in the town. Friar Remusgo had his own problems, as he explained that he would have excommunicated Sancho but was unable to do so "since I have been deprived of the weapons of the Church, with no more reason than some superior's whim in the light of a false report."[119] The audiencia subsequently ordered an investigation, in which witnesses testified that Cabrera had good relations with the other residents in the town and was in their view probably too old to rape someone. Others impugned the morality of the victim, who was around twenty years old, suggesting that she was pregnant and lived in a vice-ridden part of town.[120] It appears that the parents then abandoned the suit without ever testifying or the victim being named.

In addition to civil officials abusing their authority in order to rape local residents, clerics also preyed on their female parishioners. In 1776 in Yotala, the assistant priest Father Vicente Campusano was accused of illegally exercising civil authority by making night rounds throughout the town. Over seven years later he would also figure in the case discussed above involving Dominga Montero y Bersaín, who advanced money to gamblers and attacked him in Potosí. During his time in Yotala, however, he was accused of entering at least two women's houses, one a widow and the other whose husband was away. Father Campusano arrested them without cause and returned to assault the widow's female servant and the itinerant father's daughter, both of whom had been left alone in the houses. In the incident that precipitated the complaint against him, he had roused the residents of a home at around 10:00 p.m. but was confronted by the brother of the husband, who challenged Father Campusano's authority to make night rounds. They rightly feared that Father Campusano would arrest them to return to be alone with the couple's virgin daughter and, despite suffering a beating, were able to prevent that from occurring.[121]

Like Father Campusano, the Augustinian Matías de la Borda was also accused of raping his parishioners. In 1781, he had been held captive by the rebel Túpac Catari during his siege of La Paz and subsequently prepared a fascinating account of his captivity.[122] He was fortunate to escape with his life, although perhaps the experience affected his mental state. By 1785, he was serving as an assistant priest in Guachacalla, Carangas Province, where he was accused of "forcing and taking the virginity" of at least two Indian girls.[123] After taking the complaint of one of the victims, the local Indian governor, Manuel Quispe, urged the friar to leave the girl alone, to which Friar Borda responded by attacking Quispe and leaving him with a bloody nose. Borda had a well-deserved reputation for jealousy and violence. When a thirteen-year-old boy went to make a purchase at a store where one of Borda's victims, Ninfa Gallardo, worked, Borda took a wood saw and "broke his head in three parts and to finish off stabbed him in the arm." Civil authorities soon ordered Ninfa be sent back to her mother in Carangas, while the archbishop placed Borda in a monastery.[124]

One of the most notorious predatory priests, however, was Gregorio Josef de Merlos, a Spaniard who was transferred to various parishes as a result of recurring accusations against him. In late December 1776, he attracted attention by having a Spanish woman named Josefa as his servant, eliciting the observation from the audiencia that no other cleric had a "Spanish woman for their service, finding themselves single and without their own woman."[125] That, however, was the least of the accusations against him, which included charging his Indian parishioners exorbitant prices for funerals, not paying them for services, and raping village girls. For example, in 1770, he was accused of raping numerous teenage girls in his diocese, placing them afterward in depósito for up to a month to see whether they were pregnant, and, if so, forcing them to marry.[126]

Merlos's predecessor in Coroma, Dionicio Cortés, was also known for abducting, raping, and keeping girls prisoner in his subsequent posting in Aimaya. One, Ambrosia Rodríguez, was held for months before escaping clad only in an animal hide and ultimately offered her shackles as evidence in the case against him. In March 1781, during the Great Rebellion and only months after Ambrosia's escape, Indian parishioners would raid the house of Father Cortés, drag him to the cemetery, and beat him to death.[127] By this time, Father Merlos had begun to serve as the priest in Macha, and the rebel leader Tomás Catari was among his parishioners. Although he was accused of complicity in the rebellion, he intervened to save the lives of several *curacas*, or village chiefs, and was ultimately exonerated.[128] As he prepared to return to Spain in 1782, the audiencia described him as a priest "of the greatest merit" whose "parishioners . . . should have [treated] him with greater respect."[129]

As these cases demonstrate, violence against wives, and women in general, was not only common but socially accepted and occurred in a culture of impunity.[130] It was only when abuse crossed an ill-defined line into cruelty that some redress was possible, such as criminal charges and a divorce process. Such events took place in a wider context of physical violence against servants and Indians, and even if a man was criminally charged, generally he would spend only a short time in jail. If a wife sought a divorce on the basis of sevicia, clergy consistently and effectively urged reconciliation, thus following a policy of returning victims to their tormentors. Some cases were gruesome, with women being stabbed, having their ears severed, and commonly strung up and whipped and beaten.[131]

Parents and siblings were often well aware of spousal abuse but did little or nothing to intervene until it had reached a critical point. This reflected the social acceptance of wife abuse, a concern for familial honor if it was made public, a fear of exacerbating the situation, and the near-impossibility of doing anything about it short of filing for divorce. Despite the social climate favoring violence against women, family and neighbors did occasionally intervene. Neighbors, both within a building and next to it, sometimes came to a battered woman's aid and also substantiated accusations of abuse, concubinage, and infidelity. Beyond serving as witnesses to events, many neighbors knew through gossip and hearsay of their neighbors' activities, and such hearsay was routinely included in testimony.[132] As we have seen, some serial rapists benefitted from political protection, and the use of the night rounds provided ample opportunity for such deeds.

Even murdering a wife and her lover was legal if the husband caught them in flagrante, while in other cases authorities did not pursue wife-murderers aggressively or at all. While the dearth of cases of spousal murder would seem to indicate that it was not a common occurrence, given the climate of violence against women in colonial society, and the lack of forensics, it is likely that such crimes were, like rape and abuse, much more common and underreported.

These cases also confirm the broader trend that physical abuse and rape were the most common crimes against women in colonial Latin America. Moreover, victims tended to be of a lower class than their attackers. If they were raped, it tended to be by someone they knew, and they often lived in the same house.[133] Unlike in New Galicia, where victims appear to have tended to be Spanish or creole women, and hence of the social elite, victims in Charcas tended to be poor, mestiza, or Indian. Perhaps due to shame associated with the crime, infidelity and incest were more likely to be reported or prosecuted than rape.[134] In Charcas, it appears, however, that if a rapist was punished, he was usually fined, whereas in New Spain or New Galicia punishment usually consisted of exile and flogging.[135] Overall, a cycle of violence, reconciliation, and more violence led many women to attempt the near-impossible: divorce.

CHAPTER 5

"The Most Bitter Life One Can Conceive"

Dilatory Divorces

Under canon law, divorce is a perpetual separation of bed and board, while an annulment establishes that the marriage never existed.[1] Causes for temporary separation, which could result in permanent divorce, included sevicia, infidelity, transmissible or chronic diseases, heresy, abandonment, and inducement to commit a crime. Annulments were possible only in cases of bigamy, coercion, lack of consummation, and egregious omissions in the marriage process. The claim of coercion often depended on the idea of "reverential fear," or fear of another in a position of power over oneself and on whom one depended, to whom obedience was expected.[2]

It was such fear that induced Ylaria Romero to marry Santiago Pérez de la Parra in December 1767 in Tacopaya. Ylaria explained that Santiago appeared one day and informed her that he and her mother had "contracted" her marriage, with neither her knowledge nor her consent. Despite her reluctance to marry a complete stranger, she acceded to the plan, she explained, out of "reverential fear."[3] She insisted that she refused both arras and the wedding ring, and the marriage had never been consummated despite Santiago's forceful efforts. Santiago dismissed her statements as "ridiculous," and although Ylaria was placed in recogimiento she ultimately received divine intervention of sorts, as her husband soon died.[4]

The ecclesiastical court had exclusive jurisdiction in divorce and annulment cases, and the spouse seeking either one would file an initial petition with the vicar general, who would determine whether it merited acceptance. Although women were usually the ones to petition for divorce, this was not always the case.[5] A previous effort of reconciliation was, in practice, a necessary step for the court to accept a petition, and as we have seen this policy resulted in many battered and emotionally distressed women being returned to their abusers.[6] Once a case was accepted, the woman received a document from the vicar general enabling her to represent herself in civil court on property and child custody issues as well as sign legal documents without her husband's approval. Beyond this, a wife could also file criminal charges relating to abuse in civil court. This could give her considerable leverage, especially if the husband was imprisoned, by encouraging him to negotiate. It also gave her a means to discredit him in ecclesiastical court.[7]

When a case was admitted by the ecclesiastical court, the adverse party was notified and ordered to respond in a specified time. The woman was initially placed in depósito or recogimiento, theoretically at the husband's expense. If she was not accused of infidelity, she generally had more influence in choosing the conditions of her reclusion and whether she could see her family. Nevertheless, men generally sought to have their wives placed in recogimiento, as opposed to depósito, as a form of pressuring them to desist or negotiate. While reclusion could serve to protect a wife from an abusive husband, it also provided clergy with ample opportunity to persuade her to reconcile. Failing this, she could petition to be placed in depósito in a private home, often of relatives, or even be released to live on her own with admonitions to live honorably and chastely. In all cases, she was physically separated from her husband for the duration of the divorce process.[8]

When women initiated a divorce, they often combined a series of complaints, such as the most common charges of sevicia and infidelity, with accusations of economic or physical abandonment. Men also would group their charges, which often included infidelity, disobedience, and meddling by in-laws. The process often took years, reflecting the church's paramount desire for reconciliation, intransigence by the parties in responding to translados, requests for various extensions, and the ability to raise procedural challenges. In addition, the process was expensive not only to the honor of the parties but also in the cost of scribes, notaries, lawyers, and the reclusion of the wife in depósito or recogimiento.[9]

Because of the translado system, the process had to be urged on by the parties themselves, and if one did not respond to a translado and the other party did not complain, the ecclesiastical court was not going to urge the case forward. This is what Casilda de Urquiza, daughter of an Augustinian friar, faced in La Plata when she began her quest for divorce from Andrés Flores in October 1755. Casilda's marriage had been marked by Andrés's "intolerable cruelty," as well as his "lowly pastimes and different illicit contacts with women of the prostitutes' guild."[10] Although several witnesses supported her accusations, six years passed without Andrés responding to the charges before Casilda petitioned for a final sentence.[11] Similarly, Lusiano Zárate did not oppose the divorce petition that his Indian wife, Faustina Miranda, had submitted in January 1809 after their having been informally separated for over twenty years. Despite his lack of opposition, he refused to respond to the translado, explaining to the court, "I refuse to oppose the actions of Faustina Miranda, because I cannot leave my work, by which I survive . . . and because I have no means with which to continue the suit, and since I do not fancy her company."[12]

Given the reluctance of the church to grant divorces or annulments, and the costs and time involved, many couples initiated the process only to let it languish once the case was accepted and they had been physically separated. While such a de facto divorce was tenuous, especially when local authorities enforced spousal reunification laws, it provided an effective solution that was much more common, and attainable, than a formal divorce.

If a formal divorce was granted, neither party could remarry while the other was alive, and the party at fault faced sanctions in civil court. If the husband was found to be the guilty party in a divorce, he lost control over his wife's dowry, community property, and custody of any children and was obliged to satisfy court costs as well as to continue to financially support his wife. If the wife was found to be at fault, she would lose custody of children over three years old and the husband was not obligated to support her financially. In cases of female adultery, however, the woman would also lose her dowry and common property. If an annulment was granted both parties could then remarry, as the marriage, legally, never existed.[13]

Although many divorce cases hinged on the testimony of the spouses and their witnesses, documents, such as love letters, could play a decisive role, as the teacher Mariano Anzaldo learned in La Plata in July 1796. His wife, María Flores, had petitioned for divorce as a result of his long-standing affair with Rosa Mansilla, which had resulted in a child. Mariano was now facing the cost and ignominy of divorce in ecclesiastical court and criminal charges of abuse and economic abandonment in civil court. María's hand was strengthened when she found letters the lovers had exchanged. The discovery, however, came at the cost of a terrible beating from Mariano that, in the words of the physician who examined María, left her "well mistreated."[14] They also reveal the affection, and tensions, between the lovers.

In one, Rosa wrote:

> My dear heart Mariano:
>
> I am pleased that you are feeling better, and may God grant that you never become so ill again. May God grant also that you never get sick at all. Even though you say you love me, you deny me that favor of telling me your eyesight is better. And who believes you when you say so strongly, in order to wound me, that you are my enemy? How could you say that after so many years? . . . For my part, I do not hate you, even

> though I lack not sufficient reason to do so, God has punished me in this way, not allowing me to hate you. . . . Leave off your foolishness and try to come to me tonight, even though last night you arrived late, I will be there. Farewell, your fine [friend.]

In another, Rosa wrote:

> Mariano, woe is me, I who am so willing to please you know not what to do, because I have three [sic] masters; the first being my son who cannot be put off. The other is you, you who gives me no thought nor realizes that I am all alone, and that I must go out at night to buy the things I need. What other woman has made such a home and has been thusly so willing to please you? What I am experiencing is not life. . . . Truly you know not the nature of people, since you have to know that your son leaves me exhausted, that I can scarcely breathe for carrying him around, while you assume no responsibilities at all. It is so true what you write, you know that I have gone mad with all the things that have befallen me. Your little Julián asks how you fare; do me the favor of burning this note.

After his release from jail, and with his life now falling apart, Mariano wrote the following to Rosa:

> To my dearest life:
>
> At the present I can do no more than take advantage of the scratchings of this unhappy pen, and although I recognize that no cautious man would do so in order to reveal the sentiments that afflict his noble breast, which only strives to please you, it goes on to say to you:

On the evening of the second instant . . . at one in the afternoon, I was summoned by the Provincial Judge to respond to charges laid by my wife, during which summons I could not make myself heard, and was then remanded to jail until my wife could present her witnesses. This did not take place until Sunday, upon which I was released from said prison.

During those days of pain and suffering, I was witness to that fact that on Tuesday and Wednesday you kept me in your thoughts, as Nicolasa came bringing me sustenance, for which I thanked her effusively, since I was bereft of any other help or consolation. But I soon saw that you flagged in your zeal, since on Thursday I was no longer deserving of such consolation, and I found myself—as they say—on the moon, not knowing what to think nor to what to attribute such a sudden change. Only on Saturday did I comprehend, when Nicolasa came to tell me, on your behalf, that I should reconcile with my wife, to which I acceded, mostly because you did not experience any [compassion]. But the Lord determined otherwise, since without having to effect said reconciliation, on Sunday I left the jail.

I now am apprised that, through the influence of your sister and other persons, you have come to believe that this entire event was concocted by me and my companions to embarrass you. I am impressed by the capability, and arguments, talent and fluency of those who have caused you to believe such a thing, since in the many years that I have known you, since your infancy, you should have realized and known that I never have stooped to such chicanery, and that my manner of comporting myself is very different from that of which you accuse me on this occasion, having allowed yourself to be carried away by gossip and stories which, I say, should not find room in your heart . . . .

> Now, with regard to your charges that I sent some sort of bread to my wife, again, [you should know] that I could not send her the likes of bread, when I had nothing to eat myself, and only survived thanks to the charity of friends and comrades. . . . Perhaps it was because I gave my son a couple of biscuits which my students sent me, since at that time I was in no mood to eat, or to do anything else, because of the pressure which besieged and troubled this noble heart of mine.
>
> Upon reflecting on the state in which I found myself, and the idea that although you might be disgusted with me and all is black, all is anguish, all is total confusion, and for me now even more so [I feel] as if I were being stabbed, on the mere thought that such confusion should enter into your head. Nor do I believe the message you sent me through the jailor when he delivered to you the note in which I informed you of my release and my whereabouts. You sent word that I should never again write to you, or you would lodge a complaint with the judges using my very same notes. And that you knew for certain that this constitutes a lesson for you, and that you needed me for nothing, not even to wipe your ass. This I could not believe, given your modesty, but on the other hand you were right, because not even a poor lad or a damned man is worthy of that task. . . . Since I find myself obliged to beg you, have pity on me, but not the pity shown to a fallen bull, riven through, since I am now even more estranged than ever from my wife, which should be for you, on your part, [the chance] to want to finish me off and cause my total ruination.[15]

As was so common, there is no clear outcome to the case.

Similarly, in Santiago de Cotagaita in December 1817, Antonia Villegas sought a divorce from her husband, Juan Antonio Michel. She related that when they married seven years previously, she began to experience "the most bitter life one can conceive."[16] The vicar general accepted her petition and allowed her to live with her mother, as she had already tried to reconcile. Antonia's primary charge was infidelity, accusing Juan of having been romantically involved with Dolores Vitoria. Although Dolores had been exiled, she had returned to town and the relationship continued. While Juan Bautista Mostajo represented Antonia, Silvestre Orgáz represented Juan.[17] Juan belied his assertion that he had only innocently visited her in her home with a letter that he had written to her, which read:

> My pug-nosed young lady, my treasure:
>
> You can probably imagine the situation in which I find myself, in view of what has taken place, the only thing lacking is that they haul me before the bench. But nothing will make me cower, since I would gladly give my life for your love. I beg you . . . not to allow yourself to be seduced by Jaúregui, to treat me badly, much less to allow him to have his way with you, in which case you would see in me a lost man. I am being martyred with the utmost cruelty, but in spite of it all I will love you even more. Receive these assurances, with which you must go on, from he who loves you,
>
> *Juan Antonio*[18]

Despite his compromised position, in September 1819, he was able to have Antonia removed from her mother's house and placed in a convent, at his expense, as he insisted her mother was urging the divorce. This had the desired effect, as after about ten weeks in La Plata's Santa Clara convent, she desisted from the case.[19]

Sometimes both parties wanted a divorce but for different reasons, as in the case of Petrona Pérez and her husband, Manuel Liendo, a watchmaker in La Plata.[20] In her petition to the vicar general in 1792, Petrona described Manuel as having a "perverse spirit" and complained that he routinely abused her and her illegitimate daughters.[21] Moreover, he had abandoned her economically and lived with his lover. Manuel rejected the charge of abuse, with the customary assertion that "what is paternal correction she mistakes for cruelty." Further, he claimed that it was she who had assaulted him on several occasions, coming once "with weapon in hand where I work, spilling my honor and good reputation on the street."[22] He also suggested that, given the number of men coming and going from her house, she was pimping her daughters or was a prostitute, or both, which further eroded his honor. Petrona, and her attorney, Gregorio Nuñez, let four months go by without a response after they received the translado, and when they returned the file, they did not respond to Manuel's accusations.[23]

Under pressure from the court, on April 30 Petrona detailed his abuse, describing how he beat her, her children, and her mother and cut her brother with a knife. Moreover, she said, he had caused her to black out after he hit her on the head, humiliated her by cutting a braid from her hair, and injured her when he threw a pig's head at her chest. On one occasion, he strangled her in bed, and when she escaped and took shelter underneath it, he stabbed at her with his saber before escaping into the patio, where other residents intervened. His sword was always close at hand, as on another occasion he menaced her with it on the street before passersby interceded. Such acts, she insisted, were far from "paternal correction" and constituted sevicia, thus tacitly acknowledging the acceptability of the former.[24]

In May, the prosecutor urged the court to allow the case to proceed to the prueba, or testimonial, stage for divorce. Perhaps fearing imminent reclusion or a weak case, or believing that she did not stand a chance unless she had tried to reconcile, Petrona tried to desist the next day, in order "to honor God, the spiritual health of my soul, and avoid scandal [and] to try to attain peace and quietude." Her husband, however, had no interest in reconciliation, stating, "I recognize that her company, instead of leading me to salvation, will bring on my total ruination."[25]

Despite Petrona's change in heart, surprisingly, the court allowed the case to proceed. Manuel prodded it along, presenting their landlord, the Indian Pedro Tamayo, as a witness. He testified that Manuel treated his wife decently and that it was Petrona who abused Manuel verbally and physically. Their discord, and the frequency of late-night visitors to their quarters, had reached a point where other tenants, and even the doorman, had complained about it. As a result, Pedro had asked them to move out. One tenant, the Spanish tailor Francisco Calancha who lived above the couple, also complained about the noise. Another resident improbably described the "love and tenderness" with which Manuel treated his wife, whom he characterized as having a "sharp temperment."[26] He described how he once saw her attack Manuel, while on another occasion he encountered him with scratches on his face and a torn shirt after an argument with Petrona. Importantly, he substantiated Manuel's claim of prostitution when he described the "many men of all classes" who came to their quarters, sometimes staying until midnight.[27]

By August 8, Petrona had ignored three orders to respond to the accusations, and the prosecutor, whose job it was to preserve the matrimonial bond, was uncharacteristically sympathetic to Manuel's petition. Arguing that "the bold traits of the so-called weaker sex of womankind easily agitate the tranquility of marriage," he insisted that since Adam and Eve "society was predicated on the domination and superiority of the male."[28] Despite this, however, he reflected the prevailing view that reconciliation was always preferable to separation or divorce and urged that the court "order that the latter reenter the nuptial bed and observe married life with his wife."[29] Despite the prosecutor's view, the vicar general concluded that Petrona had brought false charges, and, to Manuel's relief, the court ruled "that the law permits, for now and until Petrona's two daughters marry, divorce and separation . . . of the marriage, for them to live apart from each other with honesty and spiritual withdrawal, as is their duty."[30] Manuel achieved the near-impossible, a temporary divorce, perhaps because his wife and her children were prostitutes. This affected Manuel's honor, made him the victim, and mitigated the weight of Petrona's claims of abuse. Manuel may have soon become a widow and been able to remarry, as in February 1793, Petrona gave her last testament.[31]

Manuel's case was indeed exceptional, as in other cases even a husband's admission of sevicia was insufficient to overcome the church's aversion to divorce. In Oropeza, Cochabamba Province, in March 1754, a pregnant María Rosa de Basuito reflected upon her fifteen-year marriage to Captain Antonio de Orozco. She was in depósito in the home of her brother, Manuel de Avilés, tending to her infant while her other children were in the custody of her husband. She petitioned the vicar general for either a divorce or annulment for "cruelty and abuse."[32] She described how, in September 1753, Antonio had humiliated her by beating her on her behind in public, leaving her with wounds "in the places which cannot be shown," and she related how her brother-in-law Nicolás had publically urged her husband to "string me up and give me two hundred lashes."[33] In a separate petition, she described how "more than thirty times I have been thrown out of my house by my husband, in many cases being dragged by the hair and dumped in the street."[34] An attempt at reconciliation failed, as in late February he had yet again expelled her from the house, "giving rise," she said, "to a serious stain on my reputation and on people's opinion of me."[35] She was especially sensitive to this, describing herself as a "noble lady" whose dowry and arras had totaled twenty-five thousand pesos.[36]

Antonio initially characterized her accusations as "fabulous words" and insisted that he was "very well known for my honorable conduct." He went on to accuse her of abusing their children and their servants. He impugned her decency by insisting that, far from her being ejected from the house, "it was her normal and everyday habit to run loose in the street."[37] He sought to have the case suspended until she gave birth, because there was evidence he wanted to provide was so incendiary that it could risk the pregnancy. By June 1754, however, he was ready to give up the fight and to return María's dowry. He wrote the court, "I recognize that everything she alleges in her petition is true and accurate, with regard to the reasons for which she was mistreated and expelled from my house. . . . Your Grace should proceed to announce your decision in her suit for divorce." By December 11, 1754, the vicar had sent the file to the vicar general in La Plata, where, despite Antonio's admissions, the prelate refused to act upon it.[38]

Sight Unseen

An arranged marriage could result in a person marrying someone they barely knew or had never even met, as was the case with Rudesinda Gallardo and Santiago Arraya in Cinti. In February 1808, she petitioned for divorce while in recogimiento in Potosí, having been sent there as a result of an accusation of adultery by Santiago. This appears to have been, at least in part, an effort to pressure her to desist. Left with no financial support despite petitioning for it in civil court, she was "experiencing great need and . . . hunger for want of support or contacts with other people."[39]

Through her attorney, Juan Bautista Mostajo, she complained of physical abuse and an unbearable stench that emanated from Santiago's body. She insisted that her health, and life, were at risk, as "sensing in our conjugal practices a fetid smell, rottenness as strange as it is unbearable emanating from his entire body, worse than a newly opened grave, to such an extreme that it has always given me the faints, so much so that constant contact with him and his odors . . . could corrupt my health, like a contagious disease that would put me away forever."[40] Looking back, she recognized that it was peculiar that, during the marriage ceremony, "they covered his face saying that they did so as the bridegroom was very short." Beyond her fears that he was contagious, and the fact that he did not work, she added that he also had "scarce knowledge of conjugal activities."[41]

In late February, the court ordered Santiago to respond directly or through an attorney within twenty-five days. When he was officially notified on March 5, he was ill in bed but alert. In his testimony, he repeated his accusation that Rudesinda had an affair with a married man, a charge she did not explicitly deny. In a subsequent filing, he asserted that the case was baseless and refused to respond to translados because he was sick, poor, and unable to hire an attorney or journey to La Plata. In so doing, he effectively put an end to the case.[42]

In 1803, like Rudesinda Gallardo, Bárbara Reyna y Pobeda married a man, Vicente Hueso, whom she had never met before their marriage. Twelve years later she knew him only too well and was seeking a divorce. She explained how she was visiting Mojocoya with her mother and had gone out at 8:00 p.m. to purchase bread. On her way home she encountered Francisco Moscoso, the cousin of her husband, who requested that she come to the home of the assistant priest. Once she was there, the priest "with great insistence . . . pushed me inside, and therein I saw several individuals, in the midst of an all-day party . . . and out of the blue, much to my surprise, the assistant curate asked me if I wanted to marry said Hueso. Thinking it was a joke, I replied 'yes, I do' so as to not displeasure them, and without further ado he had me give my hand to him, and he blessed us. . . . I still cannot believe, simple woman that I am, that such a marriage took place."

She insisted that there was not consent on her part, saying, "I was not espoused with the necessary rituals, nor were banns posted, nor was my own parish priest notified, nor my mother, nor was her permission given." She added that her husband beat her while she was pregnant, and on another occasion "he unleashed so many whippings on me from head to toe, that no part of my body was left unharmed . . . by blows, fists, the back of his hand, kicking, beatings with sticks and other abuses, while throwing at me whatever objects were within his reach."[43] Despite this, it does not appear that a divorce was granted, nor was a dispensation issued for her not marrying before her parish priest.

Although some people married strangers under pressure, others voluntarily eloped with them. Around 1784, Mariana Estrada was a "young, heedless and simple girl." She ran off to Challapata, in Paria Province, with Diego Inojosa, "whom I did not know, even by sight . . . nor from which family or where he came, and even until today I do not know his last name."[44] They married a few days later, however, Diego soon began to physically abuse her and refused to support her economically. As a result, she began to work as a servant for the interim priest, Francisco Barrios, and accompanied him to La Plata when he moved there. Perhaps under pressure from the authorities in Challapata, Diego came to La Plata and unsuccessfully urged her to live with him. From there he went on to Potosí, where, Mariana stated, he lived with a mistress, drank heavily, chewed coca, and gambled, a pastime in which he was unsuccessful and lost "even his underpants."[45] By 1798 he had refused for two years to respond to the divorce proceeding that she had begun, and as a result it was in effect abandoned.[46]

While some women married men who were near or complete strangers, in an extraordinary case, Martina Bilbao Valverde learned that her husband was not male but rather an intersex person. Not only was she bewildered, but the colonial authorities seemed to have difficulty comprehending what was by any account a tragic situation. Eighteen-year-old Martina had married the thirty-two-year-old Spaniard Antonio Yta in 1801, but they never consummated the marriage. She explained how Yta had refused "my affections and hints" by claiming that he had taken a vow of chastity.[47] Surprise turned to suspicion due to "a combination of clear signs, such as monthly menstruation, urinating in the same fashion as a woman, and, in short, for not having consummated the supposed marriage with me. . . . And what is more, he almost always slept outside the conjugal bed, and when he did sleep with me, he took the precautions of wearing underpants and many other things which modesty prohibits me from mentioning."[48]

Martina then requested that the court order a physical examination to determine Yta's sex. The court acceded to her request, and in what was no doubt a humiliating experience, two court-appointed doctors examined Yta and concluded that he was a "true woman."[49] Given this, on October 7, 1803, the court ordered the confession of "the one whom until now has been known as Antonio" Yta, which in turn raised more questions than it answered.[50] By November 1803, Martina had begun divorce proceedings, and Yta had been jailed for "concealment and simulation of gender."[51] With Yta destitute, ill, and poorly clothed, his advocate José Manuel Malavia sought to have his clothing sent to him while criticizing Martina for "contenting herself with the black satisfaction of seeing him in a dungeon."[52]

Between Yta's confession, signed as María Leocadia Yta, and a letter that his mother, Felipa Ibañez, wrote from Madrid, a tragic story emerges of a person who was punished not only for who he was but probably also for what he knew. Yta was born outside of Madrid, in Colmenar de Oreja, as María Leocadia Yta, and had come to Montevideo in 1794 from Malaga without a license. His mother explained that from a very early age María Leocadia had been rebellious and as an adult was "extremely inclined to the female sex." Although she referred to Yta as her son, he was raised as a woman. At the age of nine, Yta went to live in the household of a local duchess, who, three years later, sponsored his entrance into an Augustinian convent in Colmenar. Only two months later, and before professing, he was expelled after having been caught having sexual intercourse with a nun.[53] By February 1791, Yta had been expelled for the same reason from three more convents and placed in the custody of his sister in Madrid. There, dressed in men's clothing, Yta was caught having sex with a woman and later impregnated a woman who would die giving birth, along with the baby. From there Yta went to Valencia and Barcelona before embarking on a mail boat to Genoa, and eventually Rome, despite lacking official documents to travel.[54]

There, Yta sought the counsel of the Franciscan friar Pedro Ramos Aragones, who told him "that on orders from his Holiness [the Pope] he should dress in men's clothing from then on." Yta balked at the idea, as it would make it almost impossible to return home, where he had been known as a female. The friar responded by telling him to "take the route you choose, but in any case dress as a man," which Yta had done ever since.[55] María Leocadia then became Antonio Yta. After spending seven months in Rome, Yta returned to Barcelona and was arrested when inspectors found women's clothing in his luggage, suggesting he had not entirely abandoned his former identity. Now considered a woman again, Yta was placed in recogimiento and was released only after the death of the bishop who had ordered him there. From Barcelona, Antonio headed to Cádiz, where he impregnated Vicenta Arias de Reyna and, refusing to marry her, fled to Malaga, Montevideo, and ultimately Buenos Aires in 1794.[56]

Desperate in a foreign land, he introduced himself as Antonio Yta to Archbishop Manuel Asamor y Ramírez. Not only did Archbishop Asamor assist him, but the two lived in the same house until the prelate's death in 1796. While the documents do not reveal the nature of their relationship, it appears that Yta was bisexual. His mother remarked on his femininity and he only reluctantly began to dress as a man. While he left a trail of sexual scandal as a man in Spain, this was not the case when he came to the Americas. It is possible that while in Spain he was publicly a woman and privately a man and in the Americas became, essentially, a man by day and woman by night. Whatever the case, with his patron dead, Yta then traveled to Potosí. There, he presented a letter of introduction from the archbishop to the city's intendant, Francisco de Paula Sanz, in whose home he also lived for two years before marrying Martina. Subsequent to the marriage, Yta obtained employment as an assistant to the governor of Moxos and then as an official in the lowland town of Magdalena. A year later, he arrived in La Plata to collect his salary.[57]

Meanwhile, despite the order that Yta be confined "with the decency according to her sex," his advocate referred to him as a man. He complained that Yta was experiencing "the greatest desperation" as he was in a "hard and difficult . . . dungeon . . . without the slightest ray of light, without any ventilation, and with three strong doors."[58] He contended that no law required his incarceration for the crime of transvestism and requested that a window be left open for light and ventilation and that two of the three doors be left unlocked so that clergymen could console and counsel him. The court responded by ordering that during the day one door be left open, and a window partially so.[59]

Despite this, over the next nine months days went by when Yta saw neither a person nor the light of day. Malavia petitioned the audiencia to transfer him to the prison in the audiencia complex and to allow him to spend time in the patio during the day. It was to no avail, perhaps reflecting fears that if not held in solitary confinement he might share the details of his previous relationships with his patrons. Alone, forsaken, and despairing, Yta planned an escape by carving a hole in the prison wall. His hopes were dashed, however, when on August 1, 1804, an inspection of the dungeon revealed the effort. Things only got worse, as he was then kept in irons, and after a few days he was so sick that he could not get out of bed, had spotted, swollen feet, and was spitting blood.[60]

On September 6, 1804, the court ordered a medical examination of him by one of the doctors who had previously failed to detect that he was intersex. They also directed the jailer to do what he could to assist Yta's recovery and to allow medicines to be brought from the Hospital of San Juan de Dios, which cared for the indigent. This may have resulted in him being released from his shackles, as on September 21, 1804, at around 9:30 p.m., he escaped from the dungeon. In his report to the audiencia, the jailer Felix Cardoso insisted that after Yta's first escape attempt, he had kept watch on the prisoner every day until around 7:30 p.m. Seeking to deflect responsibility, he complained that the physical condition of the jail made it difficult to prevent a breakout and also suggested that an Indian servant had assisted the escape either through a window or with a key to the door.[61] Probably barely able to walk and wearing stained, tattered rags, perhaps Antonio Yta was seen on the streets of La Plata that evening as he disappeared from the city. He was probably not headed to Potosí, as part of the reason he was treated the way he was, apart from his being intersex and likely bisexual, may have been because of his previous relationship with the governor.

Annals of Annulment

Compared to a divorce, an annulment sought because of bigamy was a more certain process. Although bigamy does not appear to have been widespread, its presence reflected the incidence of informally separated spouses, geographical mobility, and the fact that even those who were divorced could not remarry while the former spouse was still alive. Bigamists were more likely to be men, such as the Indian Mateo Velásquez.[62] In early September 1762, he arrived in Mendoza in irons, where he was handed over by his warder to the parish priest, Pablo de Allende. He had been sent there by Father Joseph Noriega, in Soconcho, in Yamparaéz Province, after the clergyman discovered that he was a bigamist. Mateo was a dwarf muleteer who had married a slave, Juana Gamarra, in Mendoza in 1745. He later abandoned her and married María Zapata in Rio Segundo in 1757. Not long after, a local official learned that Mateo was already married and arrested him, but he escaped to Soconcho where he was soon joined by his second wife. Their tranquility there came to an end when the official located them and reported Mateo to Father Noriega.[63]

In October 1764, after two years in the Mendoza jail, the forty-something Mateo initially claimed that his first wife's mother wrote to tell him that she had died. Soon after, he confessed to providing false witnesses to attest that he was single when the priest who married him the second time gathered the información de libertad. In admitting his guilt, he also exculpated his second wife, stating that neither she nor her family knew that he was already married. His guilt reluctantly confessed, Father Allende sentenced Mateo to "a hundred lashes and a public shaming through the streets of this city . . . and that he take part personally and on a daily basis in the task of cleaning the parish Church of the city of Mendoza . . . and that he also be obliged to cohabit with his wife, complying with the obligations of matrimony."[64] María Zapata was absolved and was free to marry again. In many ways, Mateo was fortunate, as according to the Ley de Partida, he could have been sent to an island prison for five years. He was also lucky that he did not commit his crime after 1770, as he would have been subject to a new law that called for bigamists to have their property seized and to be marked on the forehead "with a hot iron with the figure of an O."[65]

In March 1800, this was what the mulato Gerónimo Suárez was facing in the town of Totora. He may not have fully understood the charges, however, as no one disputed that he was "a retard, rustic, [and an] idiot of very little reason."[66] His wife, Rosa Velásquez, testified he had abandoned her sixteen years ago, and she had recently learned from several muleteers that Gerónimo had married again in Laguna and had a child. It emerged that in the interim Gerónimo had gone to La Plata, where he encountered a former neighbor, Manuel Escalera, who told him that his wife had died. He then persuaded Gerónimo to pay him six pesos to prepare a putative legal document to that effect. Upon his return to Laguna, Gerónimo presented this fraudulent death certificate to the priest there and married. Two years later, muleteers informed him that his first wife was still alive, which he verified during a trip to Totora. In a bind, Gerónimo returned to Laguna, where he kept his dual marriages a secret until discovered by the priest in Totora a year and a half later.[67]

On December 2, 1798, Gerónimo was arrested by civil authorities on charges of bigamy, although he was also subject to ecclesiastical punishment as the crime fell under both jurisdictions. The prosecutor sought an exemplary punishment for "such an execrable" crime, which, he insisted, should include having his goods seized, exile, and having his forehead branded.[68] For his part, Gerónimo's advocate argued that it was all an innocent mistake made by someone who did not have full mental faculties. Since he had acted in "good faith and ignorance" in the belief that his wife had died, there was no crime, and, hence, there should be no punishment.[69] The prosecutor's eagerness to inflict punishment was not shared by other officials, who were loath to become involved, perhaps because they knew Gerónimo was intellectually disabled.[70]

Meanwhile, the prosecutor complained of numerous delays and insisted the only thing remaining was the sentence. The defense, however, gathered additional testimony concerning Gerónimo's mental capacity. His advocate noted that his wife in Totora had pardoned him and petitioned for his release so they could reunite. He also sought to have the author of the fake death certificate testify, however people in Totora believed that he had died. The case was then remitted to the subdelegado for sentencing, as local officials insisted they did not have the authority, nor apparently the inclination, to punish someone who was developmentally disabled. The subdelegado in turn remitted it to a judge in Totora, who accepted Gerónimo's intellectual disability and good faith and placed the blame on Escalera, who had prepared the fake death certificate. Without Escalera or testimony from the priest in Laguna, he averred that no decision could be made but that to seek additional testimony would only "eternalize" the case. Ill and broke, Gerónimo was released on April 26, 1800, after almost a year and a half in jail. Although he was not required to pay most court costs, he was required to pay the fees of the prosecutor who had sought to have him branded.[71]

While men may have dominated the ranks of bigamists, some women, such as Martina Peña y Llilo in Potosí, were also charged with the crime. She was married to Gabino Álvarez, but he had long since left her and moved to La Plata. Having convinced her priest that her husband had died, she married the mine-owner Matías Urquida. In 1779, an acquaintance of Martina, Ventura Malpartida, informed her that he had seen Gabino in the San Juan de Dios Hospital in La Plata. After ignoring Malpartida's advice to confess her misdeed to the vicar, he did so himself. The vicar dispatched a notary of the ecclesiastical court to the hospital, who located an ill and bearded Alvárez. Beyond confirming his identity, he had little else to say. The ecclesiastical prosecutor criticized the priest who had officiated the second marriage for not having demanded a copy of Gabino's death certificate, and although the case was remitted to the vicar general in La Plata as well as the Inquisition, the outcome is not indicated.[72]

Beyond bigamy, another ground for the annulment of a marriage was if a couple failed to obtain a necessary dispensation for a diriment impediment prior to their marriage. Under some circumstances, authorities could grant a dispensation and then revalidate the marriage.

Just how far ecclesiastical authorities would go to determine whether a marriage had been properly conducted was demonstrated on a mid-October day in 1818, in Pampa Ullagas. There Father Andrés Poveda, a scribe, and others sat with Pedro Ruiz to take his testimony concerning his marriage eighteen years earlier to Santusa Guayalla. Their patience was fraying, as despite their efforts, he would not talk. His advocate explained that this was because he was "mute [and] incapable of reason," and he accused Santusa of having an affair with Pedro's father. The prosecutor indicated that, beyond the impediment of incest between his wife and father, Pedro's intellectual disability raised questions as to whether he was capable of giving consent.[73]

Fourteen months later, Santusa was in depósito and scribes recorded the testimony. Apart from the priest who married them, the only living witness to the marriage was a senile man. The clergyman who officiated indicated that the sponsor of the union, who was also dead, had given consent on Pedro's behalf. In her statement, Santusa indicated that she gave consent but that Pedro "was neither asked nor did he say a word," thus indicating that he did not verbally consent to the marriage. Pedro was not entirely mute, however, as Santusa indicated that "when he is in the mood, he responds with a one or two words."[74] She also confessed that, although she had only had sex with a reluctant Pedro twice, she had six children, one of whom was the son of her father-in-law.[75]

Pedro was brought in to testify, and the vicar spent all day trying to get him to speak. Eventually, he indicated that he viewed Santusa as his mother, and he ran away when he was asked whether he wanted to be married to her. In reviewing the case, the prosecutor observed that this was a "thorny, grave and delicate issue," as most of the witnesses were dead.[76] It was clear to him, however, that Pedro neither gave consent nor wanted to be married. Despite this, for the benefit of their souls, he urged that the incest be dispensed and that the marriage be revalidated with a new ceremony as opposed to being annulled. If Pedro refused consent, he argued, they should be separated physically and disallowed from marrying while the other was alive, thus effectively granting them a divorce. In reviewing this "extremely interesting affair," the vicar general supported this view, emphasizing that Pedro should not be coerced to revalidate the marriage.[77]

Similarly, in the village of San Pedro de Turco, Carangas Province, the Indians Leandro Apasa, who was thirty-three years old and blind, and the widow Ysabel Gusman married in 1807 despite an undispensed impediment of incest. Leandro claimed that he had married under duress, as his father, the former curaca Melchor Apasa, told him he would throw him out of their home if he did not marry her. If, however, he acceded to the union, he offered to give Leandro three hundred llamas, a promise that he did not honor. Soon after their marriage, during a trip to Oruro in which the three shared a bed, Leandro discerned his father engaged in intercourse with his wife. He desisted from saying anything at the time as he was afraid of being left on the road. He later learned that they had also had sex prior to the marriage, thus putting the wife in need of a dispensation due to incest.[78]

They had been informally separated for over a decade when Leandro decided to seek an annulment, and he and his wife testified before their priest, Juan de Dios Vega, in April 1819. Isabel admitted that she and Melchor had been involved for a year prior to the marriage, which Melchor had urged as a means for them to continue the relationship. Leandro wanted nothing to do with his wife, telling Father Dios Vega that he was "ready to lose his life over any precipice before consenting to reunite."[79] In his review of the case, the prosecutor in La Plata criticized Father Dios Vega for having only one interpreter, as opposed to the required two, when Leandro's testimony was recorded. Although he sent the file back to Father Dios Vega for the testimony to be gathered correctly, there is no indication that this was done and the case appears to have been abandoned.[80]

While Leandro sought to annul his marriage on the basis of incest, Terbacia Soto was concerned that her husband, Lucas Camposano, was a priest. In a letter addressed to the vicar general, she explained how when she was a patient in La Plata's San Juan de Dios Hospital and met him, he had appeared wearing the religious habit of the order. Soon, he managed to "seduce me, with a thousand deceptions, until achieving his intent."[81] In the lead-up to their marriage, neither had obtained parental permission, the información de libertad was not gathered, and when reading the banns the priest who married them used different family names. Had the información de libertad been truthfully recorded, it would have revealed whether Lucas was a cleric, as well as the fact that Terbacia had been engaged to another man. Later, they lived in Potosí, where he battered her and then abandoned her for another woman. That affair ended when Lucas stabbed his lover three times, and then he and Terbacia reunited and fled the city. They later learned that the lover did not die and the couple returned to Potosí, where Lucas was jailed before being released on bond. The outcome of this case is unclear as the ensuing testimony, if any, was lost.[82]

A chronic or contagious illness could also serve as a basis of annulment, and it was health concerns that led Josefa López Salcedo to petition for the annulment of her marriage to Mariano Tejerina in November 1812. Through her advocate, Juan Bautista Mostajo, she related how she had grown up on a hacienda with very little contact with the outside world and was only fourteen years old when her mother yielded to Mariano's insistent propositions to marry her. She insisted she never wanted the marriage and explained how just prior to the wedding her mother-in-law made her recite exactly what to say during the ceremony. After a violent consummation, she became infected. While she acknowledged that her mother agreed to the marriage, she sought a divorce on the basis that her consent was based on ignorance, her health was imperiled, and she was unable to have intercourse. In addition, she claimed that Mariano was verbally abusive and on one occasion had strangled her. The doctor who had treated her had concluded that her condition was the result of an "excessively large penis."[83] While her case was accepted by the ecclesiastical court in early November 1812, her request to enter recogimiento was deferred.[84]

Mariano was represented by José Patricio Malavia, who denied any abuse occurred and insisted she was healthy. Josefa had meanwhile been placed in La Plata's Convent of the Virgin of Los Remedios and was to undergo a medical examination to certify her condition. She told the doctors, one of whom had treated her previously, that although she was still in pain, she did not want to be examined as it was "a repugnant act." To demonstrate that her condition had not improved, however, she showed them a shirt that she had removed a few days earlier, the bottom of which was "full of pus."[85] While her witnesses attested to her screams on her wedding night and subsequent illness, they were unable to substantiate the physical condition of her husband.[86] After some delay, Mariano claimed that Josefa wanted to reconcile but was being persuaded to the contrary by her mother or relatives. As a result, he called for her to be held incommunicado in the Santa Clara convent. Mariano then changed lawyers and was represented by Silvestre Orgáz. In late May 1814 the case was ongoing, and Josefa sought to have the testimony of her servants accepted. The outcome is unclear, however, as the file ends in mid-sentence.[87]

A lack of consummation could also be a basis for annulment, something that Nicolás Aguilera hoped would ease his fears if not his conscience. In 1769, he had come to the village of Santa Elena, in Pilaya y Paspaya Province, and had a brief intimate relationship with María Antonia Márquez. Leaving her a few days later, he journeyed to the Cinti Valley, where he met Gregoria Márquez. With the support of her mother, the two strangers married in the middle of the night. At dawn, however, Nicolás mounted his mule and was on his way. Nicolás soon learned, however, that Gregoria was María's younger sister, both fathered by the deceased assistant priest in Santa Elena, Miguel Márquez. Over the coming years, Nicolás did not see either woman, and in 1780 he began, and then abandoned, a petition for annulment. By 1791, his priest had urged him to try again to resolve the issue, and as fate would have it, he, his wife with whom he claimed never to have consummated the marriage, and her sister were all in La Plata.[88]

During the annulment proceedings, María testified that in 1769 she and Nicolás had been intimate, under verbal promise of marriage, before he left her. Far from it being an issue of conscience, she believed he had acted only after encountering both women in the city and she threatened to report him to the authorities. Gregoria stated that she had married only in an effort to please her now-deceased mother. Perhaps one of Nicolás's better decisions was to obtain the services of Gregorio Nuñez as his advocate, who, in July 1791, argued that since the marriage had never been consummated, it should be declared null. Despite Gregoria's tardiness in responding to translados, she did confirm that they had never been intimate, adding that for the past twenty-two years her conscience had been "a labyrinth of uncertainties."[89] She supported the petition for annulment, adding that she suffered from "accidents that in truth are incompatible with matrimonial life."[90] Despite the prosecutor, husband, and wife all supporting the annulment request, and after almost a year of hearings, the vicar general refused to render a decision on the basis of the declarations.[91]

The fragmentary nature of these divorce and annulment cases makes it difficult to draw conclusions. They do illuminate a world of forced marriages, unions with complete strangers, and the role that love letters could play in proceedings. They also appear to substantiate broader regional trends. As in New Spain and Chile, a previous effort of reconciliation was a necessary step for the acceptance of a divorce petition, and most cases end abruptly or are otherwise unresolved. Both of these tendencies underscore the church's doctrinal aversion to breaking the marital bond under almost any circumstance, even when a man brutally abused his wife or was married to the woman who raised him.[92]

On the basis of existing documentation concerning Charcas, between 1738 and 1778 there was, on average, one divorce case per year. This frequency, however, spiked to a high point of about three per year between 1779 and 1800, ironically coinciding with Bourbon efforts to promote spousal reunification and enhance paternal power in marriage choice. Between 1801 and 1825, the rate declined to about two cases a year, and then to one every two years between 1826 and 1855. Due to lost or destroyed documents, however, this may not be an accurate representation of the actual frequency of divorce petitions. Of approximately fifty-two divorce cases in the archbishopric of La Plata, only five divorces were actually granted, one of which was temporary. That is fewer than in Chile, where less than one-half of divorce cases actually concluded with a sentence.[93]

It appears that, barring reconciliation, many couples settled for an informal separation, or a quasi-formal one in which they were allowed to live apart pending the outcome of the usually interminable proceedings. Given the doctrinal deterrent against granting divorces, and limitations on annulments, some petitioners may have preferred a liminal life to a definitive ruling that could demand they reunite with their spouse. As a consequence, for many a de facto divorce was better than no divorce at all. In contrast to the situation in Lima and Mexico at the time, and despite the costs of a divorce, the economic elites were not overrepresented in such petitions in Charcas. As has usually been found to be the case in Mexico, Peru, Charcas, and Chile, most divorce petitions were initiated by wives on the basis of sevicia and adultery, often complemented by accusations of alcoholism, dissipation of funds, and economic abandonment. Similarly, calls for women to be placed in recogimiento, especially in a convent, were routinely used to pressure them to either desist or come to some negotiated arrangement.[94]

Conclusion

Intimate relationships in late colonial Charcas were laced with irony. Those couples who desired to be together could often only do so by violating social mores and civil and religious laws, either through concubinage, extramarital affairs, or a clandestine marriage. Those who adhered to social expectations often did so through an arranged, reluctant, or coerced marriage, sometimes to people who were near or complete strangers. Instead of affect, such unions reflected parental desires for economic and social advancement. In these circumstances, there were no self-regarding acts, especially among daughters and eldest sons. Marrying someone of lower social, ethnic, or economic standing would erode familial honor and prestige while limiting the options available for other siblings. For daughters, the "virginal jewel" was their key to a marriage that was advantageous at a familial, if not individual, level.[1]

Another level of irony was the glaring gap between laws, both civil and canon, and social practices—or between decree, doctrine, and deed. Examining late colonial society through the lens of legality provides insight into official policies and the ideals they represented but little else. Laws were selectively enforced, often contradictory, and routinely ignored by both officials and the public. Rather, it is through examining people's quotidian lives and their personal battles that we can see how society actually functioned. Despite the economic and social value associated with virginity, premarital intercourse following a verbal or written engagement was widespread, although such engagements were often unfulfilled. Similarly, despite civil and religious sanctions to discourage out-of-wedlock births, they were remarkably common, especially among the elite in Charcas. Secret pregnancies, and the acceptance of "foundlings" into the home, were common means of resolving the contradiction between personal intimacy and public appearance and the honor associated with it.[2]

In contrast to the prevalence of illegitimate births, the dearth of legal demands for child support suggests that many single mothers expected to raise their children at their own expense and were skeptical of the efficacy of bringing the father to court. Not only was a legal suit costly, but it also opened the door to a further loss of honor as the accuser would have to reveal their own actions and suffer attacks on their moral virtue by the accused. Moreover, it was very difficult to prove who the father was. Rather than civil court, the banns provided considerable opportunity, and leverage, for a single mother to extract some support from the father by claiming that they were already engaged, thus impeding the planned marriage to another.[3]

At one level, the enforcement of moral codes appears to substantiate an image of a society that demanded virtuous conduct. Night rounds rarely returned empty-handed, resulting in women sent to reclusion and the imprisonment of men after they had been caught in flagrante in sudden and often forceful searches of their or their lovers' homes. They could be effective in interrupting, if not ending, public and scandalous relationships, and it appears that in many cases authorities acted on a tip from an offended spouse. A closer look, however, reveals that such enforcement was selective and commonly reflected ongoing personal and political animosities or economic motivations, or served as a pretext for sexual predation.[4]

Given the prevalence of arranged marriages, the near-impossibility of formal divorce, and the abusive nature of many unions, it is not surprising that both men and women would yearn for, and establish, affective relationships outside of marriage. Given the greater degree of social tolerance for male infidelity and a desire to defend their honor and extract vengeance, men appear to have been more likely to take legal action against an unfaithful spouse or her lover. This was a double-edged sword, however. By seeking civil or ecclesiastical redress for his wife's infidelity, a husband's private humiliation was to a degree made public, compounding their loss of honor.[5] While a husband could kill his wife and her lover if they were caught in flagrante, legal cases concerning such events were uncommon. The practice may, however, have been more widespread than it appears given the prevalence and severity of spousal abuse, the challenges of obtaining a divorce, and the lack of forensic tools. Often husbands came to negotiated solutions that could involve exile for the male lover and a period of reclusion for the wife while clergy pressured the couple to reconcile. Exile appears to have usually been only a temporary and generally ineffective measure, although it did provide a face-saving solution. Indeed, exile, incarceration, and potentially lethal consequences failed to deter some lovers.[6] Despite the vow of celibacy, clergymen commonly had paramours, and children, and even lived with women as a family. Like priests, military men were protected from civil law by their fuero, creating additional challenges to the enforcement of moral codes.[7]

The Pragmática of 1778, and subsequent related edicts, progressively constricted the opportunities of sons and daughters to choose their mates. The frequent result was that even more potential marriages based on affect were sacrificed on the altar of patriarchal power. The decrees not only limited choice but also interjected civil authority into the ecclesiastical domain. Further, they sought to maintain the integrity of elite structures by preventing marriages between racial, and hence social, unequals. In opposing a marriage, fathers would sometimes even kidnap or sequester their offspring or their potential mates, as Francisco Barrios and Felipa Gallardo knew only too well.[8] In court, parents focused not only on racial inequality but also on economic disparity and character issues. A husband's abandonment of his wife and child could, however, mean that he in effect renounced his right to intervene in his offspring's choice of mate. Importantly, it was not just the elite who went to court to stop a marriage but also lower-class mixed-race individuals and single mothers, who often somewhat hypocritically challenged the origins of a suitor. Despite the obstacles, and range of interpretation of the law, couples could, and often did, prevail in court. This was facilitated if the woman was pregnant and sought to "cover . . . their weakness with the veil of marriage."[9] Indeed, many couples only went to court after they had become verbally engaged, eloped, and had intercourse. Often this was enough to change a parent's mind, even if reluctantly.[10]

Unlike many parents, ecclesiastical authorities were generally more accepting of a couple's desire to wed. They commonly issued dispensations and pressured parents to accept the prospective spouse, especially if the alternative was a child born out of wedlock. In a larger context, the church had long held a liberal view of marriage based on free will, and it was only subsequent to the Council of Trent (1545–1563) that a union had to be officiated by a priest. Furthermore, the Pragmáticas were only part of a much wider assault on church privileges, with regal efforts to limit saint's day celebrations, demand adherence to fee schedules for various rites, restrict the age at which a man could become a priest, prohibit clergy from drafting wills, and, in 1767, expel the Jesuits from the Americas. Beyond the doctrinal demand of free will as a basis of marriage, the assault on church privileges may also explain the relative tolerance prelates exhibited to the increase of clandestine marriages. As we have seen, while the couple was often punished, the union was in the end usually upheld if they were technically consistent with canon, if not civil, law.[11]

It is also ironic that, to some degree, enhancing a father or guardian's power to determine marriage choice exacerbated moral deviance. Forced and arranged marriages were probably more likely to be unhappy, abusive, and tainted by infidelity and result in abandonment. In some cases, such as that of Joaquín Buitrago and Francisca Torres in Cinti, a man married one person but continued a long-standing intimate relationship with another. Others simply abandoned their spouses and thus informally separated.[12] Although a husband's abandonment of his wife could lead to economic hardship for her, it also could free her of immediate male authority, and it created a broad stratum of female agency throughout society and challenged the patriarchal ideal.

A remedy to wife-abandonment had long been on the books in the form of spousal reunification laws, which the crown insistently sought to enforce in the 1770s. The result was haphazard at best, as local authorities were on the whole consistently remiss in enforcing, and sometimes even acknowledging, such directives. Even the audiencia was lax in following up and beset by poor record-keeping. Beyond that, authorities recognized that when a man who had abandoned his wife was identified and ejected from one town, there was no effective mechanism to ensure that he actually returned to, or stayed with, his wife.[13] Within this context, enforcement patterns are revealing and generally expressed elite political and personal rivalries. They were also a means of disrupting illicit relationships, especially those that had caused scandal. Enforcement of spousal reunification measures could also create economic opportunities for officials and their allies when imposed on merchants, who were often forced to sell their merchandise and settle with creditors and debtors on unfavorable terms.[14]

Men proffered many reasons for their absence from their wives, variously insisting that they were in royal service, had their wives' permission to be away, had no other economic option, or had no idea where their spouses were. Others sought to justify their absence by insisting that their wives had been unfaithful or claiming that they were widowers. Some of the most difficult situations, however, emerged in cases where a couple had begun a divorce proceeding and, once separated, abandoned the effort. This was a common practice, given the costs and time involved and the church's unwillingness to grant a divorce or annulment. Other couples informally separated without ever filing for divorce, for the same reasons. In both cases, the prospect of reuniting must have been repugnant to both husband and wife.[15]

In addition to infidelity, spousal abuse was at the root of many separations, formal or otherwise. "Correction" of a wife was socially and legally acceptable, widespread, and to some degree a consequence of arranged or involuntary marriages. Wives, and even female lovers, were frequently the victims of men's wrath, expressed through whippings and beatings, not just with their hands but also sticks, swords, knives, and other weapons. That many women complained of being tied up to a roof beam and flogged suggests that this was a common mode of abuse. Others had their ears severed, were stabbed, and were beaten to the point where one bruise was indistinguishable from the next. In some cases, parents or brothers sought, belatedly, to assist their daughters or sisters by sheltering them from their long-abusive husbands, often provoking accusations of kidnapping.[16]

Even pregnancy did not protect a woman from her husband's abuse, as Micaela Flores learned on La Plata's main plaza in April 1821. There, her husband Matías Morales beat her so severely that she bled "from below and above" and miscarried as a result.[17] It was in such cases that the protective purpose of recogimiento was most apparent, providing as it did one of the few sanctuaries from continued abuse. This was, however, usually temporary, as priests and often family members would as a matter of course urge wives to reconcile with their husbands. The emptiness of a husband's promise to moderate his ways, even under financial bond, often soon became apparent as a new, and often worse, cycle of abuse began.[18] In some cases the cruelty only came to an end with the death of the woman, whether as a direct or indirect result of such treatment.[19]

Rape was another manifestation of male power over, and abuse of, women. This was especially the case with women who were poor, who were often raped by relatives or people with whom they lived or otherwise knew. Domestic servants as well were probably frequent, and unreported, victims of rape. The most a rapist had to fear, in practice, was a modest fine and perhaps a brief period of incarceration. Night rounds provided an "official" means for rapists to separate their victims from would-be protectors. Not only was the crime difficult to prove, but the shame and dishonor that victims felt often discouraged them from reporting the assault. Furthermore, while the cases suggest that victims and perpetrators were often of similar caste, it may be that many victims did not believe they could prevail in court, especially against a man of higher social or ethnic status. The prospects were further clouded as civil authorities were often uninterested in taking action, while others, such as the alcalde pedaneo Manuel Aguilar or the justicia mayor Sancho Bracho, were complicit by protecting or assisting the rapist.[20] All of this suggests that rape, like spousal abuse, was an underreported crime.

A study of divorce cases in Charcas offers additional insights concerning colonial marriage. Beyond highlighting the frequency of infidelity and spousal abuse, it underscores the consequences of the church policy of urging reconciliation and returning wives to batterers. Further, the lack of a clear resolution of the vast majority of cases reflects the doctrinal opposition to, and often insurmountable challenges in obtaining, divorce. Despite fragmentary documentation, many cases were simply abandoned, as women with few if any other options reluctantly returned to their abusive, philandering, and often alcoholic husbands. Pressure to return came not just from clergy and family members but often also from husbands who refused to support their wives in reclusion or pay their legal bills and otherwise sought to make their lives more miserable by having them held incommunicado in a convent. Once in recogimiento, with no means to support themselves, many women sold their few valuable possessions and soon found themselves assigned to demeaning tasks. Often without a bed or belongings, many women were reduced to sleeping on a cold floor and became ill as a result of the conditions of their confinement.[21] For those accustomed to having servants in, and the comforts of, the home, all the while facing pressures inside and outside of the recogimiento to return to their husband, it must have been especially difficult.

Once a divorce petition had been accepted, many men, and occasionally women, refused to respond to translados, in essence abandoning their cases. There was a logic to this as the church allowed the couple to separate pending the outcome of the proceedings. At some point the wife would be released from recogimiento either to live in depósito, often with a family member, or allowed to live on their own. This practice led to the prevalence of de facto, as opposed to de jure, divorces, which were much less costly, time-consuming, and risky than prodding the case along to a final ruling. Not only did a divorce proceeding usually involve years of expense, but the likelihood was that it would not be granted and thus that the couple could be compelled to reunite. The dread of such a prospect was in many cases the only thing a couple could agree on, making a de facto divorce an appealing alternative. Informal separations in which a divorce petition was never filed appear to have been an even more common, affordable, and expedient approach. They were, however, fraught with risk, as without a formal order to separate pending the outcome of a divorce, couples were exposed to the lurking perils of spousal reunification laws.[22]

Divorce and annulment cases reveal not only stunning abuse but also coerced marriages and those between people who did not know or hardly knew each other. Some cause wonder, such as Rudesinda Gallardo, who married Santiago Arraya, whose obscured face she did not even see on her wedding day, or Martina Bilbao Valverde, who married Antonio Yta only to learn her husband was intersex. The latter, tragic case demonstrates the confusion, and ultimate cruelty, of colonial authorities when faced with such a situation in a society with rigidly defined gender roles, especially when an archbishop and governor were involved.[23]

In addition to revealing issues related to love and loathing in late colonial society, examining the narratives and commonalities of these cases also exposes a highly fragmented, doctrinally rigid, violent, and itinerant society where interethnic relationships were common.[24] Moreover, these court cases were in many ways exceptional, requiring time, money, patience, diligence, and usually the loss of someone's honor as a crime or transgression became public. As such, they were indicators of broader trends of which they offer only the outlines.[25] They are also illustrative in what they don't say, suggesting a tendency for negotiated and often extrajudicial settlements to disputes, frequent de facto and informal divorces, and a society where moral deviance was the norm. Beyond that, they reveal the texture of colonial society and provide a glimpse of what servants saw in households and what passersby witnessed on the streets. Domestic servants were exceptionally well-informed of the transgressions of their masters, and sometimes they were also their lovers and their victims. Servants served lovers in bed, physically protected wives from attack by enraged husbands, helped cure their wounds, and tended to women during secret pregnancies.[26] Isidro Tharifa knew that few secrets were kept from servants, for when he was discovered in bed with his married lover during night rounds, he hid behind her slave hoping not to be detected. Indeed, it was because domestic servants were so knowledgeable of such issues that people sought, and vehemently opposed, their testimony. As we have seen, domestic service was also a widely used means of concealing an illicit relationship.[27]

These cases also demonstrate that it was not just the elite who utilized the courts, as women, single mothers, mestizos, the poor, and Indians frequently sought redress. They also invite further research concerning the advocates who represented many of the protagonists. Among them are Simon Narciso de Valenzuela, most active between 1760–80; Gregorio Nuñez, prominent between 1780–92; Silvestre Orgáz, who practiced between 1794–1817; José Manuel Malavia and Juan Pablo Arias, who represented clients between 1803–5; and Juan Bautista Mostajo, active between 1807–22. Malavia, Arías, and Mostajo all served as indigent defenders, underscoring the fact that it was not just the elites who utilized the colonial judicial system.[28]

The study of colonial intimacy also paints a picture of street life and public spaces.[29] La Plata's residents saw Juan Antonio de Silva y Acuña, the corregidor of Yamparáez, march his battered wife, María Jacinta de Melo, down La Plata's streets one midafternoon in 1766 after he had caught her outside of the city following her escape from their home.[30] An even greater spectacle was on a late Saturday afternoon in Potosí in

1803 when a brutally beaten Feliciana Vásquez was carried in a macabre procession to Potosí's Virgin de los Remedios convent, escorted by her brothers, vicar, and notary, leading some to conclude she was about to die. Others walking under an arcade fronting La Plata's plaza one September nightfall encountered Isidro Villanueva and Lorenzo Coronado in a brawl, each having accused the other of having an affair with his wife. Some contemporaries would have seen an angry group of women led by the Indian Rumi Cancha shouting outside of the home of her ex-lover, Andrés Sandóval, in 1797, as his sister came out and joined in the fray. Still others saw the slave Manuel chasing his lover's husband and fellow slave Antonio through La Plata's streets shouting how he was going to "gut" him—or witnessed Maria Narcisa Miranda angrily telling off the alguacil as she refused to send her daughter's bed to her in recogimiento.[31]

Still others would have seen captured lovers, such as a shackled Roque Hurtado on mule returning under a six-person escort as he came down La Plata's streets to its jail in mid-March 1758, temporarily ending his long-standing, but illicit, relationship with Petrona Leaños.[32] Those out in the evening would have been surprised to see Mariano Zilvetti in his large white hat and cloak and his black-clad newlywed wife Melchora Estrada running as fast as they could just after they had surprised the vicar general and conducted a clandestine marriage.[33] Residents saw bullfights on plazas or people sneaking to or from their lovers' homes, perhaps to cast an amorous letter through a window. The streets and plazas were also scenes of rendezvous as lovers quietly embraced in a dark doorway or alley, hoping to avoid night rounds, led by the alcalde with his staff of office, in the company of the alguacil, soldiers, and slaves, their way illuminated by a smoky lantern.

Beyond the geographical mobility that characterized late colonial society in Charcas, these cases also underscore "categorical" mobility, in which the same people were referred to in differing social or racial terms. For example, when Manuela Berasaín was sent to recogimiento, she was referred to as a "mujer soltera," or unmarried non-virgin woman, and hence lacking honor. When she formally indicated her decision to lead a life of religious reclusion, however, a witness referred to her as "Doña," indicating that her decision had restored her honor.[34] Just as honor was subject to change, so too was ethnic status subject to interpretation based on circumstance. For example, marriage records described Patricio Ballesteros as an *español*, or Spaniard or creole, in Sacaca. In the subsequent investigation of his incestuous marriage, however, authorities described him as a mestizo.[35] Similarly, a domestic servant and rape victim, Nicolasa Merida, testified against her attacker, Gregorio Agudo. In so doing, she was referred to as an *española soltera*, or unmarried Spanish or creole woman, despite the fact that those taking her testimony recorded it with the aid of an interpreter.[36]

Like racial categories, the term *vecino* was quite malleable and, in practice, did not refer exclusively to creole and Spanish property-owners. For example, when María Ascencia Flores filed suit to prevent the marriage of her illegitimate daughter to Augustín Godoy, she claimed to be a vecina of La Plata, however she explained to the court, "I cannot express myself well in the Spanish language."[37] Similarly, a witness in the case concerning the lovers Roque Hurtado and Petrona Leaños, Nicolás Aramayo is described as a "mestizo ladino vecino" of the valley of Mojotoro, respectively underscoring his lack of racial purity, Hispanicized appearance, and elevated social status.[38]

Similarly, in his divorce proceedings, Manuel Liendo identified himself as a vecino of La Plata despite the fact that he was a renter in a property owned by Pedro Tamayo, who was classified as an Indian. Perhaps fearing he had overreached, Manuel later indicated that he was a "resident" of the city.[39] Another tenant in the same compound, the thirty-year-old Spanish tailor Juan de Dios Tapia, was also listed as a vecino.[40]

Their landlord, Pedro Tamayo, rounds out the categorical ambiguities. He was described as both a vecino of La Plata and as a *principal*, or leader of an Indian community. The thrice-married Tamayo achieved vecino status through his ownership of three houses with numerous storefronts and was also immersed in regional commercial networks that stretched to Cuzco. Well connected with La Plata's elite, he prospered politically with the independence wars and, in 1815, even served as a councilman on La Plata's city council.[41] His case underscores the fluidity, and overlapping nature, of terms used to denote race and status in the colony while highlighting the political opportunities offered by the independence movement.

The pliable nature of ethnicity raises the question as to just how rigid colonial social structures really were. Although organized as a caste society, caste distinctions were permeable. The 1778 Pragmática reflects this, as part of the reason it was decreed was to limit upward economic and social mobility through marriage, especially among mestizos. Not only were illicit relationships commonplace, but they commonly crossed caste lines, with the man generally being older and having a higher social, ethnic, and economic rank. This also contributed to the prevalence of illegitimacy in society, which in La Plata was consistently higher among Spaniards, creoles, and mestizos than among Indians. Although those born out of wedlock carried a stigma, it was attenuated by the fact that illegitimacy was prevalent in society and its effects could be minimized by paternal recognition, context, character, and, in some cases, a gracias a sacar. While the colony was predicated on upholding caste distinctions, in late colonial Charcas these ideals were considerably eroded.

Similarly, while society was organized squarely on a patriarchal basis and male power was clearly exercised in the home, state, and church, it was far from absolute. Despite the foreboding context in which they lived and harsher punishments for transgressions, women could sometimes effectively circumvent male control. Widowhood was one means to autonomy and was widespread in society.[42] One such case was that of Antonia Prudencia de Martierena, who became a widow upon the death of her first husband, Joaquín Pérez de Uriondo. She subsequently married Francisco de Guemes y Esles, the owner of a silver mine and a mill, former corregidor, and militia coronel. By 1796, she was widowed again, as were both of her daughters from her first and second marriages.[43]

It was not just widows, unmarried adult women, and divorcees who largely ran their own affairs but also married women. Many had informally divorced, were formally separated pending a divorce ruling, or had husbands who had abandoned them or were otherwise absent. This constituted a critical, and broad, stratum of women's agency and a serious challenge to the patriarchal paradigm. The road to agency was, however, often paved with agony, as women often suffered pressure to marry, years of abuse or abandonment, and confinement. While spousal reunification laws ostensibly sought to protect wives from financial abandonment, when actually applied they often resubjected independent women to direct male authority. Such laws, however, were not systematically or effectively applied, and did more to reveal woman's agency than curtail it. In the end, the patriarchy/agency issue is not a dichotomy but rather an antimony, an apparent contradiction in which both sides are true and locked in dynamic conflict.

This paradoxical situation was not lost on Simón de Aldunate y Rada, who, in 1776, was twelve years into a stalled divorce process from his wife, María Martina Bengoa.[44] Simón bitterly asserted that "it is the case that many vicars, however learned they may be, do not understand what a woman is. . . . For every hundred men who are deserted . . . in ninety cases it is or has been the women who originated the scandalous discord . . . for as their sex aspires to the greatest liberty it is more than evident . . . that to obtain it they will not leave a rock unmoved."[45] The result of a woman's desire for independence, and interminable divorce proceedings, was financial distress and, he asserted, "so many husbands without their wives."[46]

Antonio Escudero Girón also shared this view as he was facing his divorce case in La Plata, brought by his wife, María Magdalena Ortía. He recognized women's agency when he complained, "How many . . . known as divorcees . . . do not live secluded lives in any monastery, but rather the opposite, they all live in the streets, much to their delight, in plain view and much to the vexation of their poor husbands."[47]

Notes

INTRODUCTION

1. Case 1, 8–10.
2. Case 1, 9–11, 18–19.
3. Case 1, 1–2.
4. Case 1, 3–9.
5. Case 1, 8–15, 13.
6. Case 1, 16–22.
7. Case 1, 18–24.
8. This work utilizes Steve Stern's definition of patriarchy as "a system of social relations and cultural values whereby (1) males exert superior power over female sexuality, reproductive roles, and labor power; (2) such dominance confers both specific services and superior status upon males in their relationships with females; (3) authority in family networks is commonly vested in elders and fathers, thereby imparting a generational as well as sex-based dynamic to social relations; and (4) authority in familial cells serves as a fundamental metaphorical model for social authority more generally" (Stern, *Secret History of Gender*, 21). For an excellent review of the literature on patriarchy and agency in colonial Latin America, see Socolow, "Colonial Gender History"; Black, "Between Prescription and Practice," 293–94; and Black, *Limits of Gender Domination*, 275–76. See also Gauderman, *Women's Lives*, 5–7, 29, 34, 39, 41–42, 46–47; Arrom, *Women of Mexico City*, 72–73, 76–78; Seed, *To Love, Honor, and Obey*, 7; and Boyer, *Lives of the Bigamists*, 163. On women entrepreneurs, see Candlin, "Empire of Women," and Morrison, "Slave Mothers."

The degree to which women acquiesced to, and resisted, the patriarchal norms upon which social, familial, and marital relations were based in colonial and early national Latin American society is a topic of considerable debate. Steinar Saether, in "Bourbon Absolutism," argues that the application of the Royal Pragmatic on Marriage in Latin America in 1778 both highlighted and reinforced the patriarchal nature of colonial society. María Mannarelli also notes the dominance of patriarchy in her study of illegitimacy in seventeenth-century Lima, *Pecados publicos*, published in English as *Private Passions and Public Sins*. In "Women and Crime," Susan Socolow explores the way the patriarchal nature of late colonial society in Buenos Aires found expression in crimes against women. Ann Zulawski notes the patriarchal context of women's market participation in "Social Differentiation." Studies of colonial Mexico also underscore the patriarchal underpinnings of society, such as Josefina Muriel's study of the changing nature and legal issues surrounding recogimientos, in *Los recogimientos de mujeres*. Carmen Casteñeda takes a similar view of the dominance of patriarchy in her study of rape and seduction in late colonial New Galicia, in *Violación, estupro y sexualidad*, as does Christine Hunefeldt in her study of divorce in nineteenth-century Lima, *Liberalism in the Bedroom*. Hunefeldt notes the challenges patriarchy presented, along with the Catholic Church, for women seeking divorce or separation in early republican Lima.

Several scholars have, however, challenged the notion of patriarchal hegemony, emphasizing the room for maneuver for, and resistance by, women within this context. Chad Black emphasizes the customary ability of women to litigate and engage in economic activity in Quito without male permission, noting, however, increasing constraints under the Bourbon monarchs and the republican period in both "Between Prescription and Practice" and *Limits of Gender Domination*. Silvia Arrom impugns the absolutism of patriarchy in *Women of Mexico City*, while Steve Stern develops this perspective to a greater degree while focusing on underprivileged women in late colonial, and early modern, Mexico in *Secret History of Gender*. Ana María Presta also notes women's potential for autonomy in early colonial Charcas in four case studies presented in "Portraits of Four Women." Kimberly Gauderman also notes the range of women's responses to colonial patriarchy in *Women's Lives*, as does Mariló Vigil in

La vida de las mujeres en los siglos XVI y XVII. Entrepreneurialism sometimes provided a route to autonomy for colonial women, a topic explored by Kit Candlin in "Empire of Women."

Witchcraft is also viewed as a means of resistance to patriarchy in colonial Guatemala in Marth Few's *Women Who Live Evil Lives* and, to a lesser extent, by Ruth Behar in "Sex and Sin, Witchcraft and the Devil in Late-Colonial Mexico" and "Sexual Witchcraft, Colonialism, and Women's Powers." Nicole von Germeten also examines the intersections of sorcery, illicit love, and women's agency in seventeenth-century Cartagena in *Violent Delights*.

9. With a broad focus on colonial Latin America, Asunción Lavrin offers an excellent overview of the issues surrounding marriage in colonial Latin America in her "Introduction." Studies of the dynamics of marriage choice in colonial Latin America include the work of Bianca Premo, who traces the evolution of relationships between parents and their offspring in colonial Lima as the crown conferred increasing power to parents in marriage choice, underscoring a trend of increasing patriarchal power in the colony, in *Children of the Father King*. Premo also explores the application and reception of Bourbon social legislation in Lima in "'Misunderstood Love.'" Focusing on Upper Peru, Eugenia Bridikhina offers a detailed study of the multi-layered assertion of Bourbon morality in *Sin temor a dios*. With a focus on late colonial Argentina, Susan Socolow analyzes the tensions of marital decisions in "Acceptable Partners." Marriage choice in Antioquia, New Granada, is the focus of Pablo Rodríguez's "Amor y matrimonio." Focusing on New Spain, Richard Boyer explores issues of arranged and clandestine marriages, bigamy, abuse, and divorce in New Spain in *Lives of the Bigamists*. Also centered on New Spain is the work of Patricia Seed, who studies conflicts surrounding marriage choice in *To Love, Honor, and Obey*. She finds that women had considerable room for maneuver and negotiation in their choice of mate. Robert McCaa notes the relative absence of parental intervention via the courts in marriage choice in the mining city of Parral, Mexico, in "Gustos de los padres." Focusing on the national period, in *Runaway Daughters*, Kathryn Sloan studies the courting practices of working-class Mexican youth in Oaxaca. She demonstrates how they challenged, manipulated, and redefined traditional concepts of probity, familial honor, and parental control and often

found support in their marital choices from an increasingly powerful, and active, liberal state.

Other studies focus on divorce, which in colonial Latin America was limited to perpetual separation. In *Liberalism in the Bedroom*, Christine Hunefeldt examines how legal arguments concerning divorce evolved over time in early republican Lima as well as the increasing role of the state in this process. Juan Javier Pescador studies the process, and relative success, of divorce petitions in the archbishopric of Mexico in "Entre la espada y el olvido." Focusing on late colonial and early republican Mexico, Silvia Arrom offers an excellent exposition of the legal status of women, as well as of the divorce process, in *Women of Mexico City*. René Salinas Meza studies free unions, divorce, and anulments in colonial Chile in "Uniones ilegitimas y desuniones legítimas."

10. Case 2, 7; Arrom, *Women of Mexico City*, 226; Dueñas, "Adulterios, amancebamientos, divorcios y abandono," 44–45; Black, *Limits of Gender Domination*, 142; O'Day, *Women's Agency in Early Modern Britain and the American Colonies*, 9. See also World Bank, *World Development Report 2012*, 150.
11. Case 3, 1.
12. Case 4, 11–12, 19–28; case 5, 3–45; case 6, 12; case 7, 34; case 8, 647–48.
13. Familial and personal honor were tied to issues of sexuality and marriage in Latin America. Lyman Johnson and Sonya Lipsett-Rivera explore the centrality of honor in colonial Latin American society in their introduction to their comprehensive edited volume, *Faces of Honor*, as does Mark Burkholder in "Honor and Honors" in the same volume. The volume also offers the ecclesiastical perspective in Geoffrey Spurling's "Honor, Sexuality, and the Colonial Church" and in Lyman Johnson's examination of how commoners defended their honor in colonial Buenos Aires, "Dangerous Words, Provocative Gestures, and Violent Acts." In the same volume, Sonya Lipsett-Rivera focuses on how women in late colonial Mexico defended their honor in "Slap in the Face of Honor." Lipsett-Rivera also offers an incisive analysis of the linkages between honor, architecture, public and private spaces, and the human body in *Negotiation of Daily Life*. The relationships between honor, illicit love, and elopement in colonial Cartagena and early national Mexico are explored, respectively, in Nicole von Germeten's *Violent Delights* and in Kathryn Sloan's *Runaway Daughters*.

The issue of racial passing is also taken up by Joanne Rappaport, who focuses on colonial Bogotá in "Mischievous Lovers." Illegitimacy and "natural children" as well as secret pregnancies and the use of the gracias al sacar to legitimate one's status are treated regionally by Ann Twinam in *Public Lives*. Thomas Calvo also studies the prevalence of illegitimacy in New Spain in "Warmth of the Hearth."

Ann Twinam has also written extensively on the topic of honor and racial passing, in works such as *Public Lives*, "Honor, Sexuality, and Illegitimacy," and "Negotiation of Honor." Ramón Gutiérrez also offers an excellent discussion of the construction of colonial honor in "Honor Ideology." The effect of broken engagements on individual and familial honor is the topic of Juan García Gonzales's "El incumplimiento de las promeses." Focusing on Arequipa, Peru, Sarah Chambers charts the increasing value of one's virtue in determining honor as opposed to one's social or racial standing as colony was replaced by republic in *Subjects to Citizens*.

14. Case 9, 1–2; ABAS, Archivo Parroquial, Libro de Bautismos Santo Domingo, Vol. 33, 91; case 10, 96; Delgado, "Sin Temor de Dios," 109; Arrom, *Women of Mexico City*, 63; Lavrin, "Introduction," 11; Twinam, "Negotiation of Honor," 83; Twinam, "Honor, Sexuality, and Illegitimacy," 129; Lipsett-Rivera, "Slap in the Face of Honor," 191; Lipsett-Rivera, *Gender and the Negotiation*, 12–15; Sloan, *Runaway Daughters*, 4; Germeten, *Violent Delights*, 21, 147.

15. Case 11, 4; Fray, *La perfecta casada*, 60, 68, 137; Van Deusen, *Between the Sacred and the Worldly*, xi–xii, 4; Van Deusen, "Defining the Sacred and the Worldly," 444–45, 449; Gauderman, *Women's Lives*, 54; López Navarro, "Prólogo," 8–10, 12–13, 16; Socolow, "Acceptable Partners," 227–28; Gutiérrez, "Honor Ideology," 84, 86; Kuznesof, "Ethnic and Gender Influences," 161–62, 164, 168; Chambers, *Subjects to Citizens*, 3, 4, 164–66, 169; Johnson and Lipsett-Rivera, "Introduction," 1–2, 4–5, 7–8, 15; Lipsett-Rivera, *Negotiation of Daily Life*, 247; Burkholder, "Honor and Honors," 18, 42; Spurling, "Honor, Sexuality, and the Colonial Church," 93; Twinam, "Honor, Sexuality, and Illegitimacy,"123–24, 148; Seed, *To Love, Honor, and Obey*, 65–67, 140; Lewis, "'Weakness' of Women," 79; Lavrin, "La sexualidad," 500–501; Lipsett-Rivera, "Slap in the Face of Honor," 179; Mannarelli, *Pecados publicos*, 61, 257, 261; Burkholder, "Honor and Honors," 18, 23, 29.

16. Case 12, 1–4; Twinam, *Public Lives*, 65, 94; Germeten, *Violent Delights*, 16, 147, 149; Chambers, *Subjects to Citizens*, 167–68; Johnson and Lipsett-Rivera, "Introduction," 4.
17. Johnson and Lipsett-Rivera, "Introduction," 4–5, 10; Flores Galindo and Chocano, "Las cargas del sacramento," 404; Chambers, *Subjects to Citizens*, 172–73; Twinam, "Honor, Sexuality, and Illegitimacy," 127; Seed, *To Love, Honor, and Obey*, 70, 237–38, 240; Chambers, *Subjects to Citizens*, 3–4, 172–73, 179, 186, 246.
18. The diversity of experiences of religious reclusion in Lima and the multivalent meaning of recogimiento have been studied by Nancy Van Deusen in *Between the Sacred and the Worldly* and "Defining the Sacred and the Worldly." The differing forms and legal context of recogimiento in New Spain are examined with case studies by Josefina Muriel in *Los recogimientos de mujeres*. Kathryn Burns offers a study of the economic life of convents and the institution of recogimiento in colonial Cuzco in *Colonial Habits* and the role they played in the acculturation of mestizas in "Gender and the Politics of Mestizaje." In addition to the cases cited below, see also cases 13 and 14.
19. Van Deusen, *Between the Sacred and the Worldly*, xi–xii, 4; Van Deusen, "Defining the Sacred and the Worldly," 444–45, 449; Gauderman, *Women's Lives*, 54; Socolow, "Acceptable Partners," 227.
20. Van Deusen, *Between the Sacred and the Worldly*, xii, 79, 446; Van Deusen, "Defining the Sacred and the Worldly," 444.
21. Van Deusen, *Between the Sacred and the Worldly*, xii, 9, 56, 123, 151, 450; Van Deusen, "Defining the Sacred and the Worldly," 446; Premo, *Children of the Father King*, 83, 1–8.
22. Muriel, *Los recogimientos de mujeres*, 45, 217, 219; Van Deusen, *Between the Sacred and the Worldly*, xiv, 80, 98; Van Deusen, "Defining the Sacred and the Worldly," 447; Burns, "Gender and the Politics of Mestizaje," 15–16. See also Hunefeldt, *Liberalism in the Bedroom*, 152–74; and Lavallé, "Divorcio y nulidad," 440.
23. Case 15, 1–3.
24. Case 16, 1–4.
25. Case 17, 1–3; Premo, *Children of the Father King*, 89–90; Arrom, *Women of Mexico City*, 212–13, 215; Van Deusen, *Between the Sacred and the Worldly*, 98; Hunefeldt, *Liberalism in the Bedroom*, 163.

26. Arrom, *Women of Mexico City*, 214.
27. Case 18, 1–4, 7, 14.
28. Case 19, 1, 3.
29. Case 19, 4–5. See also case 20, 1–2.
30. Case 21, 1–5.
31. Case 21, 9–16, 20–27, 30–40.
32. Case 21, 43–87; case 22, 403. For more on María Francisca Barrios, see case 23, 3–5; and case 24, 292.
33. Case 25, 1.
34. Case 25, 2–5, 8, 11–12.
35. Case 26, 1; Muriel, *Los recogimientos de mujeres*, 39; Black, *Limits of Gender Domination*, 75, 80.
36. Case 27, 1; case 28, 1–15; case 29, 1–5; case 30, 1–8; case 31, 1–21; case 32, 1–5; case 33, 1–4; Boyer, *Lives of the Bigamists*, 17–22.
37. Case 34, 12; case 35, 2; case 36, 29–30; Premo, *Children of the Father King*, 30, 32, 41; Black, *Limits of Gender Domination*, 76; Van Deusen, *Between the Sacred and the Worldly*, 86.
38. Black, *Limits of Gender Domination*, 77, 79, 111, 120; Honores, "Alcalde ordinario." Concerning the use of night rounds, see also cases 16, 37, 38, 39, 40, 41, 42, 43, 44, 45, 46, 47, and 48.
39. Case 49, 1–5; case 50, 2; case 28, 2; case 51, 1; case 45, 1; case 52, 3; Black, *Limits of Gender Domination*, 77–80; Sloan, *Runaway Daughters*, 105, 128.
40. Case 53, 1.
41. Case 54, 1–3; case 45, 3; case 55, 13; case 11, 1; case 56, 17–21; case 57, 27–32, 53; case 58, 5; case 59, 10, 13–17, 51–54; Lavrin, "Sexuality," 60; Mannarelli, *Pecados publicos*, 199.
42. Case 60, 1–2; case 31, 5; case 61, 1; case 62, 3; case 63, 3; case 25, 2; case 60, 1–2; case 64, 5; case 65, 1; case 66, 16; case 47, 11; case 67, 33; case 68, 13; case 69, 3; case 70, 1; case 71, 31; case 72, 1–2; case 73, 1; case 74, 1; Black, *Limits of Gender Domination*, 78.
43. Case 75, 1; Black, "Between Prescription and Practice," 277–79, 283–85; Black, *Limits of Gender Domination*, 128–41; García Gonzales, "El incumplimiento de las promeses," 611–25; Arrom, *Women of Mexico City*, 55–56; Premo, *Children of the Father King*, 22.
44. Several studies probe the often contradictory legal context in which women operated in colonial Latin America, for instance Pilar Gonzalbo

Aizpuru's *Familia y orden colonial* and Asunción Lavrin's "La sexualidad" and "Sexuality." The degree to which women were equated legally with Indians is the topic of Laura Lewis's "'Weakness' of Women." Focusing on Ecuador is the work of Christina Borchart de Moreno, who traces how the transition from colony to republic affected how the laws applied to women in "Words and Wounds." While colonial women were with few exceptions considered minors by law, in "Between Prescription and Practice" Chad Black emphasizes the gap between theory and reality in Ecuador by demonstrating that, contrary to colonial laws, women often represented themselves before civil courts. Similarly, Jessica Delgado studies both how women represented themselves before the ecclesiastical court and how they crafted their cases in colonial Toluca in "Sin Temor de Dios."

45. Lewis, "'Weakness' of Women," 74–75; Muriel, *Los recogimientos de mujeres*, 16–17; Zulawski, "Social Differentiation," 97–98; Arrom, *Women of Mexico City*, 55, 57–58, 61–62, 64, 68, 81; Premo, *Children of the Father King*, 28, 136. See also Boyer, "Women," 252–58; Arrom, *Women of Mexico City*, 61, 76; Premo, *Children of the Father King*, 25; and Rodríguez, "Amor y matrimonio," 151–52. See also case 76. An arras was a gift to the bride-to-be that served as an expression of good faith.

46. Case 77, 1; case 78, 4; case 55, 15; case 32, 7; Black, "Between Prescription and Practice," 273–74, 277, 283–85, 293; Black, *Limits of Gender Domination*, 1–2, 5–6, 122–23, 142–43, 158, 160, 260–62; Dueñas, "Adulterios," 44–45; Lewis, "'Weakness' of Women," 75; Muriel, *Los recogimientos de mujeres*, 16–17; Zulawski, "Social Differentiation," 97–98; Arrom, *Women of Mexico City*, 55, 58, 61, 64; Premo, *Children of the Father King*, 28, 136. See also McCaa, "Gustos de los padres," 580, 586–87, 590, 592–93, 608.

47. Arrom, *Women of Mexico City*, 69; Premo, *Children of the Father King*, 26.

48. Arrom, *Women of Mexico City*, 217; Dueñas, "Adulterios," 43; Lavallé, "Divorcio y nulidad," 429; González de Riego, "Fragmentos," 203.

1. MORALITY VERSUS AFFINITY

Title: Case 79, 37.

1. Case 26, 1; case 80, 6, 7; case 81, 1–15; case 82, 26–27; Muriel, *Los recogimientos de mujeres*, 39; Salinas Meza and Goicovic Donoso, "Amor, violencia y passion," 248–50, 267–68; Twinam, *Public Lives*, 107–12; Mannarelli,

Pecados publicos, 127–28; Salinas Meza, "Uniones ilegitimas y desuniones legítimas," 175, 184–85; Lavrin, "La sexualidad,"498; Lavrin, "Sexuality," 62, 79, 192; Seed, *To Love, Honor, and Obey*, 27; Socolow, "Acceptable Partners," 220. For a discussion of moral crimes in Quito, see Black, *Limits of Gender Domination*, 100–119.

2. Twinam, *Public Lives*, 11; Saether, "Bourbon Absolutism," 491–92. See also McCaa, "Gustos de los padres," 580, 583–84; Socolow, "Acceptable Partners," 231; and Powers, *Women in the Crucible*, 195.
3. Lavrin, "Introduction," 37; Mannarelli, *Pecados publicos*, 15. See also Van Deusen, "Diasporas, Bondage, and Intimacy"; and Powers, *Women in the Crucible*, 133.
4. Bridikhina, *Sin temor a dios*, 114–15; López Beltrán, "Intereses y pasiones," 51. See also López Beltrán, "El círculo del poder."
5. Saether, "Bourbon Absolutism," 491–92; Calvo, "Warmth of the Hearth," 295; Twinam, *Public Lives*, 11; Bridikhina, *Sin temor a dios*, 115; Lavrin, "La sexualidad," 494–95; Lavrin, "Introduction," 12; Lewis, "'Weakness' of Women," 77; López Beltrán, "La buena vecindad," 229.
6. ABAS, LBSD, vol. 33, 83–104, 116–21; ABAS, LBSD, vol. 34, 6–26; ABAS, LBSD, vol. 35, 119–42; ABAS, LBSD, vol. 36, 56–71, 194–211; ABAS, LBSD, vol. 37, 140–64; ABAS, LBSD, vol. 41, 19–51; ABAS, LBSD, vol. 42, 201–40; ABAS, LBSD, vol. 43, 88–109; ABAS, LBSD, vol. 44, 1–43; ABAS, LBSD, vol. 45, 30–35, 90–97, 123–25; ABAS, LBSD, vol. 46, 270–312; ABAS, LBSD, vol. 47, 41–59; ABAS, LBSD, vol. 49, 164–92; ABAS, LBSD, vol. 50, 360–95; ABAS, LBSD, vol. 51, 1–44; ABAS, LBSD, vol. 53, 13–51; ABAS, LBSD, vol. 54, 12–21; ABAS, LBSD, vol. 36, 194–211.
7. ABAS, LBSS, vol. 5, 210–19; ABAS, LBSS, vol. 6, 116–50; ABAS, LBSS, vol. 7, 47–55; ABAS, LBSD, vol. 38, 3; ABAS, LBSD, vol. 45, 90–97, 123–25; ABAS, LBSD, vol. 49, 164–92; ABAS, LBSD, vol. 50, 360–95; ABAS, LBSD, vol. 51, 1–44; ABAS, LBSD, vol. 53, 13–51; ABAS, LBSD, vol. 54, 12–21.
8. ABAS, LBSD, vol. 34, 6–26; ABAS, LBSD, vol. 36, 56–71, 194–211.
9. ABAS, LBSD, vol. 33, 83–104, 116–21; ABAS, LBSD, vol. 34, 6–26; ABAS, LBSD, vol. 35, 83–104, 119–42; ABAS, LBSD, vol. 36, 56–57, 194–211; ABAS, LBSD, vol. 37, 140–64; ABAS, LBSD, vol. 38, 3; ABAS, LBSD, vol. 41, 19–51; ABAS, LBSD, vol. 42, 201–40; ABAS, LBSD, vol. 43, 88–109; ABAS, LBSD, vol. 44, 1–43; ABAS, LBSD, vol. 45, 30–35, 90–97, 123; ABAS, LBSD, vol. 46, 270–312; ABAS, LBSD, vol. 47, 41–59; ABAS, LBSD, vol. 49, 164–92;

ABAS, LBSD, vol. 50, 360–95; ABAS, LBSD, vol. 51, 1–44; ABAS, LBSD, vol. 53, 13–51; ABAS, LBSD, vol. 54, 12–21, 25; ABAS, LBSS, vol. 2, 203–19; ABAS, LBSS, vol. 3, 95–114, 265–80; ABAS, LBSS, vol. 4, 47–54; ABAS, LBSS, vol. 5, 45–61, 210–19; ABAS, LBSS, vol. 6, 116–50; ABAS, LBSS, vol. 7, 47–55.

10. Case 83, 1; case 75, 1–2; case 84, 1; case 85, 1; Twinam, *Public Lives*, 96; Gonzalbo Aizpuru, *Familia y orden colonial*, 58–59, 70; Seed, *To Love, Honor, and Obey*, 168; Salinas Meza and Goicovic Donoso, "Amor, violencia y passion," 244, 248, 250–53; Socolow, "Women and Crime," 40.
11. Lavrin, "La sexualidad," 493; Twinam, *Public Lives*, 82, 87, 188, 217–20; Bridikhina, *Sin temor a dios*, 112; Mannarelli, *Pecados publicos*, 198–200; Arrom, *Women of Mexico City*, 63.
12. Lavrin, "La sexualidad," 513; Lavrin, "Introduction," 12; Muriel, *Los recogimientos de mujeres*, 20; Morrison, "Slave Mothers," 34–35; Twinam, *Public Lives*, 40, 74, 128, 130, 136, 188, 276; Twinam, "Honor, Sexuality, and Illegitimacy," 147.
13. Twinam, "Negotiation of Honor," 88–90, 94; Twinam, *Public Lives*, 29–30, 183, 185, 187, 208, 260; Bridikhina, *Sin temor a dios*, 132; Rappaport, "Mischievous Lovers," 9–10, 19. For a discussion of the gracias al sacar, see Twinam, *Public Lives*, 50–55.
14. Twinam, *Public Lives*, 128.
15. Arrom, *Women of Mexico City*, 69; Twinam, *Public Lives*, 47, 118, 128, 143, 160, 166, 178, 181–82, 188, 340; Mannarelli, *Pecados publicos*, 257–59; Flores Galindo and Chocano, "Las cargas del sacramento," 418; Mannarelli, *Pecados publicos*, 308; Premo, "'Misunderstood Love,'" 241–42; Socolow, "Acceptable Partners," 227.
16. Twinam, *Public Lives*, 66–67, 69, 73, 78, 134, 137; Mannarelli, *Pecados publicos*, 199. See also Lofstrom, *Tres familias*, 34.
17. Case 64, 11.
18. Case 64, 5, 11, 36.
19. Case 64, 2. On the use of love letters in courtship and court cases, see also Sloan, *Runaway Daughters*, chapter 3; and French, "'Te Amo Muncho.'"
20. Case 64, 1–4.
21. Case 64, 61.
22. In addition to the case below concerning child support see cases 86 and 87. Concerning illegitimate children, see cases 1, 15, 45, 52, 88, 89, 90, 91, 92, 93, 94, 95, 96, 97, 98, 99, and 100.

23. Case 59, 1, 5–10, 13–37. See also case 101, 430. For a later legal dispute involving Tardío, see case 102, 688.
24. Case 59, 6.
25. Case 59, 40–44, 48, 51–58.
26. Case 59, 1, 61–66.
27. Case 59, 67–76, 79.
28. Case 103, 538; case 104, 724. Tardío and his mother exchanged considerable powers in the administration of their affairs. See case 105, 46–47; and case 106, 152–53.
29. In addition to the cases below, see also cases 40, 107, 108, 109, 110, 111, and 112.
30. Case 43, 1; Bridikhina, *Sin temor a dios*, 16, 92–96; Gauderman, *Women's Lives*, 56–57; Germeten, *Violent Delights*, 55, 71.
31. Case 53, 1.
32. Case 53, 1.
33. Case 53, 2–4, 7.
34. Case 53, 6, 8.
35. Case 53, 7.
36. Case 53, 4–5, 7.
37. Case 53, 8.
38. Case 53, 8.
39. Case 55, 1–3, 6–7.
40. Case 55, 7–8, 61.
41. Case 55, 8–13, 15–16, 52.
42. Case 55, 18–19.
43. Case 55, 20–21.
44. Case 55, 20–23, 31–34, 53.
45. Case 55, 93–98, 104.
46. Case 55, 105–6.
47. Case 55, 18, 30–41, 71–74, 105–12.
48. Case 45, 1–6. For other cases that included stakeouts see cases 55, 113, and 114.
49. Case 45, 6–15.
50. Case 114, 1, 7.
51. Case 114, 1, 7.
52. Case 114, 8–13.

53. For additional cases of male infidelity, see case 2; case 9; case 15; case 16; case 28; case 34; case 39; case 46; case 65; case 70; case 82; case 95, 1–4; case 99; case 100; case 115; case 116; case 117; case 118; case 119; case 120; case 121; case 122; case 123; case 124; case 125; case 126; case 127; case 128; case 129; case 130; case 131; case 132; case 133; case 134; and case 135.
54. Case 45, 4; Mannarelli, *Pecados publicos*, 157; Arrom, *Women of Mexico City*, 64–65; Lavrin, "Sexuality," 67–68; Socolow, "Women and Crime," 52; Powers, *Women in the Crucible*, 196; Gonzalbo Aizpuru, *Familia y orden colonial*, 63; Boyer, *Lives of the Bigamists*, 140.
55. Case 50, 1, 14.
56. Case 50, 1; case 136, 1; case 137, 6. Concerning names omitted from the record, see cases 138, 139, and 140.
57. Case 50, 1–5.
58. Case 50, 7–8; case 136, 1.
59. Case 50, 9.
60. Case 50, 14.
61. Case 50, 15–16; case 136, 1; case 137, 2, 7.
62. Case 141, 1–13.
63. Case 141, 16.
64. Case 141, 19.
65. Case 142, 1.
66. Case 142, 2–7.
67. Case 142, 6, 8.
68. Case 142, 12. For another case in which a woman successfully had her husband's lover banished, see case 143.
69. Case 143, 1–4.
70. Case 143, 6–8.
71. In addition to the cases cited below, see also cases 19, 21, 36, 60, 66, 87, 100, 118, 120, 122, 130, 131, 138, 141, 144, 145, 146, 147, 148, 149, 150, 151, 152, 153, 154, 155, 156, 157, 158, 159, 160, and 161. In *Violent Delights*, Germeten views female infidelity as a pervasive form of "sexual agency" in colonial Cartagena (4, 12, 84, 206, 232–34). Concerning female infidelity in New Spain, see Boyer, *Lives of the Bigamists*, 145–52.
72. Case 58, 4; case 143, 1–4; case 162, 1–4; case 35, 1; Lavrin, "Sexuality," 67–68; Twinam, *Public Lives*, 85; Salinas Meza and Goicovic Donoso, "Amor, violencia y pasión," 239.

73. Case 96, 1–2.
74. Case 96, 5.
75. Case 96, 6, 9.
76. Case 96, 8.
77. Case 96, 8–9.
78. In addition to the cases below, see also cases 43, 50, 52, 79, 99, 113, 119, 121, 128, 133, 136, 137, 152, 162, 163, 164, 165, 166, 167, 168.
79. Case 162, 1, 3.
80. Case 162, 1.
81. Case 162, 2–4.
82. Case 163, 1–2.
83. Case 163, 1–2. For a similar case, see case 43.
84. Case 52, 1–3, 6, 8–10.
85. Case 52, 4, 6–7, 14–15.
86. Case 128, 2.
87. Case 35, 1.
88. Case 35, 1.
89. Case 35, 1.
90. Case 35, 1–2.
91. In addition to the cases cited here, see also cases 1, 41, 50, 52, 81, 113, 126, 136, 137, 140, 160, 163, 169, and 170.
92. Case 140, 1–3.
93. Case 140, 3.
94. Case 140, 3.
95. Case 140, 3.
96. Case 140, 6–7.
97. Case 140, 7.
98. Case 140, 8.
99. Case 169, 4.
100. Case 169, 1–4.
101. Negotiations between plaintiff and defendant were a not-uncommon, if informal, part of court proceedings. See case 1; case 43; case 77, 1–5; case 96; case 113; case 142; case 171; and Black, *Limits of Gender Domination*, 100–101.
102. Case 113, 1.
103. Case 113, 4.

104. Case 113, 4–6.
105. Arrom, *Women of Mexico City*, 211; Van Deusen, *Between the Sacred and the Worldly*, 87. See also cases 1, 3, 21, 57, 66, 119, 133, 152, 165, 166, 167, 168, 172, and 333.
106. Case 113, 7.
107. Case 113, 7, 9, 11–13, 18–19.
108. Case 113, 1, 6.
109. Case 113, 11.
110. Case 113, 11–14.
111. Case 113, 14.
112. Case 113, 15–19.
113. Case 113, 25–26.
114. Case 113, 29–36.
115. Concerning jurisdictional rivalries, see also cases 21, 31, 46, 55, 79, 80, 111, 167, 173, and 174.
116. Armendáriz, "Carta de Castelfuerte," 217. See also Powers, *Women in the Crucible*, 98–100; Harrison, "Theology of Concupiscence," 147; Lavrin, "La sexualidad," 508–11; Hunefeldt, "Comunidad," 5; Mills, "Bad Christians," 206; "Representación de la ciudad," 62; Lewin, *La rebelión de Túpac Amaru*, 230; Stavig, "'Living in Offense,'" 612; Mendina, *Historia del tribunal*, 202–6, 225, 322, 328, 330, 332, 416–17; O'Phelan Godoy, *Rebellions and Revolts*, 74; Twinam, *Public Lives*, 166; Mannarelli, *Pecados publicos*, 126–27; Salinas Meza and Goicovic Donoso, "Amor, violencia y passion," 250; and Sánchez, "Pecados secretos," 128, 134–41. Concerning cases in Charcas, see cases 58, 140, 167, 170, 175, 176, and 177.
117. "El Obpo de Quito," 221. See also Serrada, "Testimonio."
118. Juan and Ulloa, *Discourse and Political Reflections*, 107, 281.
119. Juan and Ulloa, *Discourse and Political Reflections*, 282, 284.
120. Juan and Ulloa, *Discourse and Political Reflections*, 292–93.
121. Juan and Ulloa, *Discourse and Political Reflections*, 293–94.
122. Juan and Ulloa, *Discourse and Political Reflections*, 284–87.
123. "De un vecino del Cuzco," 154.
124. Case 178, 1–2; case 179, 4.
125. Case 178, 1–2; case 179, 2–4.
126. Case 86, 1–3, 6–12. For a similar case, see case 180.

127. Case 98, 1, 6–8, 31–33.
128. Case 46, 1, 2–3.
129. Case 46, 4–6, 9, 12–17.

2. PRAGMÁTICA AND PATRIARCHY

Title: Case 181, 13.

1. Case 182, 1–9; case 183, 1; Black, *Limits of Gender Domination*, 1, 2, 8, 13, 70, 102, 122–23; Saether, "Bourbon Absolutism," 475–76, 485–86, 488–89, 496; Premo, "'Misunderstood Love,'" 246; Premo, *Children of the Father King*, 2; Bridikhina, *Sin temor a dios*, 12, 15, 41, 59, 66–67; Gonzalbo Aizpuru, *Familia y orden colonial*, 47, 268; Arrom, *Women of Mexico City*, 77; Van Deusen, *Between the Sacred and the Worldly*, 309; Socolow, "Acceptable Partners," 212; Lavrin, "Introduction," 17; Seed, *To Love, Honor, and Obey*, 204; Zulawski, "Social Differentiation," 97; Stolcke, "Invaded Women," 18. For greater detail on Spanish law, and its origins, as it applied to women, couples, and families, see Saether, "Bourbon Absolutism," 475–509; Black, "Between Prescription and Practice," 273–98; García Gonzales, "El incumplimiento de las promeses," 611–42; Arrom, *Women of Mexico City*, 53–97; Lavrin, "Introduction"; and Premo, *Children of the Father King*, 17–41; Twinam, *Public Lives*, 18; Gauderman, *Women's Lives*, 24; and Seed, *To Love, Honor, and Obey*, 205. For a discussion of the differences between the more decentralized Habsburg approach to governance with its intersecting jurisdictions and emphasis on custom and conciliation versus the centralizing tendencies of the Bourbon monarchs, see Black, *Limits of Gender Domination*, 1, 8, 19, 70, 102, 122–23, 274–75.
2. Case 184, 1–3; Socolow, "Acceptable Partners," 210, 231; Gutiérrez, "Honor Ideology," 91–92; Boyer, *Lives of the Bigamists*, 64; Germeten, *Violent Delights*, 193; Socolow, "Acceptable Partners," 211; Seed, *To Love, Honor, and Obey*, 200–202, 224; Germeten, *Violent Delights*, 192; Gonzalbo Aizpuru, *Familia y orden colonial*, 81; Muriel, *Los recogimientos de mujeres*, 18; Arrom, *Women of Mexico City*, 57; Premo, *Children of the Father King*, 22; Zulawski, "Social Differentiation," 97; Twinam, "Negotiation of Honor," 85; Twinam, *Public Lives*, 36–37; Van Deusen, *Between the Sacred and the Worldly*, 83. See Premo, *Children of the Father King*, 16–24, 32–41, for a discussion of minority in Spanish America.

3. Sloan, *Runaway Daughters*, 41; Seed, *To Love, Honor, and Obey*, 128, 137, 205, 210, 220; Socolow, "Acceptable Partners," 219–21; Saether, "Bourbon Absolutism," 477.
4. Case 182, 10–13, 47; Saether, "Bourbon Absolutism," 475, 490, 494; Premo, "'Misunderstood Love,'" 238; Bridikhina, *Sin temor a dios*, 134, Socolow, "Acceptable Partners," 210, 225–26; Sloan, *Runaway Daughters*, 41.
5. Case 182, 10–18; case 185, 1, 9; Socolow, "Acceptable Partners," 211; Gauderman, *Women's Lives*, 24.
6. Case 174, 1; case 186, 1.
7. Saether, "Bourbon Absolutism," 498, 505; Twinam, *Public Lives*, 18; Gauderman, *Women's Lives*, 24; Seed, *To Love, Honor, and Obey*, 205; Socolow, "Acceptable Partners," 238.
8. The law further stipulated that in cases where only the mother survived, the age of majority for the children came a year earlier, and if only grandparents were alive, their approval was necessary, but only up to age twenty-one for women and twenty-three for men. If offspring were under guardianship, they could marry without consent upon reaching age twenty-two in the case of men and twenty in the case of women. Furthermore, any engagement that was not signed and witnessed by a notary was not legally valid. See case 187, 1; case 69, 9–12; Saether, "Bourbon Absolutism," 504; Socolow, "Acceptable Partners," 212–13; and Seed, *To Love, Honor, and Obey*, 222–23.
9. Seed, *To Love, Honor, and Obey*, 223; Socolow, "Acceptable Partners," 235.
10. Socolow, "Acceptable Partners," 214; Seed, *To Love, Honor, and Obey*, 75–76.
11. Case 188, 355. See also case 67.
12. Seed, *To Love, Honor, and Obey*, 68, 109; García Gonzales, "El incumplimiento de las promeses," 632–37; Casteñeda, *Violación, estupro y sexualidad*, 41–48; Rodríguez, "Amor y matrimonio," 163–64, 166; Lavrin, "Sexuality," 61.
13. Sloan, *Runaway Daughters*, 2, 176; Twinam, "Negotiation of Honor," 85–86; Twinam, *Public Lives*, 91–92; Lavrin, "Sexuality," 61.
14. García Gonzales, "El incumplimiento de las promeses," 627, 632–37; Casteñeda, *Violación, estupro y sexualidad*, 41–48; Rodríguez, "Amor y matrimonio," 163–66; Lavrin, "Sexuality," 63–64; Pescador, "Entre la espada y el olvido," 194, 197–200; Powers, *Women in the Crucible*, 116; Salinas

Meza and Goicovic Donoso, "Amor, violencia y passion," 248; Dueñas, "Adulterios," 36. See also cases 72, 189, and 190.

15. Case 93, 1.
16. Case 93, 6.
17. Case 93, 2.
18. Case 93, 5, 7–8.
19. Case 93, 9.
20. Case 93, 1–2.
21. Case 191, 1, 3.
22. Case 191, 2.
23. Case 191, 4.
24. Case 191, 6–7.
25. Boyer, *Lives of the Bigamists*, 65–81; Presta, "Portraits of Four Women," 245, 252; Lavallé, "Divorcio y nulidad," 438–41; González de Riego, "Fragmentos," 206–7. See also case 51; case 57; case 119; case 120; case 122; case 166; case 192; case 193; case 194; case 195; case 196, 309–13; Seed, *To Love, Honor, and Obey*, 33–34, 41; and Gutiérrez, "Honor Ideology," 88–90.
26. "Representación de la ciudad," 36.
27. "Representación de la ciudad," 37; Stavig, "'Living in Offense,'" 602–3, 606, 610–11.
28. "Representación de la ciudad," 36.
29. "Representación de la ciudad," 37–38.
30. In addition to the cases below, see also cases 91, 197, and 198.
31. Seed, *To Love, Honor, and Obey*, 84–85; Boyer, *Lives of the Bigamists*, 64; Gantier, personal communication, July 18, 2013.
32. Case 199, 1; case 200, 1; case 201, 1–36; case 202, 1–2; case 203, 1; case 201, 1–4, 15, 21, 36; case 204; Rodríguez, "Amor y matrimonio," 146–47, 154–55; Casteñeda, *Violación, estupro y sexualidad*, 160; Salinas Meza, "Uniones ilegitimas y desuniones legítimas," 175–76; Lavrin, "La sexualidad," 497–98; Lavrin, "Sexuality," 50, 55, 58; Gonzalbo Aizpuru, *Familia y orden colonial*, 64; Presta, "Portraits of Four Women," 251; Boyer, *Lives of the Bigamists*, 64; Casteñeda, *Violación, estupro y sexualidad*, 150. In addition to the cases discussed below, see case 134; case 205; case 206; and case 207, 1–3, 7–12, 13, 17, 28.
33. Case 208, 1–2.

34. For a similar case, see case 209, 1–4.
35. Case 210, 1–4.
36. Case 210, 4–7.
37. Case 210, 7–15, 23–25.
38. For a similar case, see case 211.
39. Case 194, 1–5.
40. Case 194, 10–11.
41. In addition to the cases below, see case 92.
42. Case 90, 1–3, 13.
43. Case 90, 2.
44. Case 90, 4–6, 10–13.
45. Case 212, 1–5. See also case 213; Gantier, personal communication, July 18, 2013; and case 214.
46. Case 212, 6.
47. Case 212, 6–8, 11; Gantier, personal communication, July 18, 2013.
48. Case 212, 7–8, 11, 13, 15–16.
49. In addition to the cases cited below, see case 176; case 215; case 216, 1; case 217; and case 218.
50. Gutiérrez, "Honor Ideology," 97–98; Powers, *Women in the Crucible*, 118; Socolow, "Acceptable Partners," 228; Seed, *To Love, Honor, and Obey*, 171–73. In addition to the cases below, see also case 67.
51. Case 219, 15–19, 1–8, 11–12. In addition to the cases of parental opposition discussed below, see case 220. For more on Felipa Gallardo and her marriage to Manuel Barrientos, see Lofstrom, *Tres familias*, 35–62.
52. Case 219, 15, 19; Lofstrom, *Tres familias*, 36.
53. Case 219, 18–19.
54. Case 219, 21–23; Lofstrom, *Tres familias*, 36.
55. Case 219, 23–26.
56. Case 219, 27–28.
57. Case 219, 30.
58. Case 219, 32–33.
59. Case 219, 34.
60. Case 219, 35; Lofstrom, *Tres familias*, 37.
61. Case 219, 35–36; case 182, 1–9; case 183, 1; Saether, "Bourbon Absolutism," 475–76, 485–86, 488–89, 496; Premo, "'Misunderstood Love,'" 246; Premo, *Children of the Father King*, 2; Bridikhina, *Sin temor a dios*, 12, 15, 41, 59,

66–67; Gonzalbo Aizpuru, *Familia y orden colonial*, 47, 268; Arrom, *Women of Mexico City*, 77; Van Deusen, *Between the Sacred and the Worldly*, 309; Socolow, "Acceptable Partners," 212; Lavrin, "Introduction," 17; Seed, *To Love, Honor, and Obey*, 204; Zulawski, "Social Differentiation," 97; Stolcke, "Invaded Women," 18. For greater detail on Spanish law, and its origins, as it applied to women, couples, and families, see note 1 of chapter 2 of this book.

62. Manuel Robles knew what Felipa was facing from personal experience. He was fighting his own battle concerning marriage after having become engaged to Manuela Castro, whose father, fellow attorney Juan Antonio Castro, refused to consent to the union. See case 221, 1–5.
63. Case 219, 40, 43–44; Lofstrom, *Tres familias*, 37.
64. Case 219, 43–44.
65. Case 219, 48; Lofstrom, *Tres familias*, 37–38.
66. Case 219, 54–55; case 222, 282–83; Lofstrom, *Tres familias*, 38, 54–55. See also case 223, 335–54.
67. Case 224, 1–10.
68. Case 224, 12–27.
69. Cases 225, 226, and 227.
70. Case 228, 1–2. For a similar case, see case 229, 1–7; and case 230.
71. Case 228, 3.
72. Case 231, 2, 6–7.
73. Case 231, 4–5.
74. Case 231, 9.
75. Case 231, 9.
76. Case 231, 16–20.
77. Case 69, 1–12. For a similar case in which a father objected to a very young daughter marrying, see case 217. Concerning squandered dowry, see cases 165 and 232.
78. For another case concerning maternal opposition, see case 233.
79. Case 68, 1–3.
80. Case 68, 10–11.
81. Case 68, 13–19, 23–27.
82. Case 68, 37.
83. Case 68, 30–31.
84. Case 68, 38–49.

85. Case 68, 52–54.
86. Case 68, 58–59.
87. Case 68, 60–65.
88. Case 234, 317–30, 334; Lofstrom, *Tres familias*, 53.
89. Delgado, "Sin Temor de Dios," 109; Casteñeda, *Violación, estupro y sexualidad*, 42; Sloan, *Runaway Daughters*, 9. Concerning New Spain, see Boyer, *Lives of the Bigamists*, 87–103. In addition to the cases below, see also cases 1, 12, 70, 89, 147, 218, and 235.
90. Case 236, 233–34; Bridikhina, *Sin temor a dios*, 108. For a comparative discussion of seduction laws in the United States, Canada, Scotland, France, and colonial Latin America, see Sloan, *Runaway Daughters*, 39–42.
91. Casteñeda, *Violación, estupro y sexualidad*, 43, 151–52; Premo, *Children of the Father King*, 118; Germeten, *Violent Delights*, 20.
92. Case 237, 1; Casteñeda, *Violación, estupro y sexualidad*, 44–47; Seed, *To Love, Honor, and Obey*, 100–101; Hunefeldt, *Liberalism in the Bedroom*, 188.
93. Case 58, 1, 6.
94. Case 58, 4.
95. Case 58, 6.
96. Case 58, 2–13, 25.
97. Case 58, 1, 5.
98. Case 58, 2.
99. Case 58, 6, 24–29.
100. Case 58, 17–20, 24–31, 46–47, 61–64.
101. Case 58, 69, 72–73.
102. Case 58, 73, 76, 78.
103. Case 58, 80, 127.
104. Case 238, 636, 639; case 239, 71; case 240, 624; case 8, 647–49; case 241, 603; case 242, 401; case 243, 16–17; case 100, 1–3, 4–6, 7–10.
105. Case 58, 11; case 239, 72, 91. See also case 242, 401; case 244, 444; case 245, 491; and case 246, 721–24.
106. Seed, *To Love, Honor, and Obey*, 89; Socolow, "Women and Crime," 47; Lavrin, "Sexuality," 51.
107. Lavrin, "Sexuality," 65–66; Hunefeldt, *Liberalism in the Bedroom*, 180, 183. In addition to the cases below, see also case 247 and case 248, 1–9. For a case concerning slaves who wanted to marry, see case 249.
108. Case 79, 1, 8, 9.

109. Case 79, 1, 8.
110. Case 79, 1–7.
111. Case 79, 23.
112. Case 79, 31–35.
113. Case 79, 9–10.
114. Case 79, 10–20, 87.
115. Case 79, 31–35.
116. Case 79, 37–40, 83.
117. Case 79, 17, 83.
118. Concerning clandestine marriages in New Spain, see Boyer, *Lives of the Bigamists*, 69–73.
119. Case 173, 1–2, 5–8, 11–12, 17.
120. Case 173, 17, 19, 75.
121. Case 173, 13, 19, 23–24, 69; Twinam, *Public Lives*, 309. On the Oruro rebellion see Cajías de la Vega, *Oruro 1781*, and Robins, *El mesianismo y la rebelión indígena*.
122. Case 173, 6, 8–9, 11–13, 17–18.
123. Case 173, 2–3, 18.
124. Case 173, 5.
125. Case 173, 5.
126. Case 173, 4–5, 9–10, 14–15, 18.
127. Case 173, 7, 15.
128. Case 173, 12.
129. Case 173, 19.
130. Case 173, 22–26.
131. Case 173, 27.
132. Case 173, 53.
133. Case 173, 53–59.
134. Case 173, 61.
135. Case 173, 62, 66, 69, 80–82, 85, 87, 90–94.
136. Case 173, 95–99.
137. Case 173, 100.
138. Case 173, 102.
139. Case 250, 8–9, 11.
140. Case 250, 2–6, 10–12.
141. Case 250, 3, 8–9.

142. Case 250, 10.
143. Case 250, 11.
144. Case 250, 11.
145. Case 250, 13.
146. Case 250, 14.
147. Case 250, 15–18.
148. Case 250, 18–19.
149. Case 250, 19–20.
150. Case 250, 20–21.
151. Case 181, 1, 8–9.
152. Case 181, 2–4.
153. Case 181, 5–6, 25.
154. Case 181, 25.
155. Case 181, 10.
156. Case 181, 11–13.
157. Case 181, 13.
158. Case 181, 13.
159. Case 181, 14–16.
160. Case 181, 17–24.
161. Case 181, 27.
162. Case 181, 27.
163. Case 181, 27.
164. Case 181, 27, 30–37.
165. Case 251, 1–2.
166. Case 251, 1; case 252, 1–4.
167. Case 251, 2.
168. Case 251, 1.
169. Case 251, 2.
170. Case 251, 2.
171. Case 251, 3–5.

3. MORAL IMPERATIVES

Title: Case 251, 17.

1. In addition to the cases discussed in this section, see also case 34; case 44; case 100; case 108; case 158, 1–3; case 253; case 254; case 255; case 256; case 257; case 258; and case 259, 1–3.

2. Case 260, 1–2; case 261, 1–13; Bridikhina, *Sin temor a dios*, 16, 97–104; Gonzalbo Aizpuru, *Familia y orden colonial*, 66–67; Boyer, *Lives of the Bigamists*, 124–28.
3. Case 157, 1. See also Black, *Limits of Gender Domination*, 101, 115.
4. Case 2, 2–3; case 262, 1–4.
5. Case 263, 1–2; case 260, 5–11.
6. Case 264, 1; case 157, 1; case 260, 1–2.
7. Case 265, 1–6; case 157, 1.
8. Case 2, 1; case 260, 1–2; case 266, 1–2; case 267, 1–8; case 268, 1–2.
9. Case 2, 3.
10. Ibid, 3–4.
11. Case 269, 9; case 267, 1, 9.
12. Case 269, 1–18.
13. In addition to the cases cited below, see also cases 2, 88, 130, 131, 270, 271, and 332.
14. Case 272, 1, 3, 7; case 129, 1–2, 8–9, 12–13.
15. Case 272, 1.
16. Case 272, 3.
17. Case 272, 3.
18. Case 272, 4–6.
19. Case 272, 6–11. Concerning claims of ill health and uncrossable rivers, see case 273.
20. Case 272, 12.
21. Case 274, 1.
22. Case 274, 2–3.
23. Case 274, 2–22.
24. Case 82, 1–26.
25. Case 82, 25–27.
26. Case 275, 1; case 170, 5; case 82, 1–26; case 274, 1; case 2, 3–4, 7–8; case 272, 1–7.
27. Case 275, 2–4.
28. Case 157, 123–32; case 276, 1.
29. Case 277, 1.
30. Case 277, 2–3.
31. Case 277, 2–3, 6; case 278, 202, 228.
32. Case 277, 6.

33. Case 277, 6.
34. Case 277, 9–10.
35. Case 277, 11–12.
36. In addition to the cases below, see also cases 268, 279, 280, and 281.
37. Case 158, 3–7, 9.
38. Case 158, 8–9.
39. Case 271, 1.
40. Case 271, 2–35.
41. For additional cases of this nature, see cases 159, 282, 283, 284, and 285.
42. Case 139, 2, 7, 15.
43. Case 139, 7.
44. Case 139, 7.
45. Case 139, 7–8.
46. Case 139, 16–25; case 48.
47. Case 286, 1–2.
48. Case 286, 4.
49. Case 286, 4–14.
50. Case 286, 14–16.
51. Case 286, 17.
52. Case 286, 25–26.
53. Case 286, 27–29.
54. Case 286, 31.
55. Case 132, 1, 3–4. For other cases of a woman demanding her husband return, see cases 110 and 273.
56. Case 132, 4–5.
57. In addition to the case below, concerning the role of neighbors in cases see also cases 18, 32, 36, 45, 49, 53, 54, 55, 58, 59, 66, 78, 81, 99, 113, 141, 143, 150, 153, 154, 155, 158, 287, 288, 289, and 290; Germeten, *Violent Delights*, 194; Sloan, *Runaway Daughters*, 128; and Lipsett-Rivera, *Negotiation of Daily Life*, 11, 135.
58. Case 153, 1–3.
59. Case 153, 4.
60. Case 133, 1, 4, 6.
61. Case 133, 6.
62. Case 133, 6.

63. Case 156, 1–9, 11, 16–17. Rafaela Subieta's role in running a house of depósito also figures in case 45, 7.
64. Case 156, 11, 16.
65. Ibid, 10, 17.
66. Ibid, 10, 20.
67. Ibid, 21.
68. Case 167, 1–2, 3–5, 7–8.
69. Case 167, 2, 10–11.
70. Case 291, 1.
71. Case 291, 1.
72. Case 291, 1–4.
73. Black, *Limits of Gender Domination*, 23, 31, 74, 85, 90, 100–119, 101.
74. Arrom, *Women of Mexico City*, 226.

4. DOMESTIC VIOLENCE AND RAPE

Title: Case 292.

1. Flores Galindo and Chocano, "Las cargas del sacramento," 403; Salinas Meza and Goicovic Donoso, "Amor, violencia y passion," 241, 253–55, 262–65; Black, *Limits of Gender Domination*, 260–61; Boyer, *Lives of the Bigamists*, 110–12, 132–40. In addition to the cases below, see cases 33, 61, 62, 127, 166, 253, 290, 293, 294, 295, 296, 297, and 298. See also cases 3, 16, 18, 21, 35, 39, 43, 51, 53, 54, 57, 63, 66, 71, 81, 95, 107, 112, 113, 115, 116, 117, 118, 121, 122, 123, 124, 125, 126, 129, 135, 142, 148, 154, 155, 165, 166, 175, 253, 288, 292, 297, 299, 300, 301, 302, 303, 304, and 305.
2. Case 29, 5.
3. See for example case 27; case 65; case 116, 1, 8; case 297; case 306; case 307; González de Riego, "Fragmentos," 207; Lavallé, "Divorcio y nulidad," 436–38; and Salinas Meza and Goicovic Donoso, "Amor, violencia y passion," 241, 253–55.
4. Delgado, "Sin Temor de Dios," 114; Gonzalbo Aizpuru, "Conflictos y rutinas," 574; Gonzalbo Aizpuru, *Familia y orden colonial*, 269; Arrom, *Women of Mexico City*, 72, 232, 236–37; Lavrin, "Introduction," 21; Stavig, *Amor y violencia*, 80; Stavig, "'Living in Offense,'" 600–601; Stern, *Secret History of Gender*, 67–68; Socolow, "Women and Crime," 43–44; Powers, *Women in the Crucible*, 100–108, 200; Borchart, "Words and Wounds," 139.

See also Boyer, "Women," 258–71; Flores Galindo and Chocano, "Las cargas del sacramento," 410; and Lavallé, "Divorcio y nulidad," 436–38.

5. Case 304, 10.
6. Case 56, 1, 3, 34, 42, 15–16.
7. Case 56, 1, 4, 42. Regarding de la Quintana, see case 308, 765–74.
8. Case 56, 3, 13–14.
9. Case 56, 1–4.
10. Case 56, 9.
11. Case 56, 11.
12. Case 56, 12.
13. Case 56, 34.
14. Case 56, 35.
15. Case 56, 15.
16. Case 56, 15–16.
17. Case 56, 17–21.
18. Case 56, 29–31.
19. Case 56, 31.
20. Case 56, 42–46.
21. Case 56, 36–38, 42–51.
22. In addition to the cases discussed below, see also cases 81 and 309.
23. Case 303, 1–2.
24. Case 303, 3.
25. Case 303, 3.
26. Case 303, 3.
27. Case 303, 3.
28. Case 303, 3–4.
29. Case 303, 4–5.
30. Case 28, 1. For another case in which a wife lost her ear to abuse, see case 302.
31. Case 303, 1.
32. Case 303, 4.
33. Case 303, 6, 15.
34. Case 63, 1.
35. Case 63, 1, 3–5.
36. Case 30, 3, 8. See also case 118, 17.
37. Case 30, 3–7; case 5, 3–45.

38. Case 287, 1.
39. Case 287, 1.
40. Case 287, 2–3.
41. Case 287, 3.
42. Case 287, 3.
43. Case 287, 3.
44. Case 287, 3–6.
45. Case 31, 1; case 310, 79–86; case 311, 185–88, 193.
46. Case 31, 13–16.
47. Case 31, 1–6, 16.
48. Case 31, 4–6.
49. Case 31, 3, 6.
50. Case 31, 7–12.
51. Case 31, 17–19.
52. Case 31, 20–21.
53. Case 312, 280.
54. Case 288, 1–11.
55. Case 288, 14–54.
56. Case 32, 1, 16.
57. Case 32, 2–5.
58. Case 32, 4–5.
59. Case 32, 7.
60. Case 32, 8–9.
61. Case 32, 12.
62. Case 32, 14–18.
63. Case 32, 19–20.
64. Case 313, 1.
65. Case 313, 1–2.
66. Case 313, 2.
67. Case 313, 2, 5–6.
68. Case 165, 1–2, 4–5.
69. Case 165, 1.
70. Case 165, 4.
71. Case 165, 4.
72. Case 165, 3.
73. Case 165, 15–16.

74. Case 165, 5–6, 9–14, 16–17, 22.
75. Case 123, 1.
76. Case 123, 1.
77. Case 123, 1.
78. Case 123, 1–2.
79. Case 123, 3.
80. Case 39, 1–2.
81. Case 39, 2.
82. Case 39, 2–3.
83. In addition to the cases cited below, see cases 73, 74, and 168 and Pescador, "Entre la espada y el olvido," 220. For cases where women were, apparently falsely, accused of murdering their husbands, see case 314, 1; and case 315.
84. Case 177, 1; Arrom, *Women of Mexico City*, 64–65.
85. Case 36, 1, 7–8.
86. Case 36, 3.
87. Case 36, 9.
88. Case 36, 8.
89. Case 36, 10–12, 28.
90. Case 36, 28.
91. Case 36, 30.
92. Case 36, 30.
93. Case 316, 1.
94. Case 316, 1, 4–5.
95. Stavig, *Amor y violencia*, 17, 19. For a discussion of rape and canon law, see Casteñeda, *Violación, estupro y sexualidad*, 33–39. In addition to the cases below, see also cases 21, 119, 152, 205, 304, 309, and 317.
96. Case 318, 5.
97. Case 319, 1, 3.
98. Case 319, 2.
99. Case 319, 3–4.
100. Case 318, 1.
101. Case 318, 1.
102. Case 318, 2.
103. Case 318, 5.
104. Case 318, 5.
105. Case 97, 1.

106. Case 97, 1–7.
107. Case 152, 1–3.
108. Case 152, 1, 3–5.
109. Case 320, 1–3.
110. Case 321, 1.
111. Case 321, 1.
112. Case 321, 1–4.
113. Case 78, 1–4.
114. Case 78, 5–8.
115. Case 119, 1.
116. Case 119, 1–8.
117. Case 40, 1.
118. Case 40, 2.
119. Case 40, 2.
120. Case 40, 3–19.
121. Case 139, 17; case 48, 1.
122. Case 4, 11–12, 19–28.
123. Case 322, 2.
124. Case 322, 1–2, 5, 9.
125. Case 323, 384.
126. Case 324, 2–4, 10–16, 18, 20, 22–33, 35–40, 43, 45–46, 49, 56–57, 60, 64, 67, 69–70, 72–75, 77–80, 89, 137–38; Robins, *Priest-Indian Conflict*, 52–58.
127. Case 325, 1–2; case 326, 1–9; case 6, 12; case 7, 34.
128. Case 327, 11; case 328, 19; case 329, 3; case 330; Robins, *Genocide and Millennialism*, 80–81; Robins, *Priest-Indian Conflict*, 184.
129. Case 331, 33. See also Robins, *Priest-Indian Conflict*, 151–52.
130. Dueñas, "Adulterios," 38; Johnson, "Dangerous Words," 149; Chambers, *Subjects to Citizens*, 177; Seed, *To Love, Honor, and Obey*, 80; Socolow, "Acceptable Partners"; Socolow, "Women and Crime," 43–45, 217; Hunefeldt, *Liberalism in the Bedroom*, 61–75.
131. Case 296, 3–5; case 304, 1, 20; case 71, 3; case 165, 4; case 39, 2; case 124, 1; case 95, 3; case 304, 21; Van Deusen, *Between the Sacred and the Worldly*, 87; Arrom, *Women of Mexico City*, 211.
132. Case 52, 3; case 36, 25–26; case 332, 3. See also Sloan, *Runaway Daughters*, 105, 128; and Lipsett-Rivera, *Negotiation of Daily Life*, 11, 135.

133. Socolow, "Women and Crime," 43–46, 54; Rodríguez, "Amor y matrimonio," 149; Stavig, *Amor y violencia*, 19; Casteñeda, *Violación, estupro y sexualidad*, 100–101, 144. For cases in Charcas, see cases 40, 78, 119, 152, 205, 309, 317, 318, 319, 320, and 321.

134. Casteñeda, *Violación, estupro y sexualidad*, 21, 78, 89, 99–103, 113, 115, 120–25, 143.

135. Lavrin, "Sexuality," 71.

5. DILATORY DIVORCES

Title: Case 126, 1.

1. In addition to the cases discussed below, see also cases 18, 20, 28, 29, 30, 31, 33, 62, 64, 69, 124, 125, 133, 135, 148, 156, 194, 207, 210, 213, 214, 239, 244, 261, 271, 283, 284, 289, 290, 292, 299, 313, 333, 334, 335, and 336.
2. Case 334, 1; Muriel, *Los recogimientos de mujeres*, 18–20; Salinas Meza, "Uniones ilegitimas y desuniones legítimas," 178–79, 190; Arrom, *Women of Mexico City*, 66, 208; Van Deusen, *Between the Sacred and the Worldly*, 83; Flores Galindo and Chocano, "Las cargas del sacramento," 412; Lavallé, "Divorcio y nulidad," 443–44, 449–52, 459, 460–61; González de Riego, "Fragmentos," 61.
3. Case 334, 1.
4. Case 334, 3–13.
5. See, for example, cases 118 and 337 and Dueñas, "Adulterios," 43.
6. In addition to the cases previously cited, see also cases 115 and 122.
7. Arrom, *Women of Mexico City*, 216–19, 225; Van Deusen, *Between the Sacred and the Worldly*, 86; Gauderman, *Women's Lives*, 69; Powers, *Women in the Crucible*, 120–22, 194.
8. Van Deusen, *Between the Sacred and the Worldly*, 86, 88, 92–93; Dueñas, "Adulterios," 43.
9. Arrom, *Women of Mexico City*, 228–29, 232, 240, 247; Van Deusen, *Between the Sacred and the Worldly*, 85; Arrom, *Women of Mexico City*, 216–27, 226–27; Van Deusen, *Between the Sacred and the Worldly*, 86, 88, 92–93; Gauderman, *Women's Lives*, 69; Gonzalbo Aizpuru, *Familia y orden colonial*, 68. Concerning intransigence, see cases 13, 20, 21, 25, 60, 65, 66, 107, 133, and 138.
10. Case 116, 1, 8, 10; case 117, 1, 3–6; Arrom, *Women of Mexico City*, 216–17; Van Deusen, *Between the Sacred and the Worldly*, 86.

11. Case 116, 12, 17, 21, 30–35, 38–39.
12. Case 107, 2–4, 6–7, 12–15.
13. Arrom, *Women of Mexico City*, 208–11; Van Deusen, *Between the Sacred and the Worldly*, 87; Van Deusen, *Between the Sacred and the Worldly*, 83; Premo, *Children of the Father King*, 61; Powers, *Women in the Crucible*, 114; Arrom, *Women of Mexico City*, 66, 207–8; Presta, "Portraits of Four Women," 248.
14. Case 305, 4–7.
15. Case 305, 1–5.
16. Case 126, 1.
17. Case 126, 2–3, 6–7, 10, 13.
18. Case 126, 17.
19. Case 126, 19–20.
20. See also case 120.
21. Case 66, 1. See also case 338, 198–99.
22. Case 66, 2–5, 25.
23. Case 66, 6–7.
24. Case 66, 9–12, 30.
25. Case 66, 14, 16. Her husband, however, had no interest in reconciliation, stating, "I recognize that her company instead of leading me to salvation instead prepares my ruin," especially in "the pernicious company of her daughters."
26. Case 66, 17–20, 22–25.
27. Case 66, 25, 29–30.
28. Case 66, 37, 39.
29. Case 66, 38.
30. Case 66, 39.
31. Case 339, 66–69.
32. Case 71, 1, 29. The original Spanish for "cruelty and abuse" was "sevicia crueldad, y malos tratamientos."
33. Case 71, 5–6.
34. Case 71, 3, 5.
35. Case 71, 1.
36. Case 71, 1, 3.
37. Case 71, 7–8, 17, 19.
38. Case 71, 15, 19, 21, 23–29, 32–33.

39. Case 138, 1–6.
40. Case 138, 2, 4, 6. For similar cases, see Lavallé, "Divorcio y nulidad," 456, 458–59.
41. Case 138, 6.
42. Case 138, 28.
43. Case 51, 1.
44. Case 3, 1.
45. Case 3, 2.
46. Case 3, 2–4.
47. Case 335, 1–2, 11.
48. Case 335, 1–2.
49. Case 340, 3, 11.
50. Case 335, 4.
51. Case 335, 1; case 340, 1.
52. Case 340, 4, 15.
53. Case 335, 5, 28, 29, 30.
54. Case 335, 5–7, 28–30.
55. Case 335, 7.
56. Case 335, 5–8.
57. Case 335, 7–8, 28.
58. Case 335, 9, 11, 15, 22–23.
59. Case 335, 16–17.
60. Case 335, 17–23.
61. Case 335, 25.
62. Powers, *Women in the Crucible*, 130; Arrom, *Women of Mexico City*, 226. For a study of bigamy in New Spain, see Boyer, *Lives of the Bigamists*. In addition to the cases cited below, see cases 193, 301, 341, 342, and 343 and Salinas Meza, "Uniones ilegitimas y desuniones legítimas," 180–81.
63. Case 344, 1–4. Muleteers were not uncommon among the ranks of bigamists, see Boyer, *Lives of the Bigamists*, 5.
64. Case 344, 4–8.
65. Case 344, 8; case 47, 5.
66. Case 47, 17–19, 28.
67. Case 47, 1–4.
68. Case 47, 5, 8; Black, *Limits of Gender Domination*, 75.

69. Case 47, 7.
70. Case 47, 8–15; Black, *Limits of Gender Domination*, 19.
71. Case 47, 17–28.
72. Case 345, 1–5.
73. Case 151, 1.
74. Case 151, 6–7.
75. Case 151, 7.
76. Case 151, 11.
77. Case 151, 11.
78. Case 192, 1–3.
79. Case 192, 3–4, 13.
80. Case 192, 6–8, 10–13, 15.
81. Case 175, 1–2.
82. Case 175, 1–3.
83. Case 57, 1–4, 8, 22.
84. Case 57, 5.
85. Case 57, 8, 10–11, 22.
86. Case 57, 18, 27–32.
87. Case 57, 40–42, 44–45, 53–56.
88. Case 346, 1–2.
89. Case 346, 3–12.
90. Case 346, 12–13.
91. Case 346, 14–17.
92. Case 210, 23–25; Delgado, "Sin Temor de Dios," 111; Salinas Meza, "Uniones ilegitimas y desuniones legítimas," 178–79, 188; Arrom, *Women of Mexico City*, 66, 68, 207–8, 211, 226; Van Deusen, *Between the Sacred and the Worldly*, 87; Gonzalbo Aizpuru, *Familia y orden colonial*, 68; González de Riego, "Fragmentos," 203.
93. Case 66, 39; case 239, 72; case 261, 2; case 151, 11; Salinas Meza, "Uniones ilegitimas y desuniones legítimas," 188.
94. Case 117, 1, 3–6; Arrom, *Women of Mexico City*, 208–10, 226–27; Van Deusen, *Between the Sacred and the Worldly*, 88, 92–93; Dueñas, "Adulterios," 44. See also González de Riego, "Fragmentos," 211; Pentimalli, Albornoz, and Luján, "Mirar por su honra," 162; Salinas Meza, "Uniones ilegitimas y desuniones legítimas," 179, 187–88; Pescador, "Entre la espada y el olvido,"

203; Van Deusen, *Between the Sacred and the Worldly*, 79–80; Lavallé, "Divorcio y nulidad," 434; Dueñas, "Adulterios," 43; González de Riego, "Fragmentos," 202; and Pescador, "Entre la espada y el olvido," 202–5, 208.

CONCLUSION

1. Case 114, 1; Presta, "Portraits of Four Women," 245, 252; Seed, *To Love, Honor, and Obey*, 33–34, 41; Gutiérrez, "Honor Ideology," 88–90. See also case 196, 309–13. The original Spanish for "virginal jewel" was "prenda virginal."
2. Twinam, "Negotiation of Honor," 85–86; Twinam, *Public Lives*, 66–67, 73, 91–92; Lavrin, "Sexuality," 61; Mannarelli, *Pecados publicos*, 199, 308; Premo, "'Misunderstood Love,'" 241–42; Socolow, "Acceptable Partners," 227; McCaa, "Gustos de los padres," 598.
3. Case 90, 1–6, 10–13; case 92, 1–4; Arrom, *Women of Mexico City*, 63, 67, 70; Powers, *Women in the Crucible*, 193–94; Delgado, "Sin Temor de Dios," 99–104, 102, 106–8; Black, "Between Prescription and Practice," 274–77, 283–85; Socolow, "Acceptable Partners," 210; Seed, *To Love, Honor, and Obey*, 200–202; Premo, *Children of the Father King*, 7–8.
4. Case 50, 1; case 136, 1; case 137, 6; case 40, 1; case 46, 1, 2–3; case 48, 1; case 162, 1, 4. case 112, 1–7; case 16, 1–4; case 43, 1; Bridikhina, *Sin temor a dios*, 16, 92–96; Gauderman, *Women's Lives*, 56–57.
5. Twinam, *Public Lives*, 85; Arrom, *Women of Mexico City*, 63, 67, 70; Powers, *Women in the Crucible*, 193–94; Delgado, "Sin Temor de Dios," 99–104, 106–8; Black, "Between Prescription and Practice," 274–77, 283–85; Socolow, "Acceptable Partners," 210; Seed, *To Love, Honor, and Obey*, 200–202; Premo, *Children of the Father King*, 7–8.
6. Case 126, 1–13; case 139, 16–25; case 170, 1; case 113, 1–7; case 1, 1–15; case 142, 1, 12; case 50, 15–16; case 136, 1; case 137, 2; case 162, 1–4; case 163, 1–2; case 1, 1–7; Arrom, *Women of Mexico City*, 64–65, 211; Van Deusen, *Between the Sacred and the Worldly*, 87. See also cases 99 and 160.
7. Case 86, 1–3, 6–12; case 1, 1–7. See also case 46, 1, 2–3, 4–6, 9, 12–17; case 53, 6–8; case 111, 1–2, 4–5; and case 180.
8. Case 219, 1–15, 22–23. See also case 173, 2, 10, 17, 21; case 224, 2–3; case 248, 1; and case 251, 2.

9. Case 69, 1–12; case 218, 1, 16, 27; case 218, 1–5, 11; case 216, 1; case 227, 1; case 182, 1–9; case 183, 1; case 12, 2; Saether, "Bourbon Absolutism," 475–76, 485–86, 488–89, 496; Premo, "'Misunderstood Love,'" 246; Premo, *Children of the Father King*, 2; Bridikhina, *Sin temor a dios*, 12, 15, 41, 59, 66–67; Gonzalbo Aizpuru, *Familia y orden colonial*, 47, 268; Arrom, *Women of Mexico City*, 77; Van Deusen, *Between the Sacred and the Worldly*, 309; Socolow, "Acceptable Partners," 212; Lavrin, "Introduction," 17; Seed, *To Love, Honor and Obey*, 204; Zulawski, "Social Differentiation," 97; Stolcke, "Invaded Women," 18.

10. Case 93, 1; case 92, 1; case 68, 62–65; case 216, 3; case 218, 15–27; Lavrin, "Sexuality," 65–66; Hunefeldt, *Liberalism in the Bedroom*, 180, 183; Gutiérrez, "Honor Ideology," 97–98; Powers, *Women in the Crucible*, 118. See also case 247.

11. Case 181, 13, 27; case 250, 18–20; case 173, 100, 102; Gutiérrez, "Honor Ideology," 91–92; Twinam, "Negotiation of Honor," 85; Twinam, *Public Lives*, 36–37; Van Deusen, *Between the Sacred and the Worldly*, 83; Socolow, "Acceptable Partners," 210, 231; Lavallé, "Divorcio y nulidad," 441; Robins, *Genocide and Millennialism*, 48–51. See also Brown, *Bourbons and Brandy*; Barbier, *Reform and Politics*; McFarlane, *Colombia before Independence*; Fisher, Kuethe, and McFarlane, *Reform and Insurrection*; case 181, 13, 27; and case 250, 18–20.

12. Case 158, 1–3; case 259, 1–3; case 157, 123–32; case 130, 2, 5, 10, 12; case 129, 1–13; case 275, 1; case 170, 5; case 82, 1–26; case 274, 1; case 2, 3–4, 7–8; case 272, 1–7; Arrom, *Women of Mexico City*, 226.

13. Case 267, 1–8; case 268, 1–2; case 157, 1; case 260, 1–2; case 262, 1–4.

14. Case 281, 1; case 271, 1–35. See also cases 268, 279, and 280.

15. Case 336, 1–5; case 133, 1–6; case 3, 1–4; case 69, 1–12.

16. Case 296, 1–6; case 304, 1, 20; case 71, 3; case 165, 4; case 39, 2; case 124, 1; case 95, 3; case 53, 1; case 55, 1–3; case 95, 1–4; case 113, 4; Case 358, 1–2, 5; case 111, 114; Gonzalbo Aizpuru, "Conflictos y rutinas," 574; Gonzalbo Aizpuru, *Familia y orden colonial*, 269; Arrom, *Women of Mexico City*, 72, 232, 236–37; Lavrin, "Introduction," 21; Stavig, *Amor y violencia*, 80; Stavig, "'Living in Offense,'" 600–601; Stern, *Secret History of Gender*, 67–68; Socolow, "Women and Crime," 43–44; Powers, *Women in the Crucible*, 100–108, 200; Borchart, "Words and Wounds," 139. See also case 56, 1–3, 44; case 347, 1–4; and Boyer, "Women," 258–71.

17. Case 289, 1–4. See also case 51, 1; case 56; case 63; case 115; case 290; case 302; and Flores Galindo and Chocano, "Las cargas del sacramento," 409, 411, 412.
18. Case 56, 15–16; case 303, 1–4; case 113, 6–7; case 1, 18–24; case 121, 1–3. See also Flores Galindo and Chocano, "Las cargas del sacramento," 409.
19. Case 177, 1; case 316, 1; case 36, 1, 3, 7–12, 28; case 73, 1; Pescador, "Entre la espada y el olvido," 220.
20. Case 316, 1; case 177, 1; case 73, 1; case 74, 1; case 168, 1–89; case 119, 1–8; case 321, 1–8; case 152, 1–5; case 97, 1; case 318, 1–5; case 319, 1–4; case 40, 1; Pescador, "Entre la espada y el olvido," 220.
21. Case 25, 1–12; case 15, 1–3; case 165, 15–16; case 16, 1–4; case 57, 40–42, 44–45, 53–56; case 126, 19–20; case 113, 5–6; Muriel, *Los recogimientos de mujeres*, 45, 217, 219; Van Deusen, *Between the Sacred and the Worldly*, xiv, 80, 98; Van Deusen, "Defining the Sacred and the Worldly," 447; Burns, "Gender and the Politics of Mestizaje," 15–16. See also case 165, 15–16; case 219, 1, 3; and Hunefeldt, *Liberalism in the Bedroom*, 152–74.
22. Case 56, 51; case 303, 1–5; case 113, 6–7; case 1, 18–24; case 121; case 133, 1–6; case 219, 21; case 21, 30; Arrom, *Women of Mexico City*, 226; Dueñas, "Adulterios," 43.
23. Case 138, 6; case 335, 1–2; case 340, 1, 5, 28–30.
24. Case 86, 1–3, 6–12; case 180, 3–4, 16; case 1, 1–7.
25. Bridikhina, *Sin temor a dios*, 105–7.
26. Case 55, 15; case 59, 10; case 138, 18; case 57, 53; case 30, 3; case 11, 1–2. See also Germeten, *Violent Delights*, 4.
27. Case 149, 4; case 56, 17–18; case 52, 14–15; case 59, 1, 3, 5–6; case 54, 1–3; case 53, 8.
28. On Narciso de Valenzuela, see cases 129, 135, and 348. On Gregorio Nuñez, see case 66; case 139; case 177; case 196, 309–13; case 219; case 301; and case 346. On Silvestre Orgáz, see cases 57, 123, 126, and 173. On Malavia see cases 21, 56, 68, and 340. On Arías, see cases 36, 39, 303, and 337. On Mostajo see cases 57, 107, 124, 125, 126, 138, and 290.
29. For a discussion of public space in colonial Latin America, see Lipsett-Rivera, *Negotiation of Daily Life*, and Sloan, *Runaway Daughters*, 123–28.
30. Case 30, 1–3.
31. Case 56, 1; case 141, 1–7. See also case 35, 1; case 68, 46, 49; case 77, 1; and case 111, 1–2, 4–5 .

32. Case 1, 1, 9.
33. Case 250, 1, 3, 8–9.
34. Case 79, 17, 83.
35. Case 211, 1, 2, 6.
36. Case 78, 5–6, 11.
37. Case 227, 1, 6.
38. Case 1, 5.
39. Case 66, 3, 7, 15.
40. Case 66, 24.
41. Case 66, 22, 23, 25; case 312, 280; case 349, 298; case 350, 77–81; case 351, 177; case 352, 213; case 353, 185–99; case 354, 167–68, 171–79, 181, 183; case 355, 46–48; case 352, 213.
42. Presta, "Portraits of Four Women," 237, 239–41, 249. See also McCaa, "Gustos de los padres," 607.
43. Case 356, 631; case 357, 338.
44. Case 156, 9–10, 18.
45. Case 156, 20.
46. Case 156, 20.
47. Case 135, 41.

Glossary

alcalde: mayor who also served as a magistrate
alcalde pedaneo: a rural judge
alférez real: royal standard-bearer
alguacil: sheriff
arras: gift from a future husband to his fiancée
audiencia: civil court that also had executive and administrative authority
beaterio: cloistered religious house for pious lay women
cabildo: city council or city hall
chicha: fermented corn drink
chicheria: place where chicha is sold
contestación: the response of one party to the accusation or testimony of another in a legal proceeding
corregidor: district governor, with executive and judicial powers
curaca: leader of an Indian village or district
de oficio: the initiation of a court case by a crown official who served as complainant
defensor de menores: indigent defender for minors
depósito: nonreligious place where a person is sequestered, usually in a private home
diezmo: tithe

estupro: intercourse with, or seduction of, a virgin, often involving a degree of pressure or deceit

fiscal: judicial prosecutor

fuero: independent corporate entity with its own jurisdiction

gracias al sacar: a bureaucratic means of changing one's status, for example, of race or birth

hacienda: agricultural estate

hijo expuesto: foundling

hijo natural: child born of unmarried parents

información de libertad: the collection of information prior to marriage to ensure that there are no impediments to the union

justicia mayor: magistrate with judicial, executive, and administrative authority, similar to a corregidor

ladino: Indian who has adopted Hispanic cultural traits

mestizo/a: individual of Indian and Spanish/creole descent

mita: native draft of forced labor for a specific term and with token remuneration

mitayo: Indian compelled to work for a specific term with token remuneration

mulato/a: individual of both African and European descent

obraje: vertically integrated textile production facility

principal: leader of an Indian community

protector de los naturales: government-appointed legal representative for Indians

provisor: vicar

prueba: the phase of a court proceeding where the prosecutor presents his perspective of the case

publicación de probanzas: rendering of the verdict in court proceedings

recogida: withdrawn, modest, or chaste

recogimiento: reclusion, usually in a religious house

regidor: councilman

residencia: investigation by an incoming government official of his predecessor

ronda: usually nocturnal rounds to prevent crime and enforce morality

sacrilegio: child whose father is a priest
samba: person of black and Indian descent
sentencia: court-issued sentence
sevicia: extreme cruelty, which constituted a basis for divorce
sirvinacuy: Andean trial marriage
sumaria información: initial gathering of testimony in a court case
subdelegado: lieutenant governor in charge of a subdistrict
translado: the transfer of a case file to either the defendant or plaintiff
vida maridable: moral, married life
violación: rape
vecino: property-owner in a given locale, usually but not always a Spaniard or creole
viucho: gift presented to a priest by a couple being married

Bibliography

ARCHIVAL COLLECTIONS

Archivo y Biblioteca Nacionales de Bolivia (ABNB)
Archivo de Mizque (AM)
Audiencia de Charcas, Libros de Acuerdos II (AChLA II)
Audiencia de La Plata (ALP)
Diversos Colonia, Audiencia de Charcas, Sentencias (Diver ACh Sent)
Diversos Colonia, Cabildo de Oruro (Diver Cabil. Oruro)
Escrituras Públicas (EP)
Expedientes Coloniales (EC)
EC adiciones (ECad)
EC adiciones 2 (ECad 2)
Mojos y Chuquitos (MyCh)
Provision Real (PR)
Reales Cédulas (RC)
Reales Cédulas Adiciones (RCad)
Sublevación General de Indios (SGI)
Archivo-Biblioteca Arquidiocesano Monseñor Taborga (ABAS)
Archivo Parroquial, Libro de Bautismos, Parroquia de Santo Domingo (LBSD), Españoles
Archivo Parroquial, Libro de Bautismos, Parroquia de Santo Domingo (LBSD), Mestizos
Archivo Parroquial, Libro de Bautismos, Parroquia de Santo Domingo (LBSD), Negros y Mulatos

Archivo Parroquial, Libro de Bautismos, Parroquia de San Sebastián (LBSS), Indios
Causas y Dispensas Matrimoniales
Clero, Acusaciones
Clero, Tribunal Ecclesiástico
Divorcios
Monasterios Femininas, Nuestra Señora de los Remedios
Archivo General de Indias (AGI)
Charcas

COURT CASES

Note: All cases without a title are marked as NT.

1 Querella civil y criminal entablada por Simón Tadeo Sánchez, contra don Roque Hurtado, por mantener ilícita relación con su mujer Petrona Leaños. Presto, Tomina, September 6, 1759. ABNB EC.1759.45

2 El Alcalde Ordinario de Segundo voto de la ciudad de Córdoba, informa de la providencia que dió a la pretención de Dn. Rafael Calvo, a que se declare no estar comprometido en la general expulsión de casados. Córdova, September 4, 1775. ABNB EC.1775.168

3 Demanda de Divorcio puesta pr Maria Estrada contra su marido Diego Inojosa. La Plata, February 26, 1796. ABAS, Divorcios, legajo 3, #5412

4 Diario del cerco de La Paz en 1781, por Sebastian de Segurola. Fragmento. La Paz, May 30, 1781. ABNB SGI.1781, no number

5 Causa criminal fulminada contra los agresores y autores de las muertes ejecutadas en las personas de don Juan Antonio Acuña y otros conductores del reo Tomás Catari en las inmediaciones de esta ciudad y lugar nombrado Chataquila. La Plata, February 12, 1781. ABNB SGI.350

6 Confesión de Espíritu Alonso. La Plata, April 25, 1781, in Criminales contra Nicolás Catari y otros indios. AGI, Charcas 603

7 Confesión de Bartolomé Vello. La Plata, April 21, 1781. AGI, Charcas 603

8 Arrendamiento de la hacienda de Potolo sita en la doctrina de Quilaquila, Yamparáez, que hace doña Catalina Miranda, vecina de La Plata, divorciada de don Ricardo Reynolds, su hijo legítimo don Mariano Reynolds, durante 6 años por 1.350 pesos Corrientes anualmente, revocando una anterior escritura de arrendamiento que hizo al doctor don Alejandro Pinto

y Orihuela, abogado de esta Audiencia. La Plata, October 29, 1783. ABNB EP 291

9 Feliciano Maturana, contra Cristóbal Díaz, por haber violado éste a su entenada. La Plata, n.d. ABNB EC.1769.183

10 NT, November 16, 1752. ABAS, Matrimonios, Santo Domingo, vol. 73, 96

11 Recurso de María Josefa Prado, viuda, ante la Audiencia de Charcas, contra los procedimientos del Alcalde Ordinario de 2do voto, don Felipe Peláez de la Canal, para que remita a la Audiencia de Charcas, los autos que se le sigen por ilícita correspondencia con un hombre casado. La Plata, March 16, 1763. ABNB ECad.1763.2

12 Expediente promovido por Dn Joaqn Otaso oponiendose al matrimonio qe intenta su hija con Dn Julián Balderrama. Cochabamba, November 30, 1814. ABAS, Causas y Dispensas Matrimoniales, legajo 2

13 Expediente seguido pr Da Casimira Alcerrica con su padre Dn Tomás Alcerrica. La Plata, September 27, 1804. ABNB EC.1804.52

14 Juicio criminal seguido de oficio por el alcalde de Mizque, Matías Gutiérrez, a denuncia de Jacinta Zapata, contra su esposo Nicolás Amaya y Juana Ríos, por mantener entre ambos relaciones ilícitas. Aiquile, February 1, 1771. ABNB AM.1771.13

15 NT, La Plata, January 22, 1771. ABAS, Divorcios, legajo 2, #5362

16 NT, La Plata, October 29, 1782. ABAS, Divorcios, legajo 3, #5381

17 El Monasterio de Santa Mónica (La Plata) sobre que en razón de su pobreza no puede cumplir el bando relativo al revoque y blanqueo de paredes de esta ciudad. La Plata, November 4, 1805. ABNB EC.1805.219

18 Causa que sigue doña Hilaria Díaz contra su marido don Manuel Mena. La Plata, December 15, 1764. ABNB EC.1764.10

19 NT, La Paz, June 9, 1769. ABAS, Divorcios, legajo 2, #5359

20 Recurso ante la Audiencia de Charcas, a nombre de doña Eusebia Tellería, vecina de la ciudad de La Paz, en la causa seguida contra don José Ramón de Loayza, su marido, sobre alimentos y litis de nulidad de matrimonio, solicitado por el Segundo. La Plata, August 1, 1794. ABNB ECad.1794.26

21 NT, La Plata, September 24, 1804. ABAS, Divorcios, legajo 4b, #5461

22 Venta de esclavos, una negra llamada Lucía de 24 años, con su hijo llamado Juan Crisótomo, de 1 año y medio, que hace doña Francisca Barrios,

vecina de La paz, al doctor don Antonio de Villaurrutia, del Consejo de su Majestad, por 500 pesos. April 4, 1803. ABNB EP 373

23 Venta de esclava negra nombrada Ana d 22 años de edad, que hace don Manuel Delgado Veitia, ministro contador de las Cajas Principales de La Plata, a doña María Francisca Barrios, por 500 pesos corrientes. January 3, 1803. ABNB EP 331

24 Declaración que hace don Mariano Gayozo de la Peña y Lillo, sobre las falsas declaraciones de doña María Francisca Barrios, en el pleito de divorcio que sigue con su marido don Ramón Ballivián. December 6, 1802. ABNB EP 373

25 Expediente seguido ante el Alcalde de 1er voto de La Plata, por Melchora Azurduy, reclusa en el Recogimiento de Santa Isabel, contra su esposo Manuel Arciénaga, pidiendo el divorcio y asistencia de alimentos. La Plata, November 28, 1803. ABNB, ECad.1803.60

26 Declárase tocar y pertenecer a prevención de las justicias reales y tribunal del Santo Ofico el conocimiento de las causas de los que se casan seguna vez en vida del primer consorte. Buen Retiro, March 19, 1754. ABNB RC 586

27 Expediente seguido ante la Audiencia de Charcas, por doña María Francisca Barrios, contra su marido Ramón Ballivián, sobre tropelías y extorciones. La Plata, May 4, 1805. ABNB ECad.1805.18

28 Demanda de divorcio, entablada por Melchora Flora, contra su marido Manuel Salazar, por adulterio y malos tratamientos de obra. La Plata, December 13, 1757. ABNB AM.1758.5

29 Querella criminal de doña Mónica Rodríguez, por haber tratado de herirla su marido legítimo don Carlos Vargas, del cual se hallaba separada por justos motivos. Oruro, March 17, 1763. ABNB EC.1763.12

30 María Jacinta de Melo, quejándose de los maltratos de su marido. La Plata, May 24, 1766. ABNB EC.1766.111

31 Expediente seguido pr Doña Gertrudis Mercado, sobrel diborsio en la Curia Ecleciastica de esta Diocesi, contra su Marido Dn José de Arisa, y ausilio pedido pr el Sr Provisor Vicario General al Muy Ylte Sor Presei-dente Govor Yntendte de esta Provincia de la Plata para contener a dho Arisa de los insultos qe tiene cometido. La Plata, May 31, 1796. ABNB EC.1796.42

32 Sumario criminal seguido de oficio contra Antonio Beisaga, por maltratamiento, ynjurias y malos tratamientos a su mujer Rafaela Camacho. Mizque, November 7, 1803. ABNB AM.1803.4

33 Da Ventura Utera pidiendo originales. La Plata, February 18, 1804. ABNB EC.1804.158

34 José Pimentel, a nombre de Agustín Cervantes, preso en la cárcel pública por delito de concubinato, ante el Juez Subdelegado del partido de Yamparáez, solicita se le relaje la prisión, por no habersele formado causa de oficio. August 7, 1801. ABNB ECad.1801.21

35 Antonio Merino, esclavo, se querella en contra del esclavo Manuel, por adulterio con su esposa Apolinaria Rivera, y también por tentativa de asesinato. La Plata, February 17, 1780. ABNB EC.1780.30

36 Autos criminales contra Fermin Zambrana por haberle inferido una rotura de cabeza a su muger que murió de ella. La Plata, January 3, 1807. ABNB EC.1807.47

37 NT, La Plata, June 6, 1791. ABAS, Divorcios, legajo 3, #5398

38 Querella de Andrés Torricos, cabo primero de la Escuadra de Granadores Provinciales, ante el Alcalde Ordinario de 2do voto de La Plata, contra su consorte Matiasa Sandoval, por adulterio. October 1, 1810. ABNB ECad.1810.12

39 Demanda de diborcio puesta por Margarita Niña a su marido José Gutierrez. La Plata, January 17, 1807. ABAS, Divorcios, legajo 4b, #5444

40 Josefa Villa, contra José Cabrera, por rapto de su hija menor. Poopó, July 4, 1749. ABNB EC.1750.18

41 María de tal, mujer legítima de Gregorio de la Fuente, denuncia a su marido por infiel. Mizque, December 25, 1778. ABNB EC.1776.162

42 Demanda ante el Alcalde Ordinario de 2do voto de La Plata de Manuela Fuentes, mujer legítima de Pablo Huerta, contra Hipólita Torres, por adulterio. La Plata, November 19, 1779. ABNB ECad.1779.11

43 Manuela Ferrel, contra su marido Toribio Paredes, por adulterio. Mizque, September 7, 1825. ABNB AM.1825.9

44 Expediente formado a nombre del capitán Sebastián López, comerciante en la provincia de Santa Cruz de la Sierra, vecino de la Villa de Potosí, sobre la restitución de arrobas de cera y algodón y demás bienes embargados por el gobernador de Santa Cruz de la Sierra, Pedro de Gálvez, por

transgresión y amancebamiento que le imputa. La Plata, June 21, 1709. ABNB ALP MyCh 5

45 Juicio seguido contra Catalina Vera por publico abandonamiento con José Galleguillos. Oruro, October 19, 1756. ABNB EC.1756.42

46 Dn Pascual Rodríguez sobre el asunto relativo a la separacion de su mujer. Cinti, May 6, 1806. ABNB EC.1806.115

47 Juicio criminal, seguido de oficio contra Gerónimo Suárez, por el delito de bigamia. Mizque, December 2, 1798. ABNB AM.1800.15

48 Campusano, V. La Plata, January 25, 1776. ABAS, Archivo Arzobispal, Clero, Acusaciones

49 Solicitud de Marcos Choque Tito, indio principal del pueblo de Challapata, ante el Alcalde Ordinario de 2do voto de La Plata, par que se le reciba información sumaria en la causa que sigue contra su mujer Petrona Arzabe, por adulterio. August 5, 1800. ABNB ECad.1800.11

50 Don Juan Bernardo, Alcalde ordinario, dijo que en la calle de Don Joseph Lezica, encontró a Don Pedro de Axxambide arrimado a la puerta de Don Joaquin Manrique, con una mujer casada aprovechando las sombras de la noche. Potosí, February 26, 1763. ABNB EC.1763.101

51 NT, Presto, November 25, 1815. ABAS, Divorcios, legajo 4c

52 Expediente promovido pr Da Josefa Calvimontes sobre tener amistad ylícita Da Franca Torres con su marido Dn Joachín Buitrago. La Plata, March 11, 1807. ABNB EC.1807.13

53 Testimonio remitido al Sr. Obispo de La Paz, de los autos seguidos contra don Lorenzo Farfán de los Godos, natural de Cuzco, sobre el public concubinato escandaloso con una mujer de nombre Hermenegilda, actualmente embarazada, en el pueblo de Huancané, provincia de Paucarcolla. La Paz, July 14, 1770. ABNB Ecad.1770.38

54 Juicio criminal seguido por Cruz Quinteros, contra Bernardo Centeno, por el delito de seducción y adulterio con la esposa del querellante. Mizque, March 3, 1788. ABNB AM.1788.3

55 Recurso a nombre de don José Antonio Zabala y Delgadillo, vecino y alcalde ordinario de la ciudad de Ascunción, sobre la multa de 200 pesos que le impuso el Gobernador del Paraguay, Pedro Melo de Portugal, por supuesto desacato a su autoridad, por los autos criminales que dicho Zabala siguio contra don Miguel Caldebilla, por el publico concubinato

que mantuvo éste con una mujer soltera. Asunción, September 19, 1783. ABNB SGI.1781.172

56 Expediente formado por el Vicario de la Villa de Potosí sobre el union de Da Feliciana Vasguez con su marido el alférez Rl Dn Joquí de la Quintana. Potosí, November 15, 1803. ABAS, Divorcios, legajo 4a, #5446

57 Da Josefa Lopez sobre Diborcio con su marido Don Mariano Tejerina. La Plata, November 5, 1812. ABAS, Divorcios, legajo 4c, #5451

58 Juicio criminal seguido por doña Josefa Arias de Velazco, contra don Ricardo Reynolds, por estupro, perpetrado en la persona de su hija menor Margarita Echeverría. La Plata, February 2, 1753. ABNB EC.1753.16

59 Melchora Gusman contra el Sor Alguacil Mor de Corte Dn Manl Antonio Tardío sobre que una ciratura que hubo en ella le suminstre alimentos necesarios. La Plata, July 10, 1800. ABNB EC.1800.34

60 Recurso ante la Audiencia de Charcas, a nombre de don Justo Ruiz, vecino de la Villa de Tarija, en la causa criminal seguida ante el Alcalde Ordinario de 1er voto de Tarija, contra su mujer doña Manuela Montoya y Manuel Vaca, por adulterio. La Plata, August 1, 1794. ABNB ECad.1794.25

61 NT, La Plata, April 15, 1807. ABAS, Divorcios, legajo 4b

62 NT, La Plata, August 3, 1821. ABAS, Divorcios, legajo 4d, #5458

63 NT, La Plata, February 23, 1805. ABAS, Divorcios, legajo 4b, #5441

64 NT, La Plata, November 12, 1822. ABAS, Divorcios, legajo 4d, #5457

65 Recurso de fuerza de Dn. Ramon Ballivian contra su mujer Francisca Barrios. La Plata, March 14, 1803. ABNB EC.1803.24

66 NT, La Plata, December 3, 1792. ABAS, Divorcios, legajo 3, #5403

67 Juan Heras Gandarillas, solicitando licencia judicial en defecto de la paterna para celebrar matrimonio con María Josefa Delgadillo. La Plata, April 13, 1788. ABNB EC.1788.11

68 Evaristo Tadeo Flores Porcel solicitando licencia para contraer matrimonio con Micaela Ponce. La Plata, March 5, 1805. ABNB EC.1805.76

69 Recurso de Manuela Ruíz contra su esposo Juan José Martínez por no querer dar consentimiento para que su hija tome el estado matrimonial. La Plata, April 1, 1805. ABNB EC.1805.78

70 Testimonio de la sentencia dictada por el Juez Real Subdelegado del partido de Tapacarí, y confirmación de dicha sentencia por la Audiencia de Charcas, en la causa seguida por don Tomás Terceros contra el reo

Pedro Pablo Terán, por adulterio y estupro. La Plata, June 2, 1795. ABNB ECad.1795.25

71 Autos de Demanda de Divorcio, Puesta por Da. Maria Rosa de Basuertto al Capitan Dn. Diego de Orosco, su esposo, Año de mill settesientos sinqta y quarto. Oropeza, March 5, 1754. ABAS, Divorcios, legajo 2, #5353

72 Sentencia de la Audiencia de Charcas, en la causa seguida por doña Dominga Flores de Burgos, pobre de solemnidad, vecina de la villa de Tarija con Ignacio de Echazú, regidor de aquel Cabildo, por estupro cometido bajo de esponsales. La Plata, December 5, 1798. ABNB Diver ACh Sent 690

73 Sentencia de la Audiencia de Charcas, confirma la sentiencia pronunciada pro el Alcalde Ordinario de la Villa de Potosí en la causa criminal de oficio contra el reo Juan An[gola], por la muerte de María Aldunate, su legítima mujer. La Plata, September 16, 1760. ABNB Diver ACh Sent 679

74 A la audiencia de La Plata: Con motivo de la causa de Hermenegildo Tabasque, que dío muerte a su mujer en Buenos Aires, se previene al virrey del Río de la Plata se abstenga de perdonar semejantes delitos estando ya substanciados y sentenciados. San Ildefonso, August 26, 1779. ABNB RC 722

75 En los reinos de Indias se observe puntualmente en todo su vigor la ley 82, título 16, libro 2 de la Recopilación de estos dominios que prohibe los casamientos de los ministros de las audiencias y de los de sus hijos sin licencia real. Buen Retiro, January 23, 1754. ABNB RC 584

76 Autos que sigue doña Antonia de Castro con don Pablo Urquieta, sobre que se declare por inoficiosa la dote que le dieron a doña María Eduarda de Figuroa cuando contrajo matrimonio. La Plata, December 2, 1752. ABNB EC.1752.5

77 Juicio criminal seguido por Basilia Calisaya contra su esposo Andres Camacho por adulterio cometido con Leonora Camacho, injurias y maltratamientos. Mizque, December 5, 1794. ABNB AM.1794.16

78 Juicio criminal seguido por Don Juan Terrazas contra Gregorio Agudo por intento de estupro con una criada suya. Mizque, June 10, 1808. ABNB AM.1808.11

79 Obrados de Estefa Ovando pidiendo la devolución de su hija Salomé Berasaín, raptado por Manuel Robledos. La Plata, June 8, 1750. ABNB EC.1750.37

80 Probidencia contra los casados Insestuosos. Pocoata, November 20, 1806. ABAS, Causas y Dispensas Matrimoniales, legajo 1

81 Autos contra Manuel Torres, vecino de la ciudad de La Plata, sobre las cuchilladas que dió en ella a Manuela Villca, india de Chayrapata o Aullagas (Chayanta, Potosí), por haber resistido a sus seducciones. La Plata, April 20, 1789. ABNB EC.1789.10

82 Expediente sobre que Don Antonio Poniondo, se conduzca al Reyno de Chile a hacer vida con su mujer. La Plata, December 2, 1774. ABNB EC.1774.4

83 Sobre que los gobernadores, corregidores y alcaldes mayores de las Indias no pueden casarse durante el tiempo que sirvieren sus oficios, en parte que estuviere en su jurisdicción, sin particular licencia para ello. Lisbon, February 26, 1582. ABNB RC 154

84 Se declara que las hijas de los consejeros y oidores de los reinos de las Indias, para obtener el real permiso a fin de contraer matrimonio con militares no necesitan acreditar su calidad con otro document que los títulos o copias autorizadas de semejantes empleos que hayan obtenido sus padres o abuelos. Aranjuez, April 20, 1790. ABNB RC 779

85 Real orden para que ninguno de los que están empleados en servicio de su magestad pueda contraer matrimonio sin expresa licencia del soberano. Madrid, March 24, 1791. ABNB RC 790

86 Rejas, Ramón. La Plata, December 23, 1775. ABAS, Archivo Arzobispal, Clero, Acusaciones

87 Queja de doña María Mercedes Morales, contra su marido don Eugenio Sotes. La Plata, January 10, 1788. ABNB EC.1788.70

88 Autos que sigue Da Francisca Ortiz Gallo, solicitando que por su marido Don Gregorio de Aldave y Salamanca sele contribuyan con quatrocientos ps por cia de alimento. Oruro, April 8, 1797. ABNB EC.1797.107

89 Representación de Juana Oquendo, vecina de La Plata, ante el Alcalde Ordinario de 1er voto de la misma, solicita que Mariano Muriel asista a la menor Victoria Pereira, quien se encuentra embarazada de éste y es huérfana. La Plata, June 23, 1779. ABNB ECad.2.1779.231

90 NT, Cochabamba, April 20, 1814. ABAS, Causas y Dispensas Matrimoniales, legajo 2

91 Joseph de la Cava. Tarija, July 31, 1787. ABAS, Causas y Dispensas Matrimoniales, legajo 1

92 NT, Cochabamba, September 15, 1812. ABAS, Causas y Dispensas Matrimoniales, legajo 2

93 NT, Pampa Quemada (Cinti), April 22, 1795. ABAS, Causas y Dispensas Matrimoniales, legajo 1

94 Juicio criminal seguido de oficio por el alcalde de Mizque, Matías Gutiérrez, a denuncia de Jacinta Zapata, contra su esposo Nicolás Amaya y Juana Ríos, por mantener entre ambos relaciones ilícitas. Aiquile, February 1, 1771. ABNB AM.1771.13

95 Juicio criminal seguido por Francisca Valverde, contra su esposo Tomás Arancibia, por adulterio. Mizque, October 12, 1808. ABNB AM.1808.8

96 Juicio criminal seguido por Sebastian Ferel, contra Andrés Ontiveros por adulterio conmetido con la mujer de Ferel. October 30, 1769. Mizque, ABNB AM.1769.5

97 Expediente seguida por Margarita Campero contra su amo Dn Lorenzo Cuevas pretendiendo su libertad. La Plata, July 27, 1794. ABNB EC.1794.89

98 Zorruto, Miguel. La Plata, April 3, 1777. ABAS, Archivo Arzobispal, Clero, Acusaciones

99 Denuncia de Bacilia Moreno, contra su esposo Antonio Ocaña, por el delito de adulterio. Mizque, July 29, 1793. ABNB AM.1793.17

100 Información reservada, contra don Diego de Torrez, por malentretenido con mujer casada, separación de este matrimonio, escándalo del pueblo y abandono de su mujer propia. La Plata, August 26, 1770. ABNB EC.1770.51

101 Poder que otorga doña Francisca del Risco y Agorreta, vecina de La Plata, viuda del doctor don Vicente Trardío de Guzmán, madre tutora y curadora de sus hijos menores, a favor de don Ramón de Agorreta y Miñano, official de la Dirección General de Rentas de Reino de España, vecino de Madrid, pra solicitor que su hijo don Manuel Antonio Tardío sea nombrado alguacil mayor de la Audiencia de La Plata. July 20, 1796. ABNB EP 343

102 Fianza de juzgado y sentenciado que otorga don Joaquín de Caso y Álvarez, vecino y de comercio de La Plata, a favor de don Juan José de Iturrios y Urquia, para la continuación de la causa sobre injurias que sigue con don Manuel Antonio Tardío. November 28, 1808. ABNB EP 332

103 Poder que otorga don Manuel Antonio Tardío de Agorreta, del Consejo de su Majestad, oidor honorario y alguacil mayor de Corte propietario por juro de heredad de la Audiencia de La Plata y coronel graduado de Milicias Disciplinadas, a favor de don Sebastián Parati y de don Gaspar

Soliveres, agentes de número en la Corte de Madrid, para pretensions en España. September 2, 1816. ABNB EP 379

104 Poder que otorgan los Electores de sus respectivos cantones, a favor de los Diputados elegidos para la asamblea General Constituyente del Alto Perú, a fin de que sancionen un regimen de Gobierno provisorio y deciden la suerte de las Provincias del Alto Perú. April 11, 1825. ABNB EP 381

105 Poder que otorga don Manuel Antonio Tardío de Agorreta, del Consejo de su Majestad y alguacil mayor de corte de la Audiencia de La Plata, a favor de doña Francisca del Risco y Agorreta, su legítima madre para diferentes efectos. February 20, 1811. ABNB EP 377

106 Poder que otorga doña Francisca del Risco y Agorreta, vecina de La Plata, viuda del doctor don Vicente Tardío Guzmán, a favor de su hijo legítimo don Manuel Antonio Tardío, del Consejo de su Magestad, alguacil mayor de corte de la Audiencia de La Plata, coronel graduado de milicias disciplinadas y comandante del cuerpo de voluntaries distinguidos de La Plata, para pleitos. November 10, 1817. ABNB EP 380

107 Da Faustina Miranda contra Dn Lusiano Zarate. Potosí, January 23, 1809. ABAS, Divorcios, legajo 4b, #5449

108 Diligencias remitidas por los Alcaldes Ordinarios que fueron en e año pasado de 1778 en la ciudad de la Asunción del Paraguay, sobre los casados que residen ne ella separados de sus mujeres. Ascunción, April 29, 1779. ABNB EC.1779.25

109 Juicio criminal seguido de oficio contra Ascencio Guzmán y su cuñada Bernarda Calderón, por escándalos y concubinato entre éstos. Mizque, November 10, 1783. ABNB AM.1783.11

110 Dispacho librado por el Gobierno de Cochabamba sobe que D. Jose Felix de Vargas baya a hacer vida con su mujer. Cochabamba, March 12, 1793. ABNB EC.1793.68

111 Expediente sobre la prición del soldado Miliciano Andrés Sandóval pr unos golpes qe dio a una muger llamada Rumi Cancha. La Plata, October 19, 1797. ABNB EC.1797.147

112 Testimonio del expediente formado por el alcalde ordinario de la ciudad de Misque Don Dámaso Méndez, y éste contra aquel por ilícita Amistad que mantiene con una mujer, y los excesos que ha cometido con este motivo. Mizque, March 12, 1773. ABNB EC.1773.134

113 Antonio Martínez contra Manuela Carreón por adulterio. La Plata, November 14, 1782. ABNB EC.1783.87

114 Queja entablada por Doña María de Tapia, contra don Alejandro Murillo, sobre que, con engaños y promesas de matrimonio, la sacó de su tierra. La Plata, March 25, 1760. ABNB EC.1760.22

115 Expte de diborcio entablado por Da Franca Paula Uriona, muger legitima de Dn Maro Montalvo en esta Villa de Potosí Ab de 1817. Potosí, July 22, 1816. ABAS, Causas y Dispensas Matrimoniales, legajo 2

116 Ambrosio Cabrera en nre de Da Casilda de Urquiza. La Plata, October 14, 1755. ABAS, Divorcios, legajo 2, #5355

117 NT, La Plata, March 16, 1769. ABAS, Divorcios, legajo 2, #5361

118 NT, Cinti, May 9, 1769. ABAS, Divorcios, legajo 2, #5360

119 NT, Poroma, Yamparáez, November 22, 1777. ABAS. Divorcios, legajo 2, #5374

120 NT, La Plata, November 2, 1781. ABAS, Divorcios, legajo 3, #5380

121 NT, La Plata, March 10, 1802. ABAS, Divorcios, legajo 4a, #5433

122 Camacho y Acosta sobre Divorcio. Cochabamba, March 4, 1805. ABAS, Divorcios, legajo 4b, #5439

123 Demanda de Diborcio, presta por Da Melchora Michel de Zarate, contra su marido Dn Toribio Daza. La Plata, November 25, 1807. ABAS, Divorcios, legajo 4b, #5445

124 NT, La Plata, September 28, 1807. ABAS, Divorcios, legajo 4b, #5443

125 NT, La Plata, October 17, 1808. ABAS, Divorcios, legajo 4b, #5447

126 Expediente formado sobre el divorcio promovido por Da Antonia Villegas, vecina del Pueblo de Cotagaita, contra su marido Dn. Juan Antonio Michel. Santiago de Cotagaita, December 20, 1817. ABAS, Divorcios, legajo 4c, #5453

127 Melchora Herrera contra su marido Dn Calixto Sambrana. Cochabamba, April 30, 1804. ABAS, Divorcios, legajo 4b, #5437

128 Juicio criminal seguido por Narcisa Mamani, contra Manuela Callisaya, por adulterio con su esposo. Mizque, June 22, 1808. ABNB AM.1808.10

129 Recurso de Dn. Ramón Daza, sobre habérsele precisado por el Alcalde de 20 voto de Potosí, a que pase a vivir con su mujer sin embargo de la licencia que le manifesto. Potosí, October 7, 1776. ABNB EC.1776.89

130 Recurso de Dn. José Rico, sobre motivos y causas que tiene para poder a vivir con su mujer. October 29, 1776. Cochabamba, ABNB EC.1776.94

131 Rafaela Jaldín, contra su esposo José Martínez Camacho, por abandono de su casa y no cumplir sus deberes de padre. Mizque, October 14, 1776. ABNB AM.1777.29

132 Expediente obrado a instancias de doña María León, sobre que se le precise á su marido Don Julián Velarde, á que pase a hacer vida con ella. La Plata, January 31, 1781. ABNB EC.1781.75

133 Recurso de Pastora Torres, sobre no hacer vida con su marido Feliciano Zuazo. La Plata, February 25, 1785. ABNB EC.1785.68

134 Juicio criminal seguido por Agustina Inojosa, contra su esposo Jacinto Veláquez, por adulterio. Mizque, August 1, 1766. ABNB AM.1766.2

135 Autos de diborcio y separacion perpetua declarado por el Arzobispo de esa ciudad en 22 de Deziembre 1775. La Plata, September 23, 1769. ABNB, Divorcios, legajo 21, #5370

136 El alcalde ordinario amonesta suavamente a Don Pedro Ignacio Axxambide, por las relaciones ilícitas que mantenia con mujer casada. Potosí, February 27, 1763. ABNB EC.1763.104

137 Denuncia de don José de Lecina, al Alcalde, por haber visto a don Pedro de Aranabide arrimado a la puerta de don Joaquín Monxique, con una mujer casada, aprovechando las sombras de la noche en la ciudad de Potosí. La Plata, March 10, 1763. ABNB EC.1763.7

138 NT, Potosí, February 1, 1808. ABAS, Divorcios, legajo 4b, #5448

139 Expediente seguido por el regidor de Potosí Manuel Pérez Fariños contra Dominga Montero por su conducta escandalosa. Potosí, August 13, 1783. ABNB EC.1783.149

140 Don Jaime San Gust, ordenando se restituya a su ciudad la mujer Paula Sandóval, por los escándalos que comete en la Villa Imperial de Potosí. Potosí, August 23, 1767. ABNB EC.1767.100

141 Lorenzo Coronado e Isidro Villanueva, vecinos de la ciduad de la Plata, sobre recípricos adulterios con sus propias mujeres y maltratamientos. La Plata, September 20, 1794. ABNB EC.1794.134

142 Juicio criminal, seguido por Bernardina Rojas, contra su marido Innocencio Rojas, por malos tratos y violencias. Totora, August 5, 1813. ABNB AM.1813.4

143 NT, La Plata, July 11, 1803. ABAS, Causas y Dispensas Matrimoniales, legajo 1

144 Juicio criminal seguido por el indio Pascual Quespi del pueblo de Yamparáez, contra Martín China, por el delito de adulterio. La Plata, August 23, 1753. ABNB EC.1753.75

145 Juicio seguido por Miguel Gerónimo de Bedoya contra Benito Alegre, cobrando 800 pesos, en resarcimiento de los gastos relacionados por dicho Alegre con motivo del rapto efectuado de la mujer de Bedoya. Yrupana, July 18, 1757. ABNB EC.1757.90

146 Relación que da Polonia Vargas acerca de lo procedido con el Alcalde Ordinario menos antiguo del pueblo de Tarata, por los vejámenes y perjuicios que le ha causado por la demanda de Melchora Méndez, mujer de Mariano Quiñónes, imputándole amistad adulterina con dicho su marido. La Plata, June 22, 1810. ABNB ECad.2.126

147 Compulsa de Juan Cruz, indio tributario del partido de Vallegrande, ante el Fiscal Protector General, de los autos en la causa que siguió con el reo Domingo Rojas, por el secuestro de su mujer Manuela Pantoja. October 8, 1807. ABNB ECad.1807.39

148 Criminales seguidos por Simón Galeas, contra José Morales, por adulterio. La Plata, November 17, 1768. ABNB EC.1768.45

149 Juan Jophe de Rivira, Besino y dueno de Hasienda en este Balle. Cinti, August 15, 1759. ABAS, Divorcios, legajo 2, #5357

150 Juicio criminal, seguido contra Juan Vallejos, por Dámaso Romero, por adulterio. Aiquile, June 1, 1809. ABNB AM.1809.27

151 Sobre la nulidad del matrimonio contraido pr el mudo Pedro Ruiz, con Santusa Guayalla, vecinos de la Vice-Parroquia de Pampa Ullagas. La Plata, August 26, 1817. ABAS, Divorcios, legajo 4c, #4000

152 NT, La Plata, March 26, 1784. ABAS, Divorcios, legajo 3, #5385

153 Juicio criminal seguido de oficio contra Ramón Lazarte y Paula Moreira, por mantener éstos amistad ilicita, con escándalo y mal ejemplo a los vecinos del pueblo de Aiquile. Aiquile, July 1, 1801. ABNB AM.1801.16

154 Querella de Juana Cárdenas, vecina de La Plata, ante el Alcalde Ordinario de Segundo voto de la misma, contra su marido, por maltratamientos, presenta testigos. La Plata, December 2, 1774. ABNB ECAd.2.1774.219

155 Eugenio Rojas, vecino de la ciudad de La Plata, como hermano de Matiasa Rojas, contra el marido de ésta, Esteban Lazarte, carpintero, por haberla puesto a la muerte a azotes. La Plata, April 16, 1791. ABNB EC.1791.130

156 Recurso de Dn. Simón de Aldunate y Rada, vecino de la Villa de Potosí, sobre que el alcalde de Segundo voto de esta Villa le quiere precisar a que vaya a vivir con su mujer. Potosí, December 15, 1776. ABNB EC.1776.90

157 Diligencias practicadas en virtud del auto de la Real Audiencia para que los casados vayan a hacer vidas maridables con sus mujeres a donde estas se hallacen. La Plata, March 30, 1776. ABNB EC.1776.102

158 Diligencias remitidas por el Corregidor de la Villa de Cochabamba don Pedro Rodrigo y Garralda, de las diligencias que ha practicado en orden a que los sujetos que residen en ella separados de sus mujeres, pasen al lugar donde éstas residen a vivir con ellas. Cochabamba, March 4, 1777. ABNB EC.1777.104

159 Expediente seguido sobre que Eulalia Gutíerrez haga vida con su marido Manuel Guillen. La Plata, September 16, 1786. ABNB EC.1786.80

160 Queja entablada por don Alfonso de la Fuente y Villegas, natural de España, contra el Alcalde Ordinario de Salta, por haberlo desterrado de ese lugar, alegando mantenía relación ilícita con una mujer. Salta, March 16, 1760. ABNB EC.1760.26

161 Juicio criminal seguido por Blas Umaña, contra Matías Ponce, por el delito de adulterio. Mizque, March 15, 1737. ABNB AM.1775.3

162 Juicio criminal seguido por Gabriel Durán contra Juan Bautista, por adulterio con la mujer del querellante. Challuani, May 25, 1760. ABNB AM.1770.8

163 Demanda que sigue doña María Dominga Villafañe, a su esposo don Antonio Villagómez por haber mantenido éste, amistad ilícita con Josefa Rojas, en Oruro. La Plata, May 26, 1778. ABNB EC.1778.179

164 Clemente Reano, acusa de adulterio a su esposa Estefa Renteria, con Pedro Capignata. La Plata, December 30, 1772. ABNB EC.1772.181

165 Da Maria Cartiona muger legitima de Dn Carlos Parraga. La Plata, October 26, 1756. ABAS, Divorcios, legajo 2, #5356

166 NT, Potosí, July 8, 1799. ABAS, Divorcios, legajo 3, #5425

167 Expediente de doña Gertrudis Pimentel contra su marido don Francisco Velásquez, sobre decir que no puede unirse con él, por estar siguiendo divorcio. Moscari, July 10, 1785. ABNB EC.1785.114.

168 Don Raimundo Condurgo, contra su mujer doña Petrona Barrientos, por ésta amistades ilicitas. La Plata, January 19, 1785. ABNB EC.1785.126

169 Diligencias practicadas por Sebastián de Segurola, gobernador intendente de La Paz, para que Antonia y Jacinta Barriga, hermanas, naturales de la

ciudad de La Plata, sean restituidas a esta desde la de La Paz por la vida escandalosa que llevan estando la primera de ellas en correspondencia con un sujeto casado y principal de La Paz. La Paz, March 6, 1788. ABNB EC.1789.235

170 Autos seguidos por doña Petronila Cáceres, por destierro de que se impuso de la Villa de Potosí, por suponerla mantenia relaciones ilícitas con varias personas de esa villa. Potosí, April 10, 1758. ABNB EC.1758.138

171 Juicio criminal por adulterio contra Nicolas Muñoz seguido pr su mujer Isabel Vargas. Mizque, October 27, 1809. ABNB AM.1809.14

172 Recurso de Dn. Simón de Aldunate y Rada. ABAS, Divorcios, legajo 2, #3956

173 Testimonio de los Autos Criminals obrados contra dn. Martin Medrano y dna. Maria Pasquala Yraola, por haver pasado a celebrar matrimo clandestinamte. Buenos Aires, August 23, 1794. ABAS, Causas y Dispensas Matrimoniales, legajo 1, #4174

174 Real orden comunicada por don José de Gálvez al presidente de la audiencia de La Plata: Lo que se ha de observer en orden a matrimonios de militares. Madrid, July 10, 1783. ABNB RC 753

175 Demanda de divorcio puesta por Terbacia Soto, a su marido Lucas Camposano. La Plata, January 7, 1803. ABAS, Divorcios, legajo 4a, #5436

176 Dn Thomas Pedraza, vecino del Pueblo de Santiago de Cotagayta. Chocaya, January 5, 1791. ABAS, Causas y Dispensas Matrimoniales, legajo 1

177 Nicolás Calderón sobre recusación al subdelegado de Juli (Chucuito, La Paz) en la causa que le ha fulminado por unas cuchilladas que dio a su mujer encontrándola en adulterio en fraganti con un eclesiástico. La Plata, June 5, 1789. ABNB EC.1789.55

178 Sánchez y Belzu, Luis. San Miguel de Acchilla, October 6, 1770. ABAS, Archivo Arzobispal, Clero, Acusaciones

179 Sánchez y Belzu, Luis. San Miguel de Acchilla, September 27, 1772. ABAS, Archivo Arzobispal, Clero, Acusaciones

180 Expediente criminal contra el clerigo Justo Joaquín Michel por el rapto de Evarista de Alcoser, autos seguidos por el padre de esta Pedro de Alcoser. La Plata, November 10, 1783. ABNB EC.1783.187

181 Sobre el matrimonio clandestino contraido pr D. Angl Borda con Da Juana Manuela Villegas, vecinos de la Prova. De Chichas. Cotagaita, October 19, 1821. ABAS, Divorcios, legajo 4d, #4006

182 Real cédula y pragmática expedida relative a la licencia y consentimiento que deben obtener los hijos de sus padres para contraer esponsales. El Pardo, April 7, 1778. ABNB RCad 47

183 En estos reinos se observe lo dispuesto en el inserto real decreto de 1790. XII.26 sobre varios puntos que comprende la real pragmática sobre matrimonios de 1776.III.23. Aranjuez, February 27, 1793. ABNB RC 803

184 NT, La Plata, September 28, 1789. ABAS, Causas y Dispensas Matrimoniales, legajo 1, #6050

185 Se declare que los hijos de familia mayors de veinte y cinco años, para contraer matrimonio deben pedir y obtener el consejo paterno y por su denegación el suplemento judicial prevenido en el capítulo 9 de la real pragmatica de 1776.III.23 bajo las penas establecidas en ella. Aranjuez, May 31, 1783. ABNB RC 751

186 En la real pragmática de matrimonios de 1776.III.23, deben comprenderse indistintamente los militares. Bajadoz, February 7, 1796. ABNB RC 816

187 En los reinos de Indias se publique y observe lo resuelto sobre matrimonios de los hijos de familias. Madrid, July 17, 1803. ABNB RC 873

188 Compromiso de Matrimonio entre don Mariano Arce, soltero, natural de la jurisdicción de Cochabamba, hijo legítimo del sargento mayor don Esteban de Arce y de doña Mauricia Uriona, vecinos de la misma jurisdicción, residentes en el valle deTarata y doña Lucía Taboada, natural de La Plata, soltera, hija natural de doña María Taboada. La Plata, June 11, 1796. ABNB EP 343

189 Justa Salazar, vecina de la ciudad de La Paz, sobre el cumplimento de supuestos esponsales de Manuel Campero con su hija menor Juana Calaumana. La Plata, October 27, 1789. ABNB EC.1789.205

190 Recurso de fuerza en el modo de conocer y proceder, instaurado por José Ml. Correa, contra el Provisor y Vicario General, del Arzobispado de La Plata, en la causa promovida por Felipe Cuellar padre de Micaela, por estupro y cumplimiento de esponsales. La Plata, September 2, 1792. ABNB EC.1792.36

191 Solicitud de doña María Bartolina de la Fuente, para que se le franquee testimonio de la declaración jurada de don Joaquín de la Sota, sobre su promesa de matrimonio, la misma que no ha sido cumplido. La Plata, February 11, 1760. ABNB EC.1760.68

192 Nulidad de Matrimonio por afinidad en 10 grado. Potosí, March 3, 1819. ABAS, Divorcios, legajo 4c, #4004
193 NT, La Plata, March 4, 1780. ABAS, Divorcios, legajo 3, #3965
194 Sobre el matrimonio verificado entre Manl Hidalgo y Martina Gonzales Yndios de Poopo con impedimiento de afinidad en primer grado de linea recta proveniente de copula ilicita. La Plata, July 15, 1812. ABAS, Causas y Dispensas Matrimoniales, legajo 2
195 Belsu, Luis. Acchilla, September 27, 1772. ABAS, Archivo Arzobispal, Clero, Acusaciones
196 Disolución de contrato esponsalicio que hacen el doctor don Pedro Ulloa, como apoderado del doctor don Justo Mariscal, ambos abogados de la Audiencia de La Plata y don Gregorio Núñez, procurador de causas de los del número de La Plata, para el matrimonio del citado don Justo con la hija legítima de don Gregorio, doña Petrona Núñez, menor de edad. La Plata, July 11, 1786. ABNB EP 294
197 NT, La Laguna, September 22, 1787. ABAS, Causas y Dispensas Matrimoniales, legajo 1
198 NT, Cochabamba, October 14, 1814. ABAS, Divorcios, legajo 4c, #3996
199 NT, Tarija, October 12, 1787. ABAS, Causas y Dispensas Matrimoniales, legajo 1
200 NT, Tarija, October 3, 1787. ABAS, Causas y Dispensas Matrimoniales, legajo 1
201 NT, La Plata, July 2, 1805. ABAS, Causas y Dispensas Matrimoniales, legajo 1
202 NT, La Plata, April 16, 1803. ABAS, Causas y Dispensas Matrimoniales, legajo 1
203 NT, La Plata, November 13, 1807. ABAS, Causas y Dispensas Matrimoniales, legajo 2
204 NT, Cochabamba, November 4, 1812. ABAS, Causas y Dispensas Matrimoniales, legajo 2
205 NT, La Plata, July 2, 1804. ABAS, Causas y Dispensas Matrimoniales, legajo 1
206 NT, Pocoata, 1817. ABAS, Divorcios, legajo 4c, #3999
207 Nulidad por afinidad de primer grado. Cinti, June 3, 1820. ABAS, Divorcios, legajo 4c
208 NT, La Plata, November 28, 1816. ABAS, Divorcios, legajo 4c, #3997

209 NT, La Plata, January 17, 1807. ABAS, Causas y Dispensas Matrimoniales, legajo 2
210 NT, Corquemarca, March 29, 1819. ABAS, Divorcios, legajo 4c, #4001
211 Nulidad de Matrimonio. Sacaca, October 16, 1807. ABAS, Divorcios, legajo 4b, #3989
212 Nulidad por falta de Jurisdicción. La Plata, June 5, 1816. ABAS, Divorcios, legajo 4c, #3998
213 Nulidad por bigamia y falta de Jurisdicción. La Plata, November 23, 1822. ABAS, Divorcios, legajo 4d, #4007
214 Nulidad de matrimonio, falta de jurisdiccion. Tarabuco, August 18, 1825. ABAS, Divorcios, legajo 4d, #4008
215 Licencia que solicita Dna Bernardina Monje para contraer matrimonio con Pedro Leaño. April 29, 1805. ABNB EC.1805.19
216 Representación de José Cuba, vecino de La Plata, ante el Presidente, Gobernador Intendente de la misma, entablando acción de disenso, contra Mariano Beltrán, para que no pueda casarse con su hija Clara Cuba. September 3, 1803. ABNB ECad.1803.44
217 Juicio de disenso de matrimonio seguido por los conyunges Matias Serrudo y Josefa Balas afin de impeder el matrimonio de su hija menor de catorce años. La Plata, October 13, 1806. ABNB EC.1806.63
218 Exp sobre declaración de Bernarda Martinez y Domingo Hurtado. La Plata, May 31, 1797. ABNB EC.1797.29
219 Autos seguidos por doña Felipa Gallardo y Lora, con don Francisco Barrientos, sobre que la citada mujer ocultó a un hijo suyo, menor de edad, llamado Manuel Barrientos con quien mantenía relaciones ilícitas, interpuesta la demanda por el Señor Barrientos, el alcalde ordinario de primer voto, ordenó la reclusion de Felipa Gallardo en el Monasterio de Nuestra Señora de los Remedios. La Plata, April 29, 1780. ABNB EC.1780.99
220 Nulidad de Matrimonio por falta de facultad. Pocpo, March 23, 1807. ABAS, Divorcios, legajo 4b, #3990
221 Manuel Robles contra doña Manuela Castro por que su hijo se casó con su hija. La Plata, April 24, 1780. ABNB EC.1780.149
222 Venta de una samba, Da Juliana Navarro a favor de Da Felipa Gallardo en la cantd 112ps. January 9, 1812. ABNB EP 377
223 Reconicimiento de censo en virtud de remate, que hace el licenciado don José Lorenzo García Galledos, presbitero, domiciliario del Arzobispado

de La Plata, a favor de la capellania fundada por el doctor don Antonio Diez de San Miguel y Solier por 1,00 pesos, sobre la casa ubicada en la calle de Mojotorillo que de don Francisco Barrientos, la misma que se remato en 2.700 pesos. June 1, 1808. ABNB EP 365

224 Autos seguidos por don Buenaventura Salinas, solicitan su licencia para contraer matrimonio con Bernarda Paniagua. La Plata, October 3, 1787. ABNB EC.1787.92

225 Martín Chirari y Herrera, successor al cacicazgo y gobernacíon del pueblo de indios de Moromoro (Chayanta, Potosí), sobre que se lleven a efecto los esponsales que tiene celebrados con María Manuela Toro, menor, vecina de la Plata. La Plata, March 16, 1789. ABNB EC.1789.216

226 Da Francisca Noreña viuda del Dr Dn Vicente Paniagua, contra Da Petrona Mesa por haber contraido matrimonio con su hijo, contra su voluntad. La Plata, April 28, 1792. ABNB EC.1792.168

227 Expediente sobre el dicenso que sigue Da Maria Asencia Flores, por el Matrimonio qe quiere contraer su hija Natural Da Maria Josefa Aragon con Dn augustin Godoy. La Plata, August 22, 1796. ABNB EC.1796.241

228 Solicitud de don Juan Manuel Gutiérrez, vecino de La Plata, ante el Provisor y Vicario General, dé licencia para contraer matrimonio con Doña Agueda Lora. La Plata, October 19, 1793. ABNB ECad.1793.43

229 Expediente seguido por don Basilio Rocabado sobre disenso a contraer matrimonio. La Plata, March 18, 1786. ABNB EC.1786.55

230 NT, March 2, 1786. ABAS, Matrimonios, Santo Domingo, vol. 76

231 Juicio criminal seguido por don Juan de Dios Mauje con don Benito Oquendo por el delito de rapto. La Paz, January 26, 1786. ABNB EC.1786.184

232 NT, La Paz, August 8, 1776. ABAS, Divorcios, legajo 2, #5373

233 NT, January 8, 1774. ABAS, Monasterios Femininas, Nuestra Señora de los Remedios, legajo 3

234 Reconocimiento de censo en virtud de remate, que hace don Evaristo Tadeo Flores, vecino de La Plata, a favor del Ramo de Fábrica de la Iglesia Recolección, que fue de don Mariano Molleda la misma que se remató en 1.100 pesos. May 24, 1808. ABNB EP 365

235 Querella de doña Anselma Pereira, vecina de La Plata, ante el Alcalde de 1er voto de la misma, contra don Melchor Montesinos, vecino de la Villa

de Potosí, por el rapto de su sobrina de 15 años, llamada Isabel Pereira. La Plata, December 16, 1795. ABNB ECad.1795.65

236 Desistimiento de don José de Avila, vecino de La Plata, en el peito seguido contra don Juan Manuel Gómez, por el delito de estupro que éste perpetró a Josefa Avila, hija del compareciente. La Plata, November 7, 1800. ABNB EP 329

237 En los reinos de Indias se observe la real cédula de 1796.X.30 inserta, tocante a que no se moleste con prisiones ni arrestos a los reos reconvenidos por causas de estupro. Aranjuez, May 31, 1801. ABNB RC 853

238 Imposición de censo que hace doña Catalina de Miranda, vecina de La Plata, mujer legítima de don Ricardo Reynolds a favor del dean doctor Francisco de Urquiza, sobre sus haciendas de Potolo sitas en la doctrina de Quilaquila, provincia de Yampáraez, el ingenio de Tomave, provincia de Porco, por 10.000 pesos, los cuales se subrogan a favor del Monasterio de Santa Teresa de Jesús y el Convento de San Augustín, 1.000 pesos adicionales por las mejoras que se hicieron en dicha hacienda, al maestro de campo don Diego de Torres. La Plata, December 30, 1767. ABNB EP 255

239 Venta de las haciendas de Mendoza, Chimbo y tierras del valle de Pocopoco sitos en Yamparáez y Porco que hace doña Catalina Miranda, vecina de la Plata, hija legítima y heredera de don José de Miranda y de doña María Manuela de Oretia, difuntos, divorciada de don Ricardo Reynolds a don Isidro de las Rivas, vecino de La Plata, por 3.000 pesos. La Plata, July 4, 1778. ABNB EP 304

240 Arrendamiento de la hacienda de Potolo sita en la doctrina de Quilaquila, provincia de Yamparáez, que hace doña Catalina de Miranda, vecina de La Plata, divorciada de don Ricardo Reynolds al doctor don Alejandro Pinto de Orihuela, abogado de esta Audiencia, durante 5 años, cada uno por 1.300 pesos. La Plata, October 16, 1783. ABNB EP 291

241 Venta de la hacienda Potolo, sita en Quilaquila, Yamparáez, que hace doña Catalina de Miranda, vecina de La Plata, a su hijo don Mariano Reynolds, alcalde de la Santa Hermandad de la ciudad, por 21.500 pesos, de los cuales 21.000 serán reconocidos a censo a favor de la Obra Pia fundada por el doctor don Francisco de Urquisa. La Plata, December 30, 1784. ABNB EP 313

242 Compromiso entre don Mariano y doña Isabel Reynolds, hermanos legítimos, viuda del doctor don Francisco Javier Gutiérrez de Escobar, tutora y curadora de sus hijos menores, para nombrar por árbitros y jueces a los doctors don Bonifacio Viscarra y don Esteban Agustín Gascón, abogados de la Audiencia de La Plata, en el pleito sobre la division y partición de bienes que dejó su madre doña Catalina de Miranda. La Plata, February 21, 1806. ABNB EP 352

243 Exclamación que hace doña Catalina de Miranda, mujer legítima de don Ricardo Reynolds, sobre las disposiciones que hizo su madre de los muchos bienes que dejó su padre y que como menor no percibió en ese entonces, habiendo poseído únicamente el quinto del total de dichos bienes. La Plata, January 7, 1774. ABNB EP 280

244 Revocación del poder que fue ortorgado por doña Catalina de Miranda, vecina de La Plata, a favor del que fuera su marido, don Ricardo Reynolds, con quien sigue un proceso de divorcio, para varios efectos. La Plata, March 3, 1783. ABNB EP 296

245 Venta de esclava negra bozal llamada María de 18 a 19 años de edad, que hace don José Francisco Lira, vecino de La Plata, a doña Eulalia Egusquiaguirre, mujer legítima de don Mariano Reynolds, regidor perpetuo del Cabildo, por 460 pesos. La Plata, September 2, 1812. ABNB EP 377

246 Codicilo de Don Mariano Reinolds, Vecino de esta ciudad. La Plata, March 18, 1825. ABNB EP 381

247 José Sebastian Seballos, exponiendo haberse vendido una hija suya por su mujer Josefa Durán. La Plata, September 26, 1801. ABNB EC.1801.178

248 Juicio criminal seguido por Ursula de Salazar contra Nicolás Ortega, por haber robado dinero y sacado seduciendola á la hija de la querellante, perforando paredes. Mizque, September 25, 1759. ABNB AM.1759.2

249 Solicitud del procurador general de la ciudad, ante el Alcalde de 2do voto de La Plata, relativo al matrimonio que intenta el negro José Iglesias con una negra nombrada Juana, que está a cargo de don Martín Ipiña. La Plata, August 1, 1810. ABNB ECad.1810.7

250 Expedte formado de Oficio Sre el valor del Matrimo contraido pr sorpresa entr el dd Marno Zilveti y Da Melchora Estrada. La Plata, December 14, 1819. ABAS, Causas y Dispensas Matrimoniales, legajo 2–6, #4003

251 NT, Buenos Aires, November 26, 1808. ABAS, Divorcios, legajo 4b, #3992

252 NT, La Plata, September 10, 1806. ABAS, Divorcios, legajo 4b, #3986

253 NT, Punata, September 22, 1798. ABAS, Divorcios, legajo 3, #5417
254 Demanda del Coronel don Juan Carillo, contra don Luis Solano que siendo casado vive separado de su mujer. Mohosa, December 23, 1777. ABNB EC.1777.243
255 Mandato para que los casados hagan vida con sus mujeres. Cordoba, December 24, 1777. ABNB EC.1777.265
256 Expediente para que los casados de la provincia del Paraguay que hubieren cumplido ya 3 años ausentes de sus mujeres salgan de esta provincia. Ascunción, December 23, 1779. ABNB EC.1780.136
257 Copiador de carta del Presidente Gobernador Intendente de La Plata al Alcalde Ordinario de 1er voto de la villa de Oruro, no comprende a don Juan Manuel de Medina, casado en la ciudad de La Paz, con doña Catalina de Loayza, la providencia dada por el Virrey de estas provincias, para que los casados que estuviesen separados, pasen a vivir en union con us mujeres, por razones que indica. La Plata, February 16, 1785. ABNB, Diver Cabil. Oruro 128
258 Expediente sobre que don José Pérez, salga a la villa de Oruro, a hacer vida con su mujer doña Tadea Arias. Oruro, December 27, 1785. ABNB EC.1785.70
259 Diligencias practicadas por el Corregidor de la provincia de Cochabamba, a efecto de que los casados, residentes en ella y separados de sus mujeres, pasan a hacer vida maridable, donde estas residen. Cochabamba, November 7, 1777. ABNB EC.1777.225
260 Real provision librada por la Audiencia de Charcas para que los Gobernadores, Corregidores y demás justicias de su distrito ejecuten lo mandado por real cédula de 1776.11.03, San Lorenzo el Real, sobre se continue con las diligencias con el objeto de que los sujetos casados ausentes de sus mujeres salgan de las provincias en que se hallan a hacer vida con ellas y los viudos justifiquen serlo. La Plata, July 7, 1777. ABNB, Diver ACh PR 24
261 Expediente seguido por D Jose de la Casa Nueva sobre que pase á la Ciudad de Salta a aser vida con su muger da Micaela Cabanillas. July 4, 1790. ABNB EC.1793.59
262 Expediente sobre que los sujetos que están casados en otros lugares y existen en la ciudad de la Paz, salgan de ella y pasen a hacer vida maridable con sus mujeres. La Paz, April 21, 1779. ABNB EC.1779.92

263 Expediente de la diligencias actuadas en la provincia de Mizque, en orden a que los sujetos que se hallen casados en aquella provincia de otras pasen a hacer vida maridable con sus mujeres. Mizque, December 19, 1768. ABNB EC.1768.57

264 El Señor fiscal porque los casados en España, hagan vida maridable con sus mujeres. La Plata, January 12, 1769. ABNB EC.1769.215

265 Respuestas de las autoridades locales de Poopó y la Rioja a la Audiencia de Charcas sobre el cumplimiento de la real provision que manda que los casados vuelvan a reunirse con sus consortes a los lugares donde residen. La Plata, February 20, 1773. ABNB ECad.1773.7

266 Auto de la Audiencia de Charcas para el Corregidor de Atacama, Francisco de Argumanis Fernández: Que los hombres casados que viven en dicha jurisdicción, separados de sus mujeres, se les compele y remitan, donde residen aquellas, para que hagan vida conyugal. La Plata, January 21, 1777. ABNB ECad.1777.2

267 Expediente sobre la reunion de los casados que viven separados de sus mujeres. La Plata, January 14, 1785. ABNB EC.1785.131

268 Informe del Corregidor de la Provincia de Sicasica, dando razón de los sujetos casados, separados de sus mujeres que se hallan en ella. Sicasica, June 10, 1777. ABNB EC.1777.201

269 Orden del Presidente de la Plata para la union de los casados y castigo de los blásfemos y hechiceros, buena educación del indio etc. La Plata, January 1, 1787. ABNB EC.1787.1

270 Demanda interpuesta por don Fabían Miranda, contra don Pedro García, por no haber obdecido éste a la prevención que se le hizo, de que se trasladase a Buenos Aires a vivir con su mujer. La Plata, January 25, 1772. ABNB EC.1772.3

271 Diligencias que remite el Alcalde de Santiago de Estero sobre los casados que residen en ella. La Plata, August 29, 1777. ABNB EC.1777.142

272 Obrados para impeler al General Juan José Herrera a que vaya a unirse con su esposa en Arequipa, actuados a denuncia del Corregidor de Oruro. La Plata, November 17, 1753. ABNB EC.1753.123

273 La esposa de don Gavino Quevado, para que salga de la ciudad a hacer vida con su mujer. La Plata, March 20, 1785. ABNB EC.1787.90

274 Carta y diligencias que remitío el Dr. Don Miguel Martinez de Escobar, Gobernador de Potosí, dando razón de la fuga con que eludió la

providencia de esta R.A. expedida para que fuse a hace vida con su mujer Don Juan de Herrero. Potosí, February 17, 1775. ABNB EC.1775.178

275 Doña Mauricia Delgadillo, mujer legítima de Tadeo Chacón, vecino de la Villa de Potosí, sobre que a su marido no se le declare no estar comprendido en el numero de los que viven separados de sus mujeres por las razones que expone. La Plata, October 6, 1774. ABNB EC.1774.81

276 Privaciones de separación de los casados por causas voluntarias. Buenos Aires, December 12, 1777. ABNB EC.1777.248

277 Expediente seguido por Juan Antonio Rodríguez, expresando que su mujer no quiere salir de la ciudad. La Plata, August 13, 1785. ABNB EC.1785.146

278 Fianza de haz que otorga don Clemente Lazo de la Vega, vecino de La Plata, a favor de don Juan Antonio Rodríguez, quien se halla preso en esta Cárcel Pública por encontrarse separado de su mujer, para su excarcelación, ya que su mujer, quien vivia en la ciudad de Arequipa murió en el terremoto que hubo en esta ciudad. April 11, 1785. ABNB EP 293

279 Dn. José Manzaneda, sobre se le conceda el término de un año, para ir a vivir con su mujer. La Plata, November 22, 1776. ABNB EC.1776.156

280 Diligencias que remiten los Alcaldes Ordinarios que fueron en el año de 1777 en la Ciudad de Salta en orden a los casados separados de sus mujeres y contra don Pasqual Samora. Salta, February 6, 1778. ABNB EC.1778.109

281 Don Juan de Dios Garrido, comerciante en esta ciudad sobre que se le conceda término para que pase a la ciudad de Lima, donde viva su mujer, a vivir con ella. La Plata, October 6, 1777. ABNB EC.1777.187

282 Diligencias que remite el Cabildo de la ciudad de Mizque, obradas en orden a los casados separados de sus mujeres. Mizque, June 26, 1777. ABNB EC.1777.221

283 Matiasa Fernández, vecina de la villa de Oruro (La Plata) sobre le injusta prisión y otros excesos que le ha infereido el alcalde de primer voto de dicha villa Sebastián de Campo. La Plata, June 1, 1790. ABNB EC.1790.171

284 Expediente seguido por Dn. José Martines Camacho sobre que haga vida con su mujer Dra Rafaela Faldon. La Plata, October 21, 1791. ABNB EC.1791.167

285 NT, La Plata, April 24, 1805. ABAS, Causas y Dispensas Matrimoniales, legajo 1

286 Expediente de don Lorenzo Antonio Díaz Caballero, sobre que suspende la orden que vaya a hacer vida con su mujer. La Plata, December 22, 1777. ABNB EC.1777.114
287 Josefa Vargas sobre que de separarce de su marido. La Plata, February 6, 1786. ABNB EC.1786.92
288 Toribio Terrasas contra su mujer Melchora Olmos sobre asuntos criminales. La Plata, November 15, 1798. ABNB EC.1801.149
289 NT, La Plata, April 28, 1821. ABAS, Divorcios, legajo 4d, #5456
290 NT, Cochabamba, July 10, 1822. ABAS, Divorcios, legajo 4d
291 Representación de doña Agustina Bracho y Caviedes, mujer legítima de don Manuel Valverde, separada del dicho, ante el Presidente de la Audiencia de Charcas, relativo a la custodia y posterior translado de su persona a la ciudad de Cuzco en virtud de una requisatoria del Virrey a solicitud de su madre que le atribuye defectos de fragilidad. La Plata, April 9, 1796. ABNB ECad.1796.9
292 NT, La Plata, October 31, 1809. ABAS, Divorcios, legajo 4b
293 Expediente remitido por el Corregidor de Cochabamba, sobre que el cura de Punata Dr. Don Manuel Moscoso á usurpado la Real Jurisdicón. La Plata, October 19, 1769. ABNB EC.1769.9
294 Doña Petrona Pantoja contra don Gregorio Pedraza, quien le dió muy malos tratos después de ser su esposo. La Plata, August 7, 1782. ABNB EC.1782.114
295 NT, La Plata, December 19, 1812. ABAS, Causas y Dispensas Matrimoniales, legajo 2
296 NT, La Plata, December 14, 1817. ABAS, Causas y Dispensas Matrimoniales, legajo 2
297 NT, Cochabamba, January 27, 1815. ABAS, Divorcios, legajo 4c
298 NT, La Plata, September 26, 1804. ABAS, Divorcios, legajo 4b, #5438
299 Juicio de divorcio, seguido por María Galeas, contra su esposo Lorenzo Flores, por injurias, maltratos. Mizque, December 2, 1790. ABNB AM.1790.11
300 NT, La Plata, October 14, 1755. ABAS, Divorcios, legajo 2, #5355
301 NT, Cochabamba, January 5, 1780. ABAS, Divorcios, legajo 3
302 NT, Sopachuy, Tomina, September 2, 1786. ABAS, Divorcios, legajo 3, #5387

303 Expete de Divorcio qe tiene puesta da Maria Josefa Peres de la Reynaga a su marido Dn Melchor Nuñez. Potosí, January 30, 1805. ABAS, Divorcios, legajo 4b, #5440
304 NT, Potosí, January 14, 1820. ABAS, Divorcios, legajo 4c, #5455
305 Querella de doña María Flores, ante el Alcalde de 1er voto de La Plata, contra su marido Mariano Anzaldo, por injurias y adulterio. La Plata, July 9, 1796. ABNB ECad.1796.16
306 Testimonio de los Autos segdos por Dn Domingo Maurin, con su muger Da María Manuela Azevey en la Curia Metropna de Charcas, sobre alimentos litis expensas y divorcio pedido por dha Azevey. La Plata, 1787. ABNB ECad.1787.3
307 NT, La Plata, April 2, 1806. ABAS, Divorcios, legajo 4b
308 Transacción entre el doctor don Juan José Segovia, oidor honorario de la Audiencia de La Plata, como apoderado de los herederos de don Joaquín de la Quintana, alférez real del cabildo de Potosí, en el pleito sobre la cesion de pesos que recibió el mencionado difunto en 03.01.1776. August 4, 1802. ABNB EP 303
309 Querella entablada por doña Petronila de la Reynaga, contra Venancio Carvajal, por haber contraido Amistad ilicita con una criada suya llamada Simona Nuñez. La Plata, March 4, 1758. ABNB EC.1758.163
310 Venta de las tierras de Artumayu sitas en la doctrina de San Sebastián, partido de Yamparáez, que hace el doctor José Mariano Arteaga, presbítero, a favor de doña Gertrudis Mercado de la Huerta por 1.200 pesos Corrientes, todo a censo a favor de la capellanía eclesiástica fundada por doña Josefa Arteaga, bisabuela del vendedor. March 18, 1794. ABNB EP 359
311 Venta de una casa ubicada en la esquina de San Augustín, barrio de los Tres Molles, que hacen doña Gertrudia y doña María Josefa Mercado de la Huerta, solteras, a don Pedro Tamayo, por 3.000 pesos, de los cuales 600 serán reconocidos a censo a favor del Monasterio de Nuestra Señora de los Remedios y 500 a favor de la Cofradía del Rosario. September 26, 1792. ABNB EP 355
312 Obligación de pago de don Pedro Tamayo, indio principal de la parroquia de San Sebastián de La Plata y comerciante en ella, a favor de doña Gertrudis Mercado, viuda de José Ariza, por el préstamo de 800 pesos y los réditos correspondientes. January 3, 1812. ABNB EP 377

313 Expediente formado a pedimento de da Tomasa Mariscal contra su marido D Lorenzo Mendes solicitando la separacion apoyada en los fundamtos qe alega. Cochabamba, September 20, 1812. ABAS, Divorcios, legajo 4c, #5450

314 Recurso a nombre de Rosa Nina, presa en la cárcel de la cudad de La Plata, ante la Audiencia de Charcas, en la causa seguida ante el Subdelegado del partido de Chayanta, por complicidad de la muerte de su marido. La Plata, October 19, 1808. ABNB ECad.1808.12

315 Juicio criminal, seguido contra Juana Cegido, por supuesta complicidad en la muerte de su marido. Totora, May 12, 1825. ABNB AM.1825.1

316 Criminal: sre la investigacion de la muerte executada en la Persona de Maria de tal en la Playa de Chicapilcomayo. Yamparez, December 7, 1799. ABNB EC.1799.100

317 Demanda de Rafaela, ante el Asesor de Gobierno e Intendencia de La Plata, contra su marido Alejo Ríos, sobre la division de bienes que pretende el segundo. La Plata, December 7, 1804. ABNB ECad.1804.75

318 Tomasa Rica contra Vicente Dias por abusos que cometió en su hija. La Plata, June 16, 1797. ABNB EC.1797.204

319 Juicio criminal seguido por Micaela Estrada, contra Mateo Barbero, por haber seducido a la menor Manuela. La Plata, November 19, 1772. ABNB EC.1772.50

320 Querella de Felipe Roque, indio originario del pueblo de San Pedro de Totora, provincia Carangas, ante el Fiscal de la Audiencia de Charcas, contra el indio Juan de Dios Sacama, por adulterio. La Plata, November 11, 1771. ABNB ECad.1771.88

321 Juicio criminal seguido por Gerónimo Montaño, contra Mariano Rojas, por estupro a su hija. Mizque, April 28, 1808. ABNB AM.1808.20

322 Borda, Matias. Guachacalla, November 9, 1785. ABAS, Archivo Arzobispal, Clero, Acusaciones

323 NT, La Plata, December 23, 1776. ABNB AChLA II

324 Merlos, Gregorio José. Capitulos seguidos contra el Doctor Gregorio Josef de Merlos, por algunas Yndios del Beneficio de Coroma. San Francisco de Coroma, September 22, 1770. ABAS, Archivo Arzobispal, Clero, Acusaciones

325 Incesto de Martín Choque. Coroma, January 19, 1767. ABAS, Archivo Arzobispal, Clero, Tribunal Eclesiástico

326 Cortes, Dionicio. Expediente formado sobre la querella dada á este Jusgado por la India Ambrocia Rodrigues, contra el Dr. Don Dionicio Cortés, cura y vicario del Beneficio de Aymaia. Aymaia, May 29, 1780. ABAS, Archivo Arzobispal, Clero, Acusaciones

327 Informe de Gregorio Josef de Merlos. Macha, October 7, 1780. AGI, Charcas 596

328 Informe de Tomás Catari. Macha, October 7, 1780. AGI, Charcas 596

329 Carta de Gregorio Josef de Merlos a Francisco Ramón de Herbovo y Figueróa. La Plata, January 23, 1781. AGI, Charcas 597

330 Carta de Gregorio Josef de Merlos al Licenciado Mariano de la Vega. La Plata, January 27, 1781. AGI, Charcas 597.4

331 Merlos, Josep Gregorio de. La Plata, June 8, 1782. ABAS, Archivo Arzobispal, Clero, Acusaciones

332 Diego de Estrada en virtud de su atribuciones que las leyes le acuerden, ordena que todos los casados que no estuviesen con sus mujeres, vuelvan a ellas siempre que no fueses causas de fuerza mayor. Potosí, October 25, 1778. ABNB EC.1778.62

333 El Protector de naturales de esta Ympl Villa pa la Proteccion de Joachina Velasquez. Potosí, January 9, 1758. ABAS, Divorcios, Legajo 2, #3956.

334 NT, Tacopaya, May 17, 1768. ABAS, Divorcios, legajo 2, #3958

335 Martina Vilvado y Valverde, vecina de Cochabamba, sobre el delito de disfraz de traje de Antonio Ita, español, con quien se casó en Potosí y que ha resuelto ser mujer y no varón. La Plata, May 6, 1805. ABNB EC.1805.96

336 Expediente seguida por Baltazar Miranda, para que los Alcaldes Ordinarios de la ciudad de La Plata, no les estrechen a que haga vida con su mujer Manuela Terán, por tener causa pendiente de divorcio. La Plata, August 7, 1788. ABNB EC.1788.16

337 Sobre Divorcio Urquidi. Cochabamba, January 10, 1806. ABAS, Divorcios, legajo 4b, #5442

338 Entrega que hace María Toro, mestizo, soltera, vecina de la hacienda de Yotalilla sita en Yotala, Yamparáez, de su hija natural llamada Francisca Toro, de año y medio de edad, por la pobreza extrema en la que se encuentra, a favor de don Manuel Liendo y su esposa doña Petrona Pérez. March 24, 1791. ABNB EP 338

339 Testamento de Petrona Pérez, natural de La Plata, hija legítima de don Isidro Pérez y de doña Clara Mostajo, difuntos, en el que nombra por su heredero universal a don Lucas Pérez. February 14, 1793. ABNB EP 323

340 Presidente de La Plata: Expediente seguido por Antonio Ita, preso en la cárcel de La Plata por ocultación y simulación de sexo, contra su mujer Martina Bilvao Valverde por apropiación indebida de sus efectos de ropa. La Plata, November 5, 1803. ABNB EC.1804.179

341 Autos promovidos en esta curia Arzobispal, por el sor Dor Dn Carlos de Sn Martín contra Manuel del Valle, y Miera por el matrimonio double qe se supone haver contrahido con Da. Isavel de Sn Martin. La Plata, October 7, 1791. ABAS, Causas y Dispensas Matrimoniales, legajo 1, #3977

342 NT, Cinti, November 29, 1802. ABAS, Causas y Dispensas Matrimoniales, legajo 1

343 NT, La Paz, October 25, 1818. ABAS, Divorcios, legajo 4c, #4002

344 Autos hechos de oficio en esta ciudad, contra Matheo Belazquez vecino de Mendoza sobre haberse casado dos veces. Mendoza, October 6, 1764. ABNB EC.1764.118

345 NT, Potosí, April 21, 1779. ABAS, Divorcios, legajo 3, #3964

346 NT, Salta, July 8, 1791. ABAS, Divorcios, legajo 3, #3973

347 Miguel Rojas, contra su suegro Marcelo Claros, por ocultación de su mujer y querer destruir su matrimonio. Hacienda de Conda, March 20, 1780. ABNB AM.1780.18

348 Autos seguidos por los Curas de este Arzobispdo y demas sufraganeos, sre la suspencion de la Rl. Cedula que manda que los Ynds no paguen obvenciones. La Plata, September 25, 1760. ABNB EC.1760.75

349 Obligación de pago de don Pedro Tamayo, vecino y del comercio de La Plata, a favor de doña María Morris por el préstamo de 1.200 pesos. May 16, 1811. ABNB EP 366

350 Obligación de pago de don Ignacio Risco, vecino de La Plata, a favor de don Pedro Tamayo por 1.000 pesos procedentes de la venta de ropa de la tierra. April 6, 1810. ABNB EP 371

351 Obligación de pago de don Pedro Tamayo, principal de la parroquia de San Sebastián, vecino y del comercio de La Plata, a favor del doctor don Lorenzo Fernández de Córdova, abogado y realtor propietario de la Audiencia de ella, por préstamo de 2.000 pesos. June 3, 1809. ABNB EP 376

352 Obligación de pago de don Pedro Tamayo, regidor del Cabildo de La Plata, a favor de don Manuel de Toribio Caviedes, vecino y del comercio de La Plata, por 2.051 pesos y 2½ reales procedentes de la venta de ropa de tierra. April 27, 1814. ABNB EP 379

353 Venta de casa sita en el barrio del Hospital de Santa Bárbara de La Plata, que hace doña Rafaela Apaca, viuda de don Pedro Tamayo, como tutora y curadora de sus hijos menores y albacea y tenedora de bienes de éste, al doctor don Mariano Enrique Calvo, abogado de la Audiencia de La Plata por 3.400 pesos, de las cuales 2.000 serán reconocidos a censo a favor del Monasterio de Remedios de La Plata. April 17, 1819. ABNB EP 385

354 Inventariación de los bienes fincados por fallecimiento del indio Pedro Tamayo, efectuado por el Juzgado de Segundo Voto de La Plata. March 24, 1819. ABNB EP 385

355 Testamento de don Pedro Tamayo, natural de la parroquia de San Sebastián, hijo legítimo de don Ventura Tamayo y de doña María Mónica Martínez, difuntos, casado en primeras nupcias con doña María Choque, vecina del pueblo de Condo, patido de Paria, en segundas con doña Micaela Zarate y en terceras con doña Rafaela Apaca, vecina de La Plata, hija legítima de don Manuel Apaca y de doña Ignacia Miranda, con quien procreó a Tomasa, María Mercedes y Cayetano, a quienes nombra por herederos. February 20, 1819. ABNB EP 385

356 Consentimeinto y licencia de doña Antonia Prudencia de Martierena, casada en primeras nupcias con el doctor don Joaquin Pérez de Uriondo y en segundas nupcias con el general don Francisco de Guemes y Esles, a favor de su hija doña Manuela Francisca de Guemes y Martierena, viuda de don Antonio López Carbajal, para contraer segundas nupcias con don Miguel Santiesteban, teniente del Regimiento de Infanteria fijo de Buenos Aires. La Plata, November 11, 1796. ABNB EP 343

357 Licencia que otorga doña Antonio Prudencia de Martierena viuda de primer matrimonio del doctor don Joaquín Pérez de Uriondo y de segundas del general don Francisco Guemes y Esles a favor de su hija de primer matrimonio doña María Ignacia Pérez de Uriondo, marquesa del Valle de Tojo y viuda de don Juan José Martierena, para que pueda contraer matrimonio con don José Hernández Sermeña, subteniente del Regimento de Infantería de Buenos Aires. La Plata, June 30, 1797. ABNB EP 344

358 Malingo, Nicolás. La Plata, December 16, 1775. ABAS, Archivo Arzobispal, Clero, Acusaciones

PUBLISHED SOURCES

Armendáriz, José de. "Carta de Castelfuerte a S.M." Lima, March 25, 1725. In *Estudio crítico sobre las "Noticias secretas de America" y el clero colonial (1720–1765)*, edited by Luis Merino, 217. Madrid: Consejo Superior de Investigaciones Cientificas, 1956.

Arrom, Silvia Marina. *The Women of Mexico City, 1790–1857*. Stanford: Stanford University Press, 1985.

Barbier, Jacques. *Reform and Politics in Bourbon Chile, 1755–1796*. Ottawa: University of Ottawa Press, 1980.

Behar, Ruth. "Sex and Sin, Witchcraft and the Devil in Late-Colonial Mexico." *American Ethnologist* 14 (1987): 34–54.

———. "Sexual Witchcraft, Colonialism, and Women's Powers: Views From the Mexican Inquisition." In *Sexuality and Marriage in Colonial Latin America*, edited by Asunción Lavrin, 178–206. Lincoln: University of Nebraska Press, 1989.

Black, Chad T. "Between Prescription and Practice: Licensure and Women's Legal Identity in Bourbon Quito, 1765–1810." *Colonial Latin American Review* 16, no. 2 (2007): 273–98.

———. *The Limits of Gender Domination: Women, the Law, and Political Crisis in Quito, 1765–1830*. Albuquerque: University of New Mexico Press, 2010.

Borchart de Moreno, Christina. "Words and Wounds: Gender Relations, Violence, and the State in Late Colonial and Early Republican Ecuador." *Colonial Latin American Review* 13, no. 1 (2004): 129–44.

Boyer, Richard. *Lives of the Bigamists*. Albuquerque: University of New Mexico Press, 1995.

———. "Women, La Mala Vida, and the Politics of Marriage." In *Sexuality and Marriage in Colonial Latin America*, edited by Asunción Lavrin, 252–86. Lincoln: University of Nebraska Press, 1989.

Bridikhina, Eugenia. *Sin temor a dios, ni a la justicia real: Control social en Charcas a fines del siglo XVIII*. La Paz: Instituto de Estudios Bolivianos, 2001.

Brown, Kendall W. *Bourbons and Brandy: Imperial Reform in Eighteenth-Century Arequipa*. Albuquerque: University of New Mexico Press, 1985.

Burkholder, Mark. "Honor and Honors in Colonial Spanish America." In *The Faces of Honor: Sex, Shame, and Violence in Colonial Latin America*, edited by Lyman Johnson and Sonya Lipsett-Rivera, 18–44. Durham: Duke University Press, 2001.

Burns, Kathryn. *Colonial Habits: Convents and the Spiritual Economy of Cuzco, Peru*. Durham: Duke University Press, 1999.

———. "Gender and the Politics of Mestizaje." *Hispanic American Historical Review* 78, no. 1 (1998): 5–44.

Cajías de la Vega, Fernando. *Oruro 1781: Sublevación de indios y rebelión criolla*. 2 vols. La Paz: Instituto de Estudios Bolivianos, 2004.

Calvo, Thomas. "The Warmth of the Hearth: Seventeenth-Century Guadalajara Families." In *Sexuality and Marriage in Colonial Latin America*, edited by Asunción Lavrin, 287–312. Lincoln: University of Nebraska Press, 1989.

Candlin, Kit. "The Empire of Women: Transient Entrepreneurs in the Southern Caribbean,1790–1820. *The Journal of Imperial and Commonwealth History* 38, no. 3 (2010): 351–72.

Casteñeda, Carmen. *Violación, estupro y sexualidad: Nueva Galicia, 1790–1821*. Guadalajara: Editorial Hexágono, 1989.

Chambers, Sarah. *From Subjects to Citizens: Honor, Gender, and Politics in Arequipa, Peru, 1780–1854*. University Park: Pennsylvania State University Press, 1999.

Delgado, Jessica. "Sin Temor de Dios: Women and Ecclesiastical Justice in Eighteenth-Century Toluca." *Colonial Latin American Review* 18, no. 1 (2009): 99–121.

"De un vecino del Cuzco a un ministro de Madrid." In *La verdad desnuda: o, Las dos faces de un obispo*, edited by Francisco Loayza, 154–68. Lima: Imprenta Domingo Miranda, 1947.

Dueñas, Giomar, "Adulterios, amancebamientos, divorcios y abandono: La fluidez de la vida familiar santafereña, 1750–1810." *Anuario colombiano de historia social y de la cultura* 23 (1996): 33–48.

"El Obpo de Quito informa a V.R.M. los excessos que se cometen por los Curas Regulares y por los Provinciales en sus visitas, que hazen de los Curatos, y pide para el Servicio de Dios nro. Sor Descargo de la Real concineca de V.R.M., de la de el dho. Obpo y alivio de los pobres, y miserables Yndios que se den eficazes providas para que cessen dichas extorciones." Quito,

January 8, 1728. In *Estudio crítico sobre las "Noticias secretas de America" y el clero colonial (1720–1765)*, edited by Luis Merino, 221–22. Madrid: Consejo Superior de Investigaciones Cientificas, 1956.

Few, Martha. *Women Who Live Evil Lives: Gender, Religion, and the Politics of Power in Colonial Guatemala*. Austin: University of Texas Press, 2002.

Fisher, John, Allan Kuethe, and Anthony McFarlane, eds. *Reform and Insurrection in Bourbon New Granada and Peru*. Baton Rouge: Louisiana State University Press, 1990.

Flores Galindo, Alberto, and Magdalena Chocano. "Las cargas del sacramento." *Revista Andina* 2, no. 2 (1984): 403–23.

French, William E. "'Te Amo Muncho': The Love Letters of Pedro and Enriqueta." In *The Human Tradition in Mexico*, edited by Jeffrey M. Pilcher, 123–36. Wilmington DE: Scholarly Resources, 2003.

Gantier, Bernardo, SJ. Personal communication, July 18, 2013.

García Gonzales, Juan. "El incumplimiento de las promeses de matrimonio en la Historia del derecho español." *Anuario de Historia del Derecho Español* 23 (1953): 611–42.

Gauderman, Kimberly. *Women's Lives in Colonial Quito: Gender, Law, and Economy in Spanish America*. Austin: University of Texas Press, 2003.

Germeten, Nicole von. *Violent Delights, Violent Ends: Sex, Race, and Honor in Colonial Cartagena de Indias*. Albuquerque: University of New Mexico Press, 2013.

Gonzalbo Aizpuru, Pilar. "Conflictos y rutinas de la vida familiar." In *Historia de la vida cotidiana en México*, vol. 3, edited by Antonio Rubial García and Pilar Gonzalbo Aizpuru, 553–78. Mexico City: El Colegio de México, 2005.

——— . *Familia y orden colonial*. Mexico City: El Colegio de México, 1998.

González del Riego, Delfina. "Fragmentos de la vida cotidiano a través de los procesos de divorcio: La sociedad colonial limeña en el siglo XVI." *Histórica* 19, no. 2 (1995): 197–217.

Gutiérrez, Ramón. "Honor Ideology, Marriage Negotiation, and Class-Gender Domination in New Mexico, 1690–1846." *Latin American Perspectives* 12, no. 1 (1985): 81–104.

Harrison, Regina. "The Theology of Concupiscence: Spanish-Quechua Confessional Manuals in the Andes." In *Coded Encounters: Writing, Gender, and Ethnicity in Colonial Latin America*, edited by Francisco Javier

Cevallos-Candau, Jeffrey A. Cole, Nina M. Scott, and Nicomedes Suarez-Arauz, 135–50. Amherst: University of Massachusetts Press, 1994.

Honores, R. "Alcalde ordinario." In *Diccionario Histórico de Bolivia*, vol. 1, edited by Josep Barnadas and Guillermo Calvo Ayaviri, 85. Sucre: Editorial Túpac Katari, 2002.

Hunefeldt, Christine. "Comunidad, curas y comuneros hacia fines del periodo colonial: Ovejas y pastores indomados en el Peru." *Hisla* 2 (1983): 3–31.

———. *Liberalism in the Bedroom: Quarreling Spouses in Nineteenth-Century Lima*. University Park PA: Pennsylvania State University, 2000.

Johnson, Lyman L. "Dangerous Words, Provocative Gestures, and Violent Acts: The Disputed Hierarchies of Plebeian Life in Colonial Buenos Aires." In *The Faces of Honor: Sex, Shame, and Violence in Colonial Latin America*, edited by Lyman Johnson and Sonya Lipsett-Rivera, 127–51. Durham: Duke University Press, 2001.

Johnson, Lyman, and Sonya Lipsett-Rivera. "Introduction." In *The Faces of Honor: Sex, Shame, and Violence in Colonial Latin America*, edited by Lyman Johnson and Sonya Lipsett-Rivera, 1–17. Durham: Duke University Press, 2001.

Juan, Jorge, and Antonio de Ulloa. *Discourse and Political Reflections of the Kingdoms of Peru*. Norman: University of Oklahoma Press, 1978.

Kuznesof, Elizabeth Anne. "Ethnic and Gender Influences on 'Spanish' Creole Society in Colonial Spanish America." *Colonial Latin American Review* 4, no. 1 (1995): 153–76.

Lavallé, Bernard. "Divorcio y nulidad de matrimonio en Lima (1650–1750): La desavenencia conyugal como indicador social." *Revista Andina* 4, no. 2 (1986): 427–64.

Lavrin, Asunción. "Introduction: The Scenario, the Actors, and the Issues." In *Sexuality and Marriage in Colonial Latin America*, edited by Asunción Lavrin, 1–43. Lincoln: University of Nebraska Press, 1989.

———. "La sexualidad y las normas de la moral sexual." In *Historia de la vida cotidiana en México*, vol. 2, edited by Antonio Rubial García and Pilar Gonzalbo Aizpuru, 489–517. Mexico City: El Colegio de México, 2004.

———. "Sexuality in Colonial Mexico: A Church Dilemma." In *Sexuality and Marriage in Colonial Latin America*, edited by Asunción Lavrin, 47–95. Lincoln: University of Nebraska Press, 1989.

León, Fray Luis de. *La perfecta casada*. Madrid: Ediciones Rialp, S.A., 1968. First published 1583.

Lewin, Boleslao. *La rebelión de Túpac Amaru y los origines de la independencia de Hispanoamérica*. Buenos Aires: Libreria Hachette, 1957.

Lewis, Laura. "The 'Weakness' of Women and the Feminization of the Indian in Colonial Mexico." *Colonial Latin American Review* 5, no. 1 (1996): 73–94.

Lipsett-Rivera, Sonya. "A Slap in the Face of Honor: Social Transgression and Women in Late-Colonial Mexico." In *The Faces of Honor: Sex, Shame, and Violence in Colonial Latin America*, edited by Lyman Johnson and Sonya Lipsett-Rivera, 179–200. Durham: Duke University Press, 2001.

——. *Gender and the Negotiation of Daily Life in Colonial Mexico, 1750–1856*. Lincoln: University of Nebraska Press, 2012.

Lofstrom, William. *Tres familias de Charcas: Fines del virreinato, principios de la República*. Sucre, Bolivia: Archivo y Biblioteca Nacionales de Bolivia, 2005.

López Beltrán, Clara."El círculo del poder: Matrimonio y parentesco en la élite colonial: La Paz." *Revista Complutense de Historia de América* 22 (1996): 161–81.

——. "Intereses y pasiones de los vecinos de La Paz en el siglo XVII: La élite provinciana en Charcas, virreinato del Perú." *Anuario de Estudios Americanos* 52, no. 1 (1995): 37–56.

——. "La buena vecindad: Las mujeres de élite en la sociedad colonial del siglo XVII." *Colonial Latin American Review* 5, no. 2 (1996): 219–36.

López Navarro, José. "Prólogo." In *La perfecta casada*, edited by Fray Luis de León. Madrid: Ediciones Rialp, S.A., 1968.

Mannarelli, María Emma. *Pecados publicos: La ilegitimidad en Lima, siglo XVII*. Lima: Ediciones Flora Tristán, 1993. Translated by Sidney Evans and Meredith D. Dodge as *Private Passions and Public Sins: Men and Women in Seventeenth-Century Lima* (Albuquerque: University of New Mexico Press, 2007).

McCaa, Robert, "Gustos de los padres, inclinaciones de los novios y reglas de una feria nupcial colonial: Parral, 1770–1814." *Historia Mexicana* 40, no. 4 (1991): 579–614.

McFarlane, Anthony. *Colombia before Independence: Economy, Society, and Politics under Bourbon Rule*. New York: Cambridge University Press, 1993.

Mendina, José Toribio. *Historia del Tribunal de la Inquisicion de Lima (1569–1820)*. Vol. 2. Santiago de Chile: Fondo Histórico y Bibliográfico J. T. Medina, 1956.

Mills, Kenneth. "Bad Christians in Colonial Peru." *Colonial Latin American Review* 5, no. 2 (December 1996): 183–218.

Morrison, Karen. "Slave Mothers and White Fathers: Defining Family and Status in Late Colonial Cuba." *Slavery & Abolition* 31, no. 1 (2010): 29–55.

Muriel, Josefina. *Los recogimientos de mujeres: Respuesta a una problemática social novohispana*. Mexico City: UNAM, 1974.

O'Day, Rosemary. *Women's Agency in Early Modern Britain and the American Colonies*. London: Pearson Longman, 2007.

O'Phelan Godoy, Scarlett. *Rebellions and Revolts in Eighteenth Century Peru and Upper Peru*. Cologne: Bohlau Verlag, 1985.

Pentimalli, Michela, Pedro Albornoz, and Paula Luján. "Mirar por su honra: Matrimonio y divorcio en Cochabamba, 1750–1825." *Anuario* 1997, 151–63. Sucre: Archivo y Biblioteca Nacionales de Bolivia, 1997.

Pescador, Juan Javier. "Entre la espada y el olvido: Pleitos matrimoniales en el provisorato eclesiástico de México, siglo XVIII." In *La familia en el mundo iberoamericano*, edited by Pilar Gonzalbo Aizpuru and Cecilia Rabell, 193–226. Mexico City: Instituto de Investigaciones Sociales, Universidad Nacional Autónoma de México, 1994.

Powers, Karen V. *Women in the Crucible of Conquest: The Gendered Genesis of Spanish American Society, 1500–1600*. Albuquerque: University of New Mexico Press, 2005.

Premo, Bianca. *Children of the Father King: Youth, Authority, and Legal Minority in Colonial Lima*. Chapel Hill: University of North Carolina Press, 2005.

———. "'Misunderstood Love': Children and Wet Nurses, Creoles and Kings in Lima's Enlightenment." *Colonial Latin American Review* 14, no. 2 (2005): 231–61.

Presta, Ana Maria. "Portraits of Four Women: Traditional Female Roles and Transgressions in Colonial Elite Families in Charcas, 1550–1600." *Colonial Latin American Review* 9, no. 2 (2000): 237–62.

Rappaport, Joanne. "Mischievous Lovers, Hidden Moors, and Cross-Dressers: Passing in Colonial Bogota." *Journal of Spanish Cultural Studies* 10, no. 1 (2009): 7–25.

"Representación de la ciudad del Cuzco, en el año de 1768, sobre excesos de corregidores y curas." In *Colección documental de la independencia del Perú*, vol. 1, book 2, "La rebelión de Túpac Amaru: Antecedentes," edited by Carlos Daniel Válcarcel, 3–68. Lima: Comisión Nacional del Sesquicentenario de la Independencia del Perú, 1971.

Robins, Nicholas. *El mesianismo y la rebelión indígena: La rebelión de Oruro en 1781*. La Paz: Editorial Hisbol, 1997.

———. *Genocide and Millennialism in Upper Peru: The Great Rebellion of 1780–1782*. Westport: Praeger Publishers, 2002.

———. *Priest-Indian Conflict in Upper Peru: The Generation of Rebellion, 1750–1780*. Syracuse: Syracuse University Press, 2007.

Rodríguez, Pablo. "Amor y matrimonio en la Nueva Granada: La provincia de Antioquia en el siglo XVIII." In *La familia en el mundo iberoamericano*, edited by Pilar Gonzalbo Aizpuru and Cecilia Rabell, 145–72. Mexico City: Instituto de Investigaciones Sociales, Universidad Nacional Autónoma de México, 1994.

Saether, Steinar A. "Bourbon Absolutism and Marriage Reform in Late Colonial Spanish America." *The Americas* 59, no. 4 (2003): 475–509.

Salinas Meza, René. "Uniones ilegitimas y desuniones legítimas: El matrimonio y la formacion de la pareja en Chile colonial." In *La familia en el mundo iberoamericano*, edited by Pilar Gonzalbo Aizpuru and Cecilia Rabell, 173–92. Mexico City: Instituto de Investigaciones Sociales, Universidad Nacional Autónoma de México, 1994.

Salinas Meza, René, and Igor Goicovic Donoso. "Amor, violencia y passion en Chile tradicional 1700–1850." *Anuario Colombiano de Historia Social y de la Cultura* 24 (1997): 237–66.

Sánchez, Ana, "Pecados secretos, públicas virtudes: El acoso sexual en el confesionario." *Revista Andina* 14, no 1 (1996): 121–49.

Seed, Patricia. *To Love, Honor, and Obey in Colonial Mexico: Conflicts over Marriage Choice, 1574–1821*. Stanford: Stanford University Press, 1988.

Serrada, Bernardo. "Testimonio de carta escrita al Excmo. Sor. Virrey y capn. Genl. De el Reyno del Peru por el Illmo. Sor. Obispo de la gran Ciudad de Cuzco." Cuzco, May 29, 1732. In *Estudio crítico sobre las "Noticias secretas de America" y el clero colonial (1720–1765)*, edited by Luis Merino, 223. Madrid: Consejo Superior de Investigaciones Cientificas, 1956.

Sloan, Kathryn. *Runaway Daughters: Seduction, Elopement, and Honor in Nineteenth-Century Mexico*. Albuquerque: University of New Mexico Press, 2008.

Socolow, Susan M. "Acceptable Partners: Marriage Choice in Argentina, 1778–1810." In *Sexuality and Marriage in Colonial Latin America*, edited by Asunción Lavrin, 209–47. Lincoln: University of Nebraska Press, 1989.

——— . "Colonial Gender History." *Latin American Research Review* 40, no. 3 (2005): 254–65.

——— . "Women and Crime: Buenos Aires, 1757–97." *Journal of Latin American Studies* 1, no. 12 (1980): 39–54.

Spurling, Geoffrey. "Honor, Sexuality, and the Colonial Church." In *The Faces of Honor: Sex, Shame, and Violence in Colonial Latin America*, edited by Lyman Johnson and Sonya Lipsett-Rivera, 45–67. Durham: Duke University Press, 2001.

Stavig, Ward. *Amor y violencia sexual: Valores indígenas en la sociedad colonial*. Lima: IEP, 1996.

——— . "'Living in Offense of Our Lord': Indigenous Sexual Values and Marital Life in the Colonial Crucible." *Hispanic American Historical Review* 75, no. 4 (November 1995): 597–622.

Stern, Steve. *The Secret History of Gender: Women, Men, and Power in Late Colonial Mexico*. Chapel Hill: University of North Carolina Press, 1995.

Stolcke, Verena. "Invaded Women: Sex, Race and Class in the Formation of Colonial Society." *The European Journal of Development Research* 6, no. 2 (1994): 7–21.

Twinam, Ann. "Gender, Honor, Sexuality, and Illegitimacy in Colonial Spanish America." In *Sexuality and Marriage in Colonial Latin America*, edited by Asunción Lavrin, 118–55. Lincoln: University of Nebraska Press, 1989.

——— . *Public Lives, Private Secrets: Gender, Honor, Sexuality, and Illegitimacy in Colonial Spanish America*. Stanford: Stanford University Press, 1999.

——— . "The Negotiation of Honor: Elites, Sexuality and Legitimacy in Eighteenth-Century Spanish America." In *The Faces of Honor: Sex, Shame, and Violence in Colonial Latin America*, edited by Lyman Johnson and Sonya Lipsett-Rivera, 68–102. Durham: Duke University Press, 2001.

Van Deusen, Nancy E. *Between the Sacred and the Worldly: The Institutional and Cultural Practice of Recogimiento in Colonial Lima*. Stanford: Stanford University Press, 2001.

———. "Defining the Sacred and the Worldly: Beatas and Recogidas in Late Seventeenth-Century Lima." *Colonial Latin American Historical Review* 6, no. 4 (1997): 441–77.

———. "Diasporas, Bondage, and Intimacy in Lima, 1535 to 1555." *Colonial Latin American Review* 19, no. 2 (2010): 247–77.

Vigil, Mariló. *La vida de las mujeres en los siglos XVI y XVII*. Madrid: Siglo Veintiuno, 1986.

World Bank. *World Development Report 2012: Gender Equality and Development*. Washington: World Bank Publications, 2011.

Zulawski, Ann. "Social Differentiation, Gender, and Ethnicity: Urban Indian Women in Colonial Bolivia, 1640–1725." *Latin American Research Review* 25, no. 2 (1990): 93–113.

Index

CPSIA information can be obtained
at www.ICGtesting.com
Printed in the USA
LVOW07*1940131217
559614LV00004B/193/P

9 780803 277199